Four-Color Communism

Four-Color Communism

Comic Books and Contested Power
in the German Democratic Republic

Sean Eedy

berghahn
NEW YORK · OXFORD
www.berghahnbooks.com

First published in 2021 by
Berghahn Books
www.berghahnbooks.com

© 2021, 2024 Sean Eedy
First paperback edition published in 2024

All rights reserved. Except for the quotation of short passages for the purposes of criticism and review, no part of this book may be reproduced in any form or by any means, electronic or mechanical, including photocopying, recording, or any information storage and retrieval system now known or to be invented, without written permission of the publisher.

Library of Congress Cataloging-in-Publication Data

Names: Eedy, Sean, author.
Title: Four-Color Communism: Comic Books and Contested Power in the German Democratic Republic / Sean Eedy.
Description: 1st. | New York: Berghahn Books, 2021. | Includes bibliographical references and index.
Identifiers: LCCN 2020054287 (print) | LCCN 2020054288 (ebook) | ISBN 9781800730007 (hardback) | ISBN 9781800730014 (ebook)
Subjects: LCSH: Comic books, strips, etc.—Germany (East)—History and criticism. | Literature and society—Germany (East)
Classification: LCC PN6755 .E37 2021 (print) | LCC PN6755 (ebook) | DDC 741.5/9431—dc23
LC record available at https://lccn.loc.gov/2020054287
LC ebook record available at https://lccn.loc.gov/2020054288

British Library Cataloguing in Publication Data
A catalogue record for this book is available from the British Library

ISBN 978-1-80073-000-7 hardback
ISBN 978-1-80539-336-8 paperback
ISBN 978-1-80539-445-7 epub
ISBN 978-1-80073-001-4 web pdf

https://doi.org/10.3167/9781800730007

For Debbie, my *Liebling*

Contents

List of Illustrations	viii
Acknowledgments	ix
List of Abbreviations and Terms	x
Introduction. Comics at the Intersection of State Power and Childhood	1
1. Comics and the Crisis of *Kultur* in the SED State	21
2. State Power and the East German Zeitgeist	64
3. Power, *Eigensinn*, and the Construction of Space through Comics	96
4. Escape, Escapism, and the Cultural Imperialism of Comic Book Travel in *Mosaik* and *Atze*	132
5. Western Influence, Popular Taste, and the Limitations of the FDJ's Publishing Regime	160
Conclusion. Contesting SED Power in the Comic Book Space	188
Bibliography	194
Index	211

Illustrations

1.1. Map of the *Römer-Serie*, *Mosaik von Hannes Hegen* 24 (November 1958).   25

1.2. "In Grauer Zeit" (In the Stone Age), *Mosaik von Hannes Hegen* 73 (December 1962): 23.   40

1.3. *Fix und Fax* 348, *Atze* 12 (1986).   50

1.4. "Das Gespenst auf dem Fahrrad" (Spirit on the Bicycle), *Atze* 12 (1986).   55

2.1. "Notlandung auf dem Mars" (Emergency Landing on Mars), *Mosaik von Hannes Hegen* 26 (January 1959): 12.   72

2.2. "Die Entführung ins All" (The Abduction into Space), *Mosaik von Hannes Hegen* 25 (December 1958): 10.   74

2.3. "Die Entführung ins All" (The Abduction into Space), *Mosaik von Hannes Hegen* 25 (December 1958): 12.   76

2.4. *Fix und Fax* 116, *Atze* 9 (1967).   82

2.5. Gojko Mitić at the Frösi-treff, March 1981.   86

3.1. *Pats Reiseabenteuer* 240: "Das schönste Fest" (The Most Beautiful Celebration), *Atze* 12 (1986).   103

3.2. *Max und Maxi* 75, *Atze* 12 (1986).   104

4.1. "Das Turnier zu Venedig" (The Tournament in Venice), *Mosaik von Hannes Hegen* 90 (May 1964): 15.   137

4.2. "Die Grosse Herausforderung" (The Great Challenge), *Mosaik von Hannes Hegen* 153 (August 1969): 9.   138

4.3. *Fix und Fax* 32: "Ballonfahrt" (Balloon trip), *Atze* 8 (1960).   148

Acknowledgments

The author would like to thank the following for their assistance, their suggestions, their criticisms, and their support for my earlier work and with the completion of this book: José Alaniz, John D. Benjamin, James Casteel, Chris Chapel, Cristina Cuevas-Wolf at the Wende Museum, Jennifer Evans, Jane Freeland, Martina and Günther Fuhlbrügge, Mel Gibson, Michael Goodrum, Mykelin Higham, David Hall, Gregor Hock and Petra Schmiech at Tessloff Verlag, Carolyn Kay, Sonja Klocke, Martha Kuhlman, the Kunow family, Peter Lorenz at Comicbibliothek Renate, Paul M. Malone, Dominique Marshall, Jennifer Rodgers, Corey Ross, Philip Smith, Ewa Stańczyk, Brett Sterling, Neil Thornton, Guido Weißhahn, Benjamin Woo, my readers at Berghahn, and the staff at the Bundesarchiv-Berlin-Lichterfelde.

Abbreviations and Terms

Abbreviations

CCA	Comics Code Authority
DEFA	German Film Joint Stock Company (Deutsche Film-Aktiengesellschaft)
DFD	Democratic Women's League of Germany (Demokratischer Frauenbund Deutschlands)
DFF	East German Television Broadcasting (Deutsche Fernsehfunk)
DM	Deutsche Mark
FDGB	Free German Trade Union Federation (Freier Deutsche Gewerkschaftsbund)
FDJ	Free German Youth (Freie Deutsche Jugend)
FRG	Federal Republic of Germany (West Germany)
GDR	German Democratic Republic (East Germany)
HV	Office of Publishers and Booksellers (Hauptverwaltung Verlage und Buchhandel)
JP	Ernst Thälmann Young Pioneers (Junge Pioniere, also Thälmann Pioniere)
KPD	Communist Party of Germany (Kommunistische Partei Deutschlands)
M	East German Mark (Ostmark)
SBZ	Soviet Zone of Occupation (Sowjetische Besatzungszone)
SED	Socialist Unity Party of Germany (Sozialistische Einheitspartei Deutschlands)

SMAD	Soviet Military Administration in Germany (Sowjetische Militäradministration in Deutschland)
SPD	Social Democratic Party of Germany
USSR	Union of Soviet Socialist Republics, Soviet Union
Vopo	People's Police (Volkspolizei)
ZPL	Central Party Leadership (Zentrale Parteileitung)

Terms

Alltag: everyday life

Durchherrschte Gesellschaft: thoroughly ruled society

FDJ-ler, FDJ-lerinnen: members of the Free German Youth (masculine, feminine)

Frösi, Fröhlich sein und singen: Be Happy and Sing (children's magazine)

Mosaik, Mosaik von Hannes Hegen: Mosaik by Hannes Hegen (comic)

Nischengesellschaft: niche society

Schund und Schmutz: trash and filth

Verlag Junge Welt: Young World Publishing

Verlag Neues Leben: New Life Publishing

Verordnung zum Schutz der Jugend: Regulations for the Protection of Youth

INTRODUCTION
Comics at the Intersection of State Power and Childhood

In the immediate aftermath of World War II in Europe, concerns over the acceptability and supposed harmfulness of comics were bolstered by the effects of Americanization on youth and how these issues affected the nation state, European civilization, and culture (*Kultur*).[1] In the United States, Dr. Fredric Wertham, a German-American psychologist and one of the comic industry's most vocal opponents, suggested that comics "indoctrinated children against the accepted rules of decency," comparing these publications to propaganda under European dictatorships. Although his science was questionable and less than objective, Wertham was not entirely wrong in this instance as comics were used by those very same dictatorships, just as they were by governments and the Church in the West. Wertham's thoughts on comics sided with the social theory and philosophy of the Frankfurt School, associated with the Institute for Social Research at the Goethe University Frankfurt. "Mass culture," the Frankfurt School contended, was used for the purposes of "homogeniz[ing] society with false class consciousness and capitalist aspirations."[2] In Wertham's estimation, comics served this same function in Western society. Comics produced in North America, Europe, and even the Soviet Bloc during the 1950s, the latter being the subject of this book, were hotly contested sites of power between educators, parents, politicians, and their constructions of the state and of childhood and how those two interacted and related to one another. As spaces typically uncontrolled and unmonitored by adults, comics gave children a site in which to demonstrate their desires and make meaning of the spaces they created. In effect, children themselves, and the state's perception of those children and their desires, were responsible in affecting the production of these comics and exerting their own modes of power over their contents.

Comics in the German Democratic Republic (GDR), published by the Free German Youth's (FDJ) state-owned publishers, provided spaces in which the regime and children came together and defined what was thought to be "childhood" and what that meant to notions of belonging within the state itself. Although, this was certainly not limited to the East German state or even to the Soviet Bloc, and it may just as easily be applied to the Western world. In this instance, the state as a political body and the state's publishing regime exercised obvious demonstrations of power. But the consumption of the comics themselves and children's interactions with those publications were indicative of the readership's own methods of control and how the contents of those comics were understood and digested by that readership. As such, comic books in the GDR provided an intersection between the various institutions and bodies of state power and the development and *Alltag* (everyday life) of the comics' child-readership. Comics provided a site of interaction and negotiation between children and that which was expected of them by the regime, despite these publications being indicative of the Socialist Unity Party's (SED) authority. These publications were power constructions of the state and in this purpose served the state well. They were also power fantasies, escapist, and constructive of the childhood experience. In effect, East German comics were spaces within which the state, the FDJ, the publishers, and the children for whom these comics were published enacted and exercised their various independent and individual definitions and constructions of childhood and what it meant to be a child living and growing up under East German socialism. While these comic publications were most assuredly sites of state power, they were necessarily negotiated through the lens of the child's understandings of state and society. Additionally, as comics were read and consumed within the domestic space, they became associated with privacy and the ersatz public sphere, becoming sites of children's criticisms of the state via the state's own cultural production. Comics allowed children the opportunity to interact with the FDJ and the SED regime on a level that was both engaging and entertaining, operating to increase their own political awareness. In so doing, comics enabled and encouraged dialogue between the child-citizen and the state for the perpetuation of the participatory dictatorship.[3] Through comics, these child-readers were entangled in the state's educational and ideological regimes. At the same time, they found themselves participatory to the East German culture of complaint afforded by perceptions of privacy associated with the niche society.

Comics and *Kinderzeitschriften* (magazines for children), as with much other mass media and entertainment oriented toward youth in the GDR, occupied a problematic middle-ground between the state and the children for whom they were intended. As an aspect of the FDJ's publishing regime and unofficial extension of the state's educational systems, comics as a medium suffered from the influence of its Western forebears. The FDJ wanted to publish comics because of their popularity with children on both sides of the postwar ideological divide. To ensure their own popularity, however, the publishing regime needed comics that, for all intents and purposes, mirrored those found in the West. The Berlin Wall made possible the reorientation of the East German comic market, allowing the inclusion of education and ideology to a greater degree. But these publications were never able to include as much propaganda as the FDJ wanted. This was particularly true of *Mosaik von Hannes Hegen*.[4] Children consumed these comics in ways similar to how they understood Western publications prior to the implementation of regulations curtailing their availability in 1955. As such, children as consumers negotiated what was permissible within the pages of those publications. This does not suggest that children ignored or removed ideology from comics. Instead, the ways children consumed comics and *Kinderzeitschriften* suggested that, though the ideology and education was understood and the comics themselves were considered part of the socialist education, children recognized comics as private entertainment, making their own meanings of the content, regardless of the state's intention to provide a socialist alternative to the Western *Schund und Schmutz* (trash and filth).

From at least the Brezhnev era in the Soviet Union forward, East German society and politics were in a perpetual state of transition. As suggested elsewhere by historian Mary Fulbrook, this transformation "was not intended to be ... democratic in the Western sense" as it lacked the popular support for SED policy. Rather, the East German state and society was indicative of "real existing socialism" or "developed socialism" whereby society's transitional state was directed by the Marxist-Leninist "dictatorship of the vanguard party." As some of those among the oppressed classes whom the SED sought to liberate may still suffer from their perceived "false consciousness" lingering from their long experience with capitalism, they may yet be prone to active protest and opposition. This meant that it was the responsibility of the state, of this "dictatorship of the vanguard party," to enact communist policy, sometimes despite the wishes of the population, until that population was politically conscious through the development of the socialist personality to ascend to the Marxist "dictatorship of the proletariat."[5] While SED rhetoric often employed the term "socialism" to describe the GDR's state and society, the SED was a communist party and often used "socialism" interchangeably with "communism" as the terms were employed in the nineteenth century. The title of this book uses a similarly conflated terminology. Throughout, I discuss the GDR in terms of its socialist character. That said, the SED was a communist party building the socialist German Democratic Republic as a Soviet-style communist state.

Fulbrook continues, describing the power exercised by the SED as both benign and malign in her conceptualization of East Germany as a "honeycomb state." This suggests that the GDR was a state in which the activities of the population were compartmentalized. Arguably, the division and overlap of the public and private spheres exonerates the vast numbers of civilians who willingly participated in the SED-system. At the same time, this notion maintains the perception of separation from and victimization by those same structures of governmental authority. Malign power often refers to the obvious means of coercion employed by the state against its own population. The most apparent perpetrators here are the Stasi, the East German secret police whose tendrils ran deep in the FDJ's publishing houses as with all aspects of the SED state. However, the conceptualization of malign power also refers to threats made by state officials against individuals and groups, such as the East German church, to secure their demonstrations of loyalty to the Party or the state in exchange for better housing, employment opportunities, or the ability to send one's child to pursue a university education over manual labor in the lignite (brown coal) mines.[6] It was in these malign modes of SED power that writer and researcher Phil Leask suggests the SED employed methods of humiliation, as the unjustified use of power seemingly at random and without reason. These demonstrations of state-power against Party members secured loyalty through the individual's desire to conform as a means of attaining their own ideals.[7] Often, direct interference in the lives of the East German citizenship, conceived as a carrot-and-stick approach to policy formation, saw the SED regime offer the population incentives in exchange for their loyalty or, particularly after 1971, the outward demonstration of conformity over a dyed-in-the-wool belief in the SED Party-line. If these incentives proved ineffective in generating the desired conformity or conviction, the stick was applied to produce loyalty by force.[8] The carrot-and-stick approach to the perception of the SED's malign demonstrations of power is clear, largely in those social areas without a consistent policy to deal with a problematic population.[9]

Benign power, as the term suggests, is more difficult to detect. Fulbrook suggests that the benign was more completely woven into the fabric of the East German *Alltag* and was found in many nebulous forms. Benign power shaped the reality of everyday life from shopping to entertainment to the perceived acceptability of the East German culture of complaint that was generated through the practice of *Eingaben* (citizen petitions).¹⁰ These letters of complaint provided something of a pressure valve for the pent-up problems and desires of the population. At the same time, the individualistic nature of these letters atomized voices that could lead to popular protest.¹¹ Andrew Port characterizes the GDR as a "grumble society," effectively as a state defined by controlled confrontation and condoned interaction with the state through the official endorsement of complaints issued to the local, regional, and national SED-authorities.¹² Meanwhile, Fulbrook suggests that those of the working class demonstrating left-wing tendencies or sympathies could "grumble," typically through the use of those *Eingaben*, without being admonished or punished by the regime.¹³ Likewise, Corey Ross argues that the East German population had its own agendas, its own sense of self (*Eigensinn*), that contradicted and clashed with the state. The accommodation negotiated between state authority and the desires of the population effectively consolidated the regime, at least for a time.¹⁴ Benign power structures were those invisible to the life lived in the GDR as they affected not only the ways in which the population related to the state, but how people interacted with each other.¹⁵ Through these power structures, East Germans normalized their interactions and senses of self, sometimes acting against the state that was itself responsible for the creation of those power structures. The population internalized these everyday modes of power, producing their own meanings of East German life and society.¹⁶ Although this internalization was not divorced of the SED regime's carrot-and-stick approach, these benign power structures provided the illusion of freedom from the regime's authority; authority that was understood solely in terms of those obvious and malign demonstrations of power.¹⁷ The population's conscious and willful ignorance of the state's benign power created the illusion that the state stopped at the door of the home, the domestic space. This provided people a sense of freedom from the state's malign presence and of one's own ability to lead a "normal" life; a question broached by West German bureaucrats assessing the value and legacy of the GDR in the wake of (re)unification in 1990. In the minds of many East Germans, the private sphere was construed as an area safe from the state's malign power structures regardless of the truth of the matter.¹⁸ The importance of this distinction between the malign and the benign modes of SED authority allowed the creation of the perceived *Eigensinn* in the East

German subconscious, generating meaning in the *Alltag* beyond the simple binary offered by narratives of state power and victimization.

Michel Foucault's conceptualization of the Panopticon provides an interesting lens through which to view the effects of the SED state's malign and benign constructions of power and how those were incorporated into the East German *Alltag*. Panopticism proposes a perpetual state in which prison inmates are assumed to be watched, regardless of the truth of the matter. As such, individual behavior is modified to adhere to the perceived laws and rules of the prison as institution.[19] In terms of the GDR, citizens conducted processes of self-regulation and self-censorship while acting in the public space under the assumption of state and Stasi surveillance. In his study on forensic psychology, deviation, and the socialist self as subject, Greg Eghigian suggests that the SED defined the socialist personality and asocial deviation through the linguistics of direction (i.e., to steer [*Steuerung*], to divert [*ableiten*], derailings [*Entgleisungen*], etc.). Contrary to Western perceptions of deviation as deviation from a statistical norm, the GDR understood deviation as that from "a path of natural development, a path by which all socialist subjects should invariably converge" into the socialist personality.[20] Eghigian contends that demonstrations of conformity in the GDR were part of a project to educate the psychology of the self (psycho-pedagogical) as much as they were a political impetus. This rationale implies that observation in the East German state and the population's subsequent self-regulation were parts of the socialist utopian project, demonstrated in instances of socialist science fiction novels, comics, and films. Comics were used by the SED as aspects of this Panopticism and of the levers of power employed by the state. As with other mechanisms of SED power, comic books were set upon the population for the express purposes of the self-regulation of youth, their perceived conformity to the state, and the associated retreat into the private sphere that allowed for the legitimization of SED authority.[21] This modification of behavior becomes a defense mechanism to avoid discipline by the state while acknowledging the state's authority to enact that discipline.[22] It should be noted, however, that this approach is hardly new to the study of the SED– and the Stasi state, and it is often used in connection with studies of the East German *Alltag* and the perception of the private sphere.[23]

One such mode of SED power was the Free German Youth, a mass organization re-founded in 1946 by the Soviet Military Administration in Germany (SMAD) to combat fascism among youth. This was of particular importance given the recent history of children's involvement in the

Hitler Youth and the Volkssturm (a militia organized by the Nazi Party as Germany's last line of defense against the Allied Forces encroaching on German territory) in the Soviet Zone of Occupation (SBZ).[24] Subordinated to the SED following the marriage of the East German Social Democrats (SPD) and the German Communist Party (KPD) in 1946 and, in a more official capacity, after the foundation of the GDR in 1949, the FDJ acted in parallel with the official educational regime of the SED state, largely responsible for the organization of the free time of youth, effectively educating children in their responsibilities and the ways in which they were to act in service to the socialist state.[25] As free time, not to mention the notion of a leisure society (*Freizeitgesellschaft*), was on the rise generally among the postwar population, it was the FDJ's responsibility to turn this arguable waste of youthful energies toward the construction of East German socialism and society. Not only did the idea of children and youth left to their own devices threaten the controls and conformity of the fledgling East German state, but the organization of leisure activities and time subverted the influence of Western capitalism that transgressed the GDR's borders both before and after construction of the Wall. Mass culture and the organization of leisure time became prominent features of both Germanies during the postwar. When individuals were not acting directly in service to the state, free time was dominated by state-run agencies delivering state ideology through organized activities to such an extent that there developed a close, almost indistinguishable association between free time and mass culture, or more precisely "the mass consumption of culture."[26] Comics, children's magazines, and other publications produced by the FDJ and the state-owned publishing houses served this function of organizing children's free time, time that was not dominated by the structures and institutions of education or of the FDJ, in an unofficial capacity. The portability of these publications and their goal to fill that leisure time away from the obligations to school, parents, or other institutions and figures of authority penetrated the perceived sanctity of the domestic space, the private sphere and last bastion of East German life free from the state. As comics proved immensely popular with children not only in Germany, but throughout Europe and North America, they provided a platform by which the FDJ continued to loosely organize sites of leisure in a way that was equally educational and ideologically acceptable to the motives and agendas of the East German educational and political regimes.

The unofficial steering of children's free time through comics proved more important following the construction of the Berlin Wall. As a means of keeping youth closely in line with the socialist cause after the perceived suspension of West German and American influence and all that entailed, including Western comic books, the SED regime under the leadership of Walter Ulbricht initiated the relative liberalization of the FDJ's and the SED's youth policies. Policy related to comics, however, regardless of the unevenness in the implementation of that policy from comic to comic and across the larger scope of children's magazines and publications, moved in the other direction as controlling leisure time became of greater importance for the FDJ and the SED regime.[27] In this, comics were considered both a part of the regime's state-socialist education and of larger developments surrounding children's literature in the GDR, improving the content and quality of publications for children to compete with perceived Western influence.[28] With the *Verordnung zum Schutz der Jugend* (Regulations for the Protection of Youth) in 1955 outlawing the possession and sale of Western comics and children's publications, and the Berlin Wall supposedly making these materials inaccessible, the FDJ and their publishing house for children's books and magazines, Verlag Junge Welt, put aside perceived competition with Western publications that previously, albeit arguably, determined much of the direction, presentation, and content of East German comics prior to the beginning of the 1960s.[29] The Berlin Wall not only created a captive audience for these publications but allowed the comics published in the East to be more than derivative clones of West German and American publications, attaching themselves to the burgeoning children's literature movement in the GDR, and evolving into quality publications that exceeded the cheapness and disposability that defined and glutted the medium in the postwar period.[30] In the post-Wall space, East German comics were sites in which the FDJ and the editorial regime attempted to control children's leisure time in a way that operated hand-in-hand with the East German educational systems in constructing children and childhood as a developmental space for the socialist personality.[31]

At the same time, comics were typically read in the home, in spaces considered part of the private sphere, and in those moments that were arguably unregulated by both parents and the FDJ. Comics were often purchased by the children themselves and with their own money, bypassing the permissions and authorities of parents or institutions, the FDJ included. The assumed absence of authority made the child-reader's sense of ownership over their leisure time and their private space total and empowering.[32] Moreover, the awareness that thousands of others were making the same purchases and for the same reasons created kinship among children necessary for the establishment of a comic culture.³³ For this reason, comics were important to the regime from an ideological standpoint to control children's free time and those sites of leisure.

In the mid-1980s, Günter Gaus articulated the GDR as a "niche society" (*Nischengesellschaft*) in that its population retreated into the private as an escape from the incessant ideology and politicization of society rendered by the SED.³⁴ Moreover, historian Anna Saunders suggests that the niche is useful to highlight the importance of privacy and the interactions occurring within the home as a space supposedly removed from the regime's influence. However, the concept of the niche fails to recognize the significance of interactions between the public and the private spheres, maintaining a certain rigid impenetrability between the two. While the niche is important in constructing ideas of East German identity and *Eigensinn*, it should not be implied that the private space is one entirely free from the state's politics.³⁵ Since Gaus, then, historians have come to understand the private space in a socialist society as an ersatz public sphere.³⁶

In *The Structural Transformation of the Public Sphere*, Jürgen Habermas suggests that the bourgeois order emerging with the Enlightenment created a distinction between the public and the private. Within this private realm, a bourgeois public sphere developed as a space where the critical engagement with politics and society was possible. This public sphere shifted from the private to the public realm with the mobilization of mass society in the late nineteenth and early twentieth century as divisions between the two blurred and intertwined with the rise of the modern social welfare state.³⁷ Typically, the public sphere was inconsistent with the lived experience of the GDR as the state did not permit criticisms aimed at the Party, socialism, or the successes and failures of socialist society. As a socialist state, the GDR and the entire Soviet Bloc for that matter, lacked the bourgeoisie and political structure and freedoms upon which Habermas based his notion of a public sphere as providing space for the formation of rational and critical public opinion.

That said, Habermas himself suggests that the public sphere is "a realm of our social life in which something approaching public opinion can be formed. Access is guaranteed to all citizens. A portion of the public sphere comes into being in every conversation in which private individuals assemble to form a public body."³⁸ He characterizes the "public sphere as a sphere which mediates between state and society, in which the public organizes itself as the bearer of public opinion, accords with the principle of the public sphere."³⁹ This would suggest that the public sphere exists anywhere citizens are allowed to gather and where the practice of open conversation is allowed to foment public opinion of rational criticism of the political state. In the GDR, the occurrence of this sphere of critical public opinion, as Habermas understood it, appeared in the perpetual ersatz public sphere conducted within the privacy of the domestic space.[40] When this idea is coupled with Fulbrook's conceptualization of the East German normalization and internalization of the supposed omnipresence of the SED and Stasi power, allowing those citizens to pursue a "normal" everyday life, the domestic space is transformed into an ersatz public sphere free from state power.[41] Not only this, but as state power was internalized, the citizen's perceived ability to construct the home as an ersatz public sphere provided de facto stability to the SED regime in that rational criticisms were conducted in such a way, employing language acceptable to the regime, that there was no real challenge to the structures of the state as a result.[42] Everyday experiences of life under Soviet-style regimes, including the GDR, caused citizens to become "organizationally passive and detached" from the regime exercising power over them.[43] The transformation of the private into an ersatz public sphere politicized the domestic space. As this transformative process was unofficially permitted if not encouraged by the regime, the ersatz public sphere and the incomplete freedoms permitted through the domestic practices of *Eigensinn* were themselves constructions of the SED state's exercised power. Although these practices were prevalent during the Ulbricht era of GDR history, this was more frequently the case after Erich Honecker's rise to power in 1971 as outward demonstrations of loyalty became unofficial SED state policy. The socialist personality no longer warranted genuine loyalty to socialism as it did under Ulbricht. Instead, and insofar as citizens demonstrated adherence to state laws and conventions in public, they were arguably left to their own devices in the domestic or private space of Gaus's "niche society."

Often this ersatz public sphere was given voice through the East German practice of the *Eingaben*. GDR citizens were afforded the legal right to complain about problems of the state through these petitions written into Article 3 of the GDR's 1949 Constitution. Ulbricht argued this right created a binding force between state and citizen, providing citizens a legal outlet to engage with the state in a way nonthreatening to SED power.[44] This right was not exclusive to the GDR, but it stemmed from a pre-Soviet Russian tradition whereby peasants believed the leadership to be on their side; if the leadership knew the plight of peasants, surely their problems would be solved.[45] The implication here was that the problems experienced by the citizens were not the fault of the leadership, as the leadership was obviously and apparently on the side of the peasantry, but the fault of petty bureaucrats, absolving the Party of perceived injustices to the citizenship. This practice continued into post-revolutionary Russia and, arguably, found its greatest expression in the Soviet Union during the reign of Joseph Stalin.[46] Nonetheless, the practice of *Eingaben* in East German society was one of the most prolific and common means constructing this ersatz public sphere, giving citizens the perception of having a voice in socialist society.[47] This firmly associated the ersatz public sphere in East Germany with the domestic and the feminization of space as the act of petition-writing established the home as the site of exchange between the authors of these *Eingaben*, their neighbors, and friends sharing similar complaints.[48]

It was, however, the *Eigensinn* that permitted the construction of the domestic as a space supposedly free from the state and thus free to foster this ersatz public sphere, provided that dialogue and negotiation with state power was arguably left at the door. More than simply doing things one's own way, *Eigensinn* implied the marginalization of state structures of power to make meaning of everyday life in ways that expressed the normalcy of those meanings.[49] The marginalization of official power is equivalent of Fulbrook's process of normalization. This is important in the consideration of *Eigensinn*'s effect on Gaus's construction of the "niche society." The niche is an effective tool describing the lived experience of citizens in the German Democratic Republic. However, this same niche ignores the reality of state authority and power beyond their initial purposes of atomizing and controlling society, though there is debate surrounding the perceived atomization of East German society.[50] *Eigensinn* nuances the niche society in that it accounts for this exercise of state power. It recognizes the constructed nature of the domestic space and the entire notion of privacy in the GDR. This notion allows East Germans the pretense that the regime does not transgress the boundaries and threshold of the home despite the constant presence of television, radio, print publications, and other forms of mass media. Of course, this says nothing of the Stasi presence, the FDJ, the trade union (FDGB), or even the women's league (DFD) pervading the home in an ethereal, if not a very concrete, way. But the concept of *Eigensinn* suggests an approach to daily life that marginalized that state power, negotiating the citizen's place within East German society with a supposed voice provided by engagement with the ersatz public sphere. In this way, *Eigensinn* effectively allowed citizens to interact with and criticize the regime through means permissible to both citizen and state. This interaction then proposes a negotiation between notions of power and the conceptualization of a public sphere, albeit a public sphere necessarily transposed onto a society lacking a liberal bourgeoisie. *Eigensinn* understands state power's engagement with the ersatz public sphere while acknowledging that public sphere as another yet unofficial institution of that same power.

Chapter One examines the birth of *Mosaik von Hannes Hegen* and the early development of issues surrounding the comics medium in the GDR, more generally. Following the appearance of these problems in the creation of *Mosaik* and more broadly across East German comics publishing, the chapter turns to a proposal for and the implementation of changes to the comic magazine *Atze*, submitted to the FDJ Central Committee in 1966 by then-Editor-in-Chief (*Chefredakteur*) Wolfgang Altenburger. Of the two dedicated comics in the GDR, *Atze* was a distant second in terms of both quality and sales to the more popular and consistent *Mosaik*. While *Mosaik* was allowed, within reason, to follow trends borrowed from Western European and American comics, Altenburger suggested changes to *Atze* to improve the overall quality of the publication and bring the comic in line with the ideological and educational objectives developing in children's literature with the implementation of the *Bitterfelder Weg* in 1959. This proposal spoke to larger trends in East German children's literature, elevating the mediums, both literature and comics more generally, to compete with the best adult literature produced in the socialist state as well as with the literary canons of the Western world. At the same time, attentions focused on *Atze* suggest a relative hands-off approach to *Mosaik*, for a time at least, due in no small part to the comic's overall popularity and sales. Moreover, this chapter argues that Western trends, notably the anti-comics campaigns of the 1950s as a conflict over cultural power in East Germany, revealed flaws in the East German comics industry at large.[51] As such, the East German variation of the anti-comics campaign highlighted the importance and potential of these types of *Kinderzeitschriften* for the FDJ and the SED state.

Chapter Two turns on those notions of power projected through the comics and *Kinderzeitschriften* themselves and how the FDJ employed children's interests within those constructions of power. Through the concept of benign power, this chapter expands upon discussions in the first chapter through an analysis of the operation of power constructions in *Atze* and the rationale for the comic's new profile proposed in the mid-1960s. The chapter then turns to *Mosaik*, specifically the *Weltraum-* (outer-space) and *Amerika-Serie* as stories devised to harness the cultural zeitgeist of their respective decades, turning their backdrops toward decidedly ideological approaches to storytelling without sacrificing the entertainment that initially drew children to the publications. This dual approach created tensions between children and the educational and publishing regimes as children perceived these stories in terms arguably different than those intended by the FDJ. Invoking many of these same elements and the societal zeitgeists that accompanied them again in the early-1980s, the FDJ and Verlag Junge Welt hosted a meet-up between the child-audience and the creators of one of these publications (*Frösi*, in this case). Here the FDJ used comics and the culture created around those *Kinderzeitschriften* to generate the perception of youth enthusiasm toward the state as legitimizing East German socialism.

Chapter Three picks up on threads of the previous chapters, bringing the comics as constructions of state power into the home as the home itself constituted the ersatz public sphere. In doing so, this chapter looks toward the transformation of these comics from the constructions of authority as the FDJ and the state-owned publisher, Verlag Junge Welt, intended them to be, to sites of children's criticisms through the understanding of what these comics meant to those children as both consumers and citizens in the East German state. Through an analysis of letters written to the FDJ's publishing regime and reports drafted by the publishers to determine trends among the letters themselves, this chapter suggests that comics created sites of interaction and negotiation between the state and the readership over whom the state enacted their modes and methods of control. Of course, children did not consciously ignore these modes of authority, nor were they oblivious to them. Instead, East German children, viewed through the lens of the experience of childhood, created their own meanings and significations across these publications based on what they themselves deemed important. In the domestic space and the perceived ersatz public sphere constructed therein, children reconstituted comics as sites of *Eigensinn*; spaces in which children redefined the experience of childhood and belonging in the socialist state. This does not suggest that children necessarily understood their own senses of self or that they understood their reading of comics in a particularly critical way. Children reading these publications foregrounded and prioritized their own interests and desires within the provided ideological content. This practice did, however, enable children to critically evaluate promises made to them in those publications and by the FDJ and to indirectly confront the FDJ's perceptions and definitions of childhood within socialism.

Chapter Four returns to the stories of *Mosaik* and of *Pats Reiseabenteuer* (Pat's Travel Adventures, appearing in *Atze* since the mid-1960s) and their dependence on Western comic book tropes and the visual language of travel to construct an image of the GDR and of Eastern European socialism in a form easily digestible to children reading these comics. Comics permitted the readership opportunity for the "inner emigration" that the regime considered so problematic among citizens who consumed West German media and culture. It also allowed the FDJ opportunity to demonstrate an idealized socialist state in order to generate the socialist personality among youth, to foster participation within the structures and constructions of the state that were necessary for the continuation of the GDR. By necessity, depictions of travel in these comics and the required ideological objectives of the state represented socialism through Western tropes. Arguing in favor of the superiority of East German socialism, these travel and Western tropes often led to the agents of socialism and capitalism being portrayed as virtually indistinguishable as each enacted their will over others. In the context of a supposed historically accurate past, travel in these comics did not actively address issues of German division or of the GDR as an enclosed society, thus effacing the lived reality of East German citizens. Instead, comics idealized socialism in spite of its perceived failings. This chapter goes on to suggest that comics and the representation of the socialist experience through travel opened a window onto the possibilities and potentials of European Communism that the lived reality of life in the divided and walled state could never hope to achieve. As a result, and despite the stories' attempts to create genuine enthusiasm toward the state and socialism, these stories had the opposite effect, building unrealistic expectations among the children reading these comics.

The final chapter then turns to the problems between Hannes Hegen, creator of the popular comic *Mosaik*, and the publishers of these comics from 1955 until his departure from the Mosaik-Kollektiv (Mosaic Collective) twenty years later. Initially hired to develop a comic providing a counterpoint, a socialist alternative, to the comic books accompanying American GIs during World War II and flooding the German marketplace in the aftermath, Hegen created the Digedags as direct competition to the American "funny animal" genre embodied by Disney comics published by Dell in the United States, licensed to Ehapa Verlag in West Germany.[52] This aspect was important and necessary for *Mosaik* to carve its own niche in the marketplace of the mid-1950s.[53] Following the authors and publishers conference held in the industrial town of Bitterfeld in 1959 and the subsequent implementation of the *Bitterfelder Weg* as a new direction for East German literature, dedicated to the depiction of the lived experiences of average workers in the socialist state,

Hegen was attacked by the FDJ's educational regime. Although it was adherence to Western tropes that popularized *Mosaik* upon its debut in December 1955, by the turn of the decade those same conventions were accused of disregarding historical accuracy, educational value, and ideological content, proving harmful to the development of the socialist personality among the publication's readership. Essentially, *Mosaik* was charged with too closely emulating the *Schund und Schmutz* from which it originated. This chapter explores Hegen's changing relationship with the editorial regime and the tensions that developed in the widening gap between the two. Here, Hegen exercised his own control over the publication and the direction of the stories despite the interference of the FDJ. This dynamic ultimately proved too much, forcing Hegen's departure. But during his tenure, the publication's popularity provided Hegen the space necessary to resist, if only marginally, the power constructions of the state. While this arguable and limited opposition is not intended to speak to larger conversations of resistance in the GDR or elsewhere in the Soviet Bloc, it is demonstrative of trends developed throughout this book. Specifically, it addresses the benign and malign machinations of the FDJ and SED state authority and individual abilities to carve spaces within and make their own meanings of East German socialism and socialist society.

Taken as a whole, this book questions power as a construction in publications for children and as a means of conditioning those child-readers to act in ways devised to perpetuate the East German socialist state. It is hoped in demonstrating the state's apparent benign methods of coercion, children's resistance to or acceptance of those *Kinderzeitschriften* will be made clear as letter columns, reader taste, and consumption patterns made East German comic books sites of dialogue between children and the state. This book also addresses the comics themselves—*Mosaik* and *Atze*, and to a lesser extent the magazine *Frösi*, the title of this latter being a contraction of *Fröhlich sein und singen* (Be Happy and Sing)—across the divide in socialist representation created by the *Bitterfelder Weg* and the construction of the Berlin Wall from the mid-1950s to the mid- to late-1960s as means of demonstrating the limitations imposed by both the readership and Western influence on the state's ability to publish ideological material in a supposedly insular society. Moreover, *Mosaik* and *Atze* allow for larger comparisons and discussions of Western influence in the GDR as these comics came to be as a result of the availability of similar Western publications, particularly at a time when questions of comics' potentially harmful effects on childhood development infiltrated the GDR from Western Europe and the United States.

Notes

1. James Chapman, *British Comics: A Cultural History* (London: Reaktion Books, 2011), 9–11; Richard Ivan Jobs, "Tarzan under Attack: Youth, Comics, and Cultural Reconstruction in Postwar France," *French Historical Studies* 26, no. 4 (Fall 2003): 688–95; Goran Jovanovic and Ulrich Koch, "The Comics Debate in Germany: Against Dirt and Rubbish, Pictoral Idiotism, and Cultural Analphabetism," in *Pulp Demons: International Dimensions of the Postwar Anti-Comics Campaign*, ed. John A. Lent (Cranbury: Associated University Presses, Inc., 1999), 95–102; Peter Lee, "Decrypting Espionage Comic Books in 1950s America," in *Comic Books and the Cold War, 1946–1962: Essays on Graphic Treatment of Communism, the Code and Social Concerns*, ed. Chris York and Rafiel York (Jefferson: McFarland & Company, Inc., 2012), 30–44.
2. Bradford W. Wright, *Comic Book Nation: The Transformation of Youth Culture in America* (Baltimore: John Hopkins University Press, 2001), 159.
3. Mary Fulbrook, *The People's State: East German Society from Hitler to Honecker* (New Haven: Yale University Press, 2005), 12.
4. The comic created in 1955 by Johannes Hegenbarth and featuring the Digedag characters was officially titled *Mosaik von Hannes Hegen* (this being Hegenbarth's pseudonym). This title remained in place until the introduction of the Abrafaxe characters, developed by Lothar Dräger and Lona Rietschel, at the beginning of 1976. At this point, Hegen's name was removed from the masthead and the comic officially became known as, simply, *Mosaik*. Throughout this book, I use the title *Mosaik* to refer to both the Digedags and the Abrafaxe eras, though not interchangeably. When it is necessary to draw distinction between the two for the purposes of analysis, I revert back to the titling employed by Verlag Junge Welt. It should also be noted that Hegenbarth assumed the official title of the comic to be *Mosaik* and, after his departure, sued for use of the word as a recognizably associated and copyrighted aspect of his comic publications.
5. Fulbrook, *People's State*, 5–6.
6. Fulbrook, 235–49.
7. Phil Leask, "Humiliation as a Weapon within the Party: Fictional and Personal Accounts," in *Becoming East German: Socialist Structures and Sensibilities after Hitler*, ed. Mary Fulbrook and Andrew I. Port (New York: Berghahn Books, 2013), 237–56.
8. David Childs, *The GDR: Moscow's German Ally* (New York: Routledge, 2015), 281. See also, Andrew I. Port, *Conflict and Stability in the German Democratic Republic* (Cambridge: Cambridge University Press, 2007), 2–10.
9. Where this notion of the carrot and stick is applied with regard to East German authors, see Patrick Major, *Behind the Berlin Wall: East Germany and the Frontiers of Power* (Oxford: Oxford University Press, 2010), 176–88; in relation to youth and the Free German Youth, see Alan McDougall, *Youth*

Politics in East Germany: The Free German Youth Movement 1946–1968 (Oxford: Clarendon Press, 2004); in relation to East German gender and sexuality, see Josie McLellan, *Love in the Time of Communism: Intimacy and Sexuality in the GDR* (Cambridge: Cambridge University Press, 2011).
10. Fulbrook, *People's State*, 235–49.
11. Peter Grieder, *The German Democratic Republic* (Houndmills: Palgrave, 2012), 5.
12. Port, *Conflict and Stability*, 115.
13. Fulbrook, *People's State*, 4–5.
14. Corey Ross, *Constructing Socialism at the Grass-Roots. The Transformation of East Germany, 1945–65* (Houndmills: Palgrave, 2000), 8–9. See also, Mary Fulbrook, "Putting the People Back In: The Contentious State of GDR History," *German History* 24, no. 4 (November 2006): 618 and Grieder, *German Democratic Republic*, 2–6.
15. Fulbrook, *People's State*, 235–49.
16. Mary Fulbrook, "The Concept of 'Normalisation' and the GDR in Comparative Perspective," in *Power and Society in the GDR 1961–1979: The 'Normalisation of Rule'?* ed. Mary Fulbrook (New York: Berghahn Books, 2009), 1–30.
17. Robert Darnton, *Censors at Work: How States Shaped Literature* (New York: Norton, 2014), 149–227.
18. Paul Betts, *Within Walls: Private Life in the German Democratic Republic* (Oxford: Oxford University Press, 2010), 1–18, 119–47, and 173–92.
19. Michel Foucault, "Discipline and Punish, Panopticism," in *Discipline & Punish: The Birth of the Prison*, ed. Alan Sheridan (New York: Vintage Books, 1977), 195–228.
20. Greg Eghigian, "The Psychologization of the Socialist Self: East German Forensic Psychology and its Deviants, 1945–1975," *German History* 22, no. 2 (2004): 203.
21. Eghigian, "Psychologization," 200–4.
22. Foucault, "Discipline," 195–228.
23. Governmentality and Panopticism form the theoretical backbone of numerous studies of the East German *Alltag* in relation to both the modes of state power and how the population worked within and normalized that power including but not limited to: Betts, *Within Walls*; Donna Harsch, *Revenge of the Domestic: Women, the Family, and Communism in the German Democratic Republic* (Princeton, NJ: Princeton University Press, 2008); McLellan, *Love in the Time of Communism*; Mark McCulloch, "The Sword and Shield of Consumption: The Police-Society Relationship in the Former East Germany," *Past Tense: Graduate Review of History* 1 (2012): 67–83; Port, *Conflict and Stability*; and Judd Stitziel, "Shopping, Sewing, Networking, Complaining: Consumer Culture and the Relationship between State and Society in the GDR," in *Socialist Modern: East German Everyday Culture and Politics*, ed. Katherine Pence and Paul Betts (Ann Arbor: University of Michigan Press, 2008), 253–86.

24. McDougall, *Youth Politics*, 2–5.
25. Fulbrook, *People's State*, 121–28; Anna Saunders, *Honecker's Children: Youth and Patriotism in East(ern) Germany, 1979–2002* (Manchester: Manchester University Press, 2007), 11–13.
26. Konrad H. Jarausch and Michael Geyer, *Shattered Past: Reconstructing German Histories* (Princeton, NJ: Princeton University Press, 2003), 286.
27. Ross, *Constructing Socialism*, 174–75.
28. Jeanette Z. Madarasz, *Conflict and Compromise in East Germany, 1971–1989: A Precarious Stability* (Houndmills: Palgrave, 2003), 62–66; Gaby Thomson-Wohlgemuth, "About Official and Unofficial Addressing in East German Children's Literature," *Children's Literature Association Quarterly* 30, no. 1 (Spring 2005): 34–35; and Gaby Thomson-Wohlgemuth, *Translation under State Control: Books for Young People in the German Democratic Republic* (New York: Routledge, 2009), 1–4. Madarasz approaches this material from the position of the FDJ's mandates in drawing youth into the socialist fold. Meanwhile, Thomson-Wohlgemuth suggests that East German children's literature underwent a period of transformation as the FDJ attempted to raise it to levels enjoyed by adult literature and in keeping with the *Bitterfelder Weg* and tenets of Socialist Realism mapped out by the regime in 1959. However, both meet in the middle to suggest the importance of children's literature published by the FDJ and its educational mandate in the development of the socialist personality and the construction of German socialism given the perceived significance of youth participation to the future of the SED state.
29. Jan Palmowski, "Between Conformity and Eigen-Sinn: New Approaches to GDR History," *German History* 20, no. 4 (2002): 499–500.
30. Wright, *Comic Book Nation*, 1–29.
31. Dorothee Wierling, "Youth as Internal Enemy: Conflicts in the Educational Dictatorship of the 1960s," in *Socialist Modern: East German Everyday Culture and Politics*, ed. Katherine Pence and Paul Betts (Ann Arbor: University of Michigan Press, 2008), 166–73.
32. Roger Sabin, *Comics, Comix & Graphic Novels: A History of Comic Art* (New York: Phaidon Press, 1996), 28.
33. Matthew J. Pustz, *Comic Book Culture: Fanboys and True Believers* (Jackson: University Press of Mississippi, 1999), 155–56. Though Pustz is writing to the American experience, the experience of childhood may be understood as a universal and it is not difficult to imagine East German school children discussing comics before and after class, particularly as the FDJ encouraged connections between comics and the classroom.
34. Günter Gaus, *Wo Deutschland liegt* (Munich: Deutscher Taschenbuch Verlag, 1986).
35. Saunders, *Honecker's Children*, 10.
36. See Betts, *Within Walls*; Karl Christian Führer and Corey Ross, "Mass Media, Culture, and Society in Twentieth-Century Germany: an Introduction," in

Mass Media, Culture, and Society in Twentieth-Century Germany, ed. Karl Christian Führer and Corey Ross (Houndmills: Palgrave, 2006), 1–22; Fulbrook, *People's State*; and Uta G. Poiger, *Jazz, Rock, and Rebels: Cold War Politics and American Culture in a Divided Germany* (Berkeley: University of California Press, 2000); Wierling, "Youth as Internal Enemy," 157–82.

37. Jürgen Habermas, *The Structural Transformation of the Public Sphere: An Inquiry into a Category of Bourgeois Society* (Cambridge, MA: MIT Press, 1991), 175–77.
38. Jürgen Habermas, "The Public Sphere: An Encyclopedia Article (1964)," *New German Critique* no. 3 (Autumn 1974), 49.
39. Habermas, "Public Sphere," 50.
40. For more on the development of the public sphere in a liberal society, closer to that conceptualized by Habermas, existing in the Soviet Bloc and how that public sphere affected the collapse of Soviet-style communism, not only in East Germany but throughout Eastern Europe, see Stephen Kotkin, *Uncivil Society: 1989 and the Implosion of the Communist Establishment* (New York: Modern Library, 2009); Michael Meyer, *The Year That Changed the World: The Untold Story Behind the Fall of the Berlin Wall* (New York: Scribner, 2009); and Mary Elise Sarotte, *1989: The Struggle to Create Post-Cold War Europe* (Princeton, NJ: Princeton University Press, 2009).
41. A "normal" everyday life is here implied to mean the ability to live under the assumption that the state was not always watching or else to act in such a way that practices of self-censorship became normal in and of themselves.
42. Fulbrook, "Concept of 'Normalisation,'" 1–16.
43. Marc Morjé Howard, *The Weakness of Civil Society in Post-Communist Europe* (Cambridge: Cambridge University Press, 2003), 153.
44. Betts, *Within Walls*, 174–75.
45. Leonid Heretz, "Petitions from Peasants," in *From Supplication to Revolution: A Documentary History of Imperial Russia*, ed. Gregory Freeze (Oxford: Oxford University Press, 1988), 170–79. This made the practice of *Eingaben* completely in line with socialist society and the Party line of loyalty and participation of the socialist personality as integral to the continuation of the state.
46. Sheila Fitzpatrick, *Everyday Stalinism: Ordinary Life in Extraordinary Times: Soviet Russia in the 1930s* (Oxford: Oxford University Press, 1999), 175–89.
47. Betts, *Within Walls*, 175.
48. Roland Barthes, *Mythologies*, trans. Richard Howard and Annette Lavers (New York: Hill and Wang, 1957), 58. In "Novels and Children," Barthes argues that the domestic is a space from which men, and thus the state as the masculinized political and public sphere, are absent. Yet, pressure is exerted on the domestic by men on all sides. This suggests that within the domestic, the individual is free, relatively speaking, so long as they acknowledge the authority of the state and their obligations to that authority. Interactions with the state are permitted from within the domestic so long as they are subordinated to those authorities and obligations.

49. Alf Lüdtke, "Wo blieb die 'rote Glut?' Arbeitererfahrungen und deutscher Faschismus," in *Alltagsgeschichte, Zur Rekonstruktion historischer Erfahrungen und Lebensweisen*, ed. Alf Lüdtke (Frankfurt: Campus Verlag, 1989), 224–82; Thomas Lindenberger, "Alltagsgeschichte und ihr möglicher Beitrag zu einer Gesellschaftsgeschichte der DDR," in *Die Grenzen der Diktatur: Staat und Gesellschaft in der DDR*, ed. Richard Bessel and Ralph Jessen (Gottingen: Vandenhoeck & Ruprecht, 1996), 298–325.
50. Konrad H. Jarausch, "Care and Coercion: The GDR as Welfare Dictatorship," in *Dictatorship as Experience: Toward a Socio-Cultural History of the GDR*, ed. Konrad H. Jarausch, trans. Eve Duffy (New York: Berghahn Books, 1999), 47–69 and Port, *Conflict and Stability*, 87–94.
51. Wright, *Comic Book Nation*, 87.
52. Wright, 31. Bradford Wright suggests that at least thirty-five thousand copies of *Superman* were received and read by American GIs every month during World War II. American comics were an identifiable, if not synonymous, part of GI culture during the war. This led to assumptions by European observers of "American immaturity and unsophistication."
53. Indeed, Hegen and members of the Mosaik-Kollektiv were allowed to read, and take home for study, Western comics confiscated at the border. This enabled and encouraged the Kollektiv to draw inspiration and influence from these "harmful" publications. See, Thomas Kramer, "Donald, Asterix and Abrafaxe: Die Verarbeitung amerikanischer und französischer Comic-Serien in den Mosaik-Bildgeschichten der DDR (1955–1990)," in *Kinder- und Jugendliteraturforschung 1999/2000*, ed. Hans-Heino Ewers, Ulrich Nassen, Karin Richter, and Rüdiger Steinlein (Stuttgart: Verlag J.B. Metzler, 2000), 40–66.

CHAPTER 1
Comics and the Crisis of *Kultur* in the SED State

Comic books as a cultural product of the German Democratic Republic arguably began with the adoption of the *Verordnung zum Schutz der Jugend* on 10 April 1955. Similar in function to the French Commission for the Oversight and Control of Publications intended for Children and Adolescents (16 July 1949), the West German Law on the Distribution of Writings Harmful to Young People (9 June 1953), and the British Children's and Young Persons' Harmful Publications Act (6 June 1955), the East German Regulations targeted Western, largely American, comics. These comics were perceived to threaten socialist values and the literary canon that arguably defined Germany's status as a *Kulturstaat* (nation of culture). Unlike the US campaign against comics spearheaded by the crusading Dr. Fredric Wertham and which targeted violent and sexual content in comics as the supposed leading cause of juvenile delinquency, European sentiment rallied around notions of US cultural imperialism and the destruction of national and cultural identities.[1] This was problematic for both halves of divided Germany as each state claimed rightful inheritance of Germany's cultural legacy. Ironically, this also implied that socialist East Germany adopted, at least early on, a bourgeois conceptualization of High and Low Art that was entwined with nineteenth-century perceptions of Germanness and the construction of German nationhood. Despite Germany's own history with comic publications during the Weimar Republic and the longer history of children's publications that were the arguable precursors to the modern comics tradition like *Max und Moritz—Eine Bubengeschichte in Sieben Streichen* (Max and Moritz: a Story of Seven Boyish Pranks) by Wilhelm Busch (1865), both Germanies considered comic books a quintessentially American product. Not only were comics considered lowbrow and read exclusively by children or those adults of limited intelligence, they were also inferior to any form of literature due to the incorporation of images into the text that actively, so the claim was made, hindered literacy.[2] Moreover, and of particular importance in Soviet-controlled East Germany, the comics popular and available in Germany at the time were indicative of capitalist imperialist influence dangerous to the fledgling socialist state.

As was the case with similar laws in Western Europe, the *Verordnung* provided a bulwark against the American and capitalist threat of comic books, restricting or banning the sale and distribution of *Kinderzeitschriften*, comics, and other publications intended for consumption by children. Western children's periodicals already in hand were to be turned over to the local offices of the Volkspolizei (People's Police or Vopo).[3] Through these regulations, the Free German Youth sought to control what children read and to educate those children, fostering the socialist personality among those children in so doing. The FDJ meant to teach children to be socially active citizens. At the same time, those children were to demonstrate a Marxist scientific worldview regarding historical and economic development and social relations appropriate to life under state socialism.[4] The *Verordnung* did not curb children's desire or enthusiasm for comic books nor was that the intention of these laws. Rather, the *Verordnung*, created a void in the reading material available to East German children that publishers, controlled through the FDJ and the Ernst Thälmann Young Pioneers (JP), then filled with their own periodical publications.

Literal days before the SED adopted the *Verordnung*, the state-controlled publishing house Verlag Junge Welt (Young World Publishing) launched the first issue of *Atze*. Verlag Junge Welt already published the children's periodical *Frösi* since 1953 and launched other monthly periodicals, *Bummi* (taking its name from the eponymous yellow teddy-bear featured within the magazine) and *Trommel* (Drum), in 1957 and 1958, respectively. Though these publications regularly contained comic strips, they all published educational and ideological entertainment articles of interest to children, targeting a range of age groups. *Atze*, however, was the first comic magazine published in the German Democratic Republic. An anthology comic featuring different stories and characters, the arguable star of which was the eponymous blond boy from Berlin, created by Jürgen Kieser. Those early issues featured the Atze character in the banner logo, first posing before a brick wall background which was later replaced by a globe more indicative of Atze's adventures. Over the next decade, Atze and his sister explored the far-off year of 1990 to articulate the technological revolution and societal welfare in the GDR, the Soviet Union, and across the Soviet Bloc.[5] Other characters included the well-received Wattfraß, a little black devil (*Teufel*) with electrode horns and a plug at the end of his tail, encouraging energy conservation among the children reading.[6] But as the years passed, these characters occupied increasingly less page space as Verlag Junge Welt introduced more political stories about topics such as the Russian October Revolution (1917), Soviet friendship, and the biographies of socialist heroes and martyrs in addition to adaptations of classic literature of both domestic and foreign origin. *Atze*'s publication, though, was inconsistent at best. Even at a meager eight pages, the comic suffered paper shortages and saw only sporadic publication. Moreover, the quality was questionable. The FDJ criticized the art for experimenting with the latest artistic trends and telling stories with muddied, ineffectual, and wordy language. As far as the FDJ and the Thälmann Pioneers were concerned, the irregularities of *Atze*'s production hindered its ability and, some would suggest, primary task to adequately deliver the educational content necessary of children's periodicals.[7]

Before 1955 was out, the FDJ's publisher Verlag Neues Leben (New Life Publishing) released the first issue of *Mosaik von Hannes Hegen*. This would become a concern later in the decade as Verlag Neues Leben, typically a book publisher and mouthpiece for the FDJ, intended its publications for those youth aged fourteen and older. At the time, and because of the predominance of the "funnies" to the virtual exclusion of other genres in the medium, comics bore the stigma of being intended exclusively for children.[8] Arguably, this is a burden the medium continues to bear. Comics were considered inappropriate reading material once youths aged out of the Thälmann Pioneers, advancing into the ranks of the FDJ.[9] That said, in the mid-1950s, the FDJ's Central Committee sought a competitive voice for comics published in the United States and popular in West Germany, namely those comics published by Walt Disney. When the FDJ instructed the editors at Neues Leben to develop a new comic book publication, it was their intention to create a socialist alternative to Mickey Mouse, calling the imperialist enemy by name.[10] Coincidentally, a young cartoonist by the name of Johannes Hegenbarth, adopting the pen name Hannes Hegen, was developing his own comic characters around the same time. Educated at the University of Applied Arts in Vienna and then the University of Visual Arts Leipzig, Hegenbarth sought a unique style for his creations, finding it in the Donald Duck and Uncle Scrooge comics by Carl Barks and the Marcinelle School in Belgium from which would emerge the popular *Asterix* comics a few years later.[11] The characters created through this fusion of American and European inspiration, Hegenbarth named *die Digedags*.

First appearing in the story "Auf der Jagd nach dem Golde" (On the Hunt for Gold) in December 1955, the FDJ considered the Digedags goblin-like (*die Kobolde*) in appearance. The characters lacked any real origin, emerging from pots brought before a bearded and rotund Shah with a jeweled turban and scimitar stereotypical of Middle Eastern kings of the time. It was not until the post-unification era when Ulf S. Graupner, an artist of the modern run of *Mosaik* comics, created an official origin for the characters in *Mosaik für Hannes Hegen 0: Die Geburt der Digedags* (Mosaic for Hannes Hegen 0: The Birth of the Digedags) for Hegen's sixty-fifth birthday in 1990. With a naming convention that was in no way confusing, the characters Dig, Dag, and Digedag were also physically alike, relatively speaking. Dig was short and stalky with wisps of black hair curling away from the sides of his head. Dag was taller, though by no means the tallest of the trio, with blond hair and a bit of a belly not unlike numerous Disney designs. Digedag, whose name was also shared by the group collectively, was the tallest with red hair, resembling an elongated version of Dag. Not coincidentally, the hair of these characters reflected the East German tricolor as the Digedags were agents of socialism, necessarily bringing their Marxist values on their adventures. Possessed of similar personalities and temperaments, there was never friction between them and, to the outsiders from the FDJ, the only thing differentiating the characters was the shape of their bulbous noses.[12] The FDJ criticized these characters as being unable to develop individual personalities as they were not characters unto themselves but templates (*Typen*).[13] Their first adventures, the *Orient-Südsee-Serie*, were published quarterly and were written and illustrated almost exclusively by Hegen himself. The first twelve issues saw the Digedags transported from the Middle East to the South Seas, and finally delivered to the Roman Empire by issue thirteen. Problematic for the FDJ's publishing regime, this also saw the Digedags rub shoulders with royalty, nobility, and criminals as they attended court and royal balls, fought pirates, and joined the circus. And though the distances travelled from one location to the next, and from one story to the next, made a kind of geographic logic, there were temporal inconsistencies between their fantastic adventures.

This built the idea of travel into the Digedags conceptualization, creating them as adventurers in the same vein as Donald Duck, his Uncle Scrooge, and their nephews Huey, Dewey, and Louie. At the same time, Hegen was allowed the freedom to draw inspiration from those

Figure 1.1. Map of the *Römer-Serie* (November 1958). The map not only described the course of the Digedags' journey through the story, but it also included the magical whirlwind that brought them from the previous narrative arc. This created the illusion of an unbroken narrative despite the Digedags' apparent movement through time. From *Mosaik by Hannes Hegen,* Heft-Nr. 24, © Tessloff Verlag, Nürnberg, Germany.

historical periods and events that were visually stimulating, that were interesting to children, and that were indicative of the Disney stories that influenced them. In this, perhaps, the Digedags were a little too on point as their quests for treasure led them in conceptual pursuit of Barks' Ducks. The *Sammelbände* (collected volumes) "auf der Jagd nach dem Golde" (issues 1–4), "die Rassende Seemühle" (The Frantic Fan-Boat, issues 5–8), and "Aufruhr im Dschungel" (Uproar in the Jungle, issues 9–12) had the Digedags arguably following in Donald's and Scrooge's wake. East German children were aware of the Disney comics available in West Germany and, despite the *Verordnung*, continued to access those comics through the relatively open state of Berlin's zonal borders and the inner-German border between the GDR and the western Federal Republic of Germany (FRG). Given the FDJ's insistence that Verlag Neues Leben create socialist counterparts to those Disney comics, similarities between the Digedags' early stories intentionally resembled the treasure hunting adventures of Disney's Duck characters. As noted elsewhere by Thomas Kramer, the FDJ permitted the creators of *Mosaik* the opportunity to read those confiscated Western comics in order to draw inspiration for their own socialist variations.[14] The cross-pollination of comic influence and ideas was particularly apparent in stories such as "Donald Duck finds Pirate Gold" (Four Color Comics #9, 1942), in which a pirate parrot named Yellow Beak leads Donald and his nephews in a race for treasure against the dastardly Black Pete; and the Uncle Scrooge story "Race to the South Sea" (March of Comics #41, 1949), wherein Scrooge is stranded on a South Seas island and begins running the island as a business while the indigenous people wait on him as servants. Here, Barks's comics created horizontal levels in society without hierarchic order except for the order imposed by money. The society in which the characters lived was one without solidarity, almost entirely defined by competition.[15] Although the central conflicts in *Mosaik's* stories were often not so obviously framed, the comic effectively followed the Ducks demonstrating how the problems of imperialism could be overcome through cooperation, as the Digedags were apt to do. The Digedags' cooperation was also part of the rationale behind the similarities between the characters and their personalities.

Regardless of the FDJ's problems with the comic, *Mosaik* enjoyed almost immediate and overwhelming success. At least compared to its sister publication, JP publisher Verlag Junge Welt's, *Atze*. Of course, *Atze* was not unpopular, but it suffered problems that prevented the publication from meeting the new bar set by *Mosaik*.[16] Launching in December 1955, *Mosaik von Hannes Hegen* introduced East German children, innocuously enough, to the Digedags. Early issues saw *Mosaik* split page space between the adventures of the Digedags and other stories of the "funny animal" genre of comics.[17] These comics emerged from a tradition of anthropomorphized animal cartoons wherein the animalistic characters of the figures were subsumed by oftentimes slapstick humor and the character's own humanity.[18] Disney's stable embodied this trope as the animalistic traits of characters such as Mickey Mouse, Goofy, or Donald Duck rarely, if ever, dominate their performance of humanity and humanness. The Digedags themselves, influenced by Disney as they were, emerged from this comics tradition as their own goblin like appearance and demeanor is ignored by the more realistically rendered characters surrounding them. *Mosaik*'s popularity was not foreseen by Verlag Neues Leben despite the popularity of comics more generally among East German children. Initially appearing on a quarterly publication schedule to allow Hegen the bulk of the responsibilities associated with the comic's production, *Mosaik*'s first issue had a print run of only one hundred fifty thousand copies. This number nearly doubled by the third issue, "die Bimmel-Bummelbahn" (the Ringing-Rambling Train) in June 1956, and by 1957 the publisher created the Mosaik-Kollektiv to publish the comic on a monthly basis beginning in July of that year, much to Hegen's chagrin.[19]

And though the sudden and immediate popularity of *Mosaik* is difficult to explain, it may be the result of Hegen's embrace of the Disney model, the FDJ's tacit endorsement of that model, and *Mosaik*'s own resemblance to the Western *Schmutzliteratur* (filth literature) the publishing regime hoped to avoid. Capitalizing on the popularity of comics in both East and West Germany in the mid-1950s and, supposedly, providing children a socially acceptable alternative to the comics readily available in the Federal Republic, SED ideology played a very small role in early issues of *Mosaik*. Even *Atze*, designed to be superior in its demonstration of ideology, failed to deliver ideology in any real way. In each case, this stemmed from the German perception of the comic book medium itself. Despite Germany's history of comics publications in the 1920s and 1930s, the socialist regime understood comics to be an American medium. The language was considered sloppy, employing the basest slang. The images were thought unclear as to the meaning they depicted, cluttered with speech bubbles as they were.[20] Comics are, after all, a hybrid medium wherein the drawings convey the narrative as much as the written word.[21] This says nothing of the capitalist influence and violence thought inherent to comics.[22] But the medium itself was indicative of childhood and was consequently overlooked by the FDJ and its publishers in terms of comics' educational potential. East German comics bore the medium's stigmas and failed to create themselves as a legitimate alternative to Western comics in any concrete way. *Mosaik* provided counterparts to Mickey Mouse, or more accurately to Donald Duck and Uncle Scrooge, but given the stigmas attached to the medium and the regime's notion that comics were an inferior literary form without educational value, East German comics' ability to deliver the socialist worldview was initially overlooked by those institutions responsible for their creation. As such, preconceived ideas about the comics medium served only to reinforce perceptions of the medium as trashy, pulp, and more importantly, Western literature.[23]

Prior to the formation of the Mosaik-Kollektiv in 1957, Hannes Hegen was largely left to his own devices with those earliest issues of the comic. Despite working with letterers and colorists, Hegen wrote and illustrated the first few issues himself. And though Hegen's name remained on the comic's masthead, the *Kollektiv*, of which Hegen remained an editor and creative voice, was gathered for two reasons. First, Verlag Neues Leben wanted *Mosaik* published on a regular, monthly basis. This could capitalize on the comic's immediate popularity among East German children. A more frequent publication schedule could also address the FDJ's lingering concern over the potential influence of children's periodicals; one that would reappear in the early 1960s as a criticism of *Atze*. Namely, an ongoing comic-story series with regularly appearing characters that was available in shops and at magazine stands at regular intervals, such as a monthly publication cycle, was better able to relay educational information and have that information retained by the readers.[24] Second, the Mosaik-Kollektiv was meant to rein in Hegen's creative voice, despite Hegen delivering the exact Disney-clone demanded by the FDJ in 1955. Prior to the *Kollektiv's* influence on the comic, and even afterward for that matter, *Mosaik* was criticized for its apparent lack of the socialist worldview. Until the proposal for the *Amerika-Serie* passed the JP Central Committee in 1968, *Mosaik* suffered supposed problems of the stories' settings, to say nothing of its perceived (mis)use of history, historical representation, and the Digedags interactions with the past.[25] Under Hegen's guidance, *Mosaik* was a comic about hobnobbing with capitalist-imperialism, falling in with the bourgeoisie to which *Mosaik* supposedly provided an alternative.

The second storyline after the formation of the Mosaik-Kollektiv was the *Weltraum-Serie* started in the December 1958 issue, titled "die Entführung ins All" (the Abduction into Space). As both the FDJ and Verlag Neues Leben hoped, this issue was published according to the comic's new monthly schedule and began a story that was more ideologically aware than previous stories. The *Weltraum-Serie* opens in the Sahara Desert with Dig, Dag, and their travelling companion, Sinus Tangentus—a scientifically-minded Roman named for two of the three main trigonometric functions as though to demonstrate this trait—searching for a crashed meteor.[26] Sinus is tall and scrawny, dressed in robes (stereo)-typical of Roman philosophers, and bald with fine hair in a ring like an olive wreath. Digedag left the group some time earlier to help the circus animals brought with them at the beginning of the *Römer-Serie* (the Roman series) that were threatened by the Emperor. As Dig, Dag, and Sinus search the desert for their crashed meteor, they instead find a puzzling structure which none could identify. Even Sinus, supposedly the most intelligent of the three was at a loss, calling it "a strange architecture! Not Greek, not Babylonian or Assyrian, hmm—I also don't know what to make of it" ("Eine seltsame Arkitektur! Nicht griechisch, nicht babylonisch oder assyrisch, hm—ich weiß auch nicht, was ich davon halten soll.").[27] And being from Imperial Rome, Sinus has no reason to suspect that the structure is a golden rocket ship from the planet Neos, specifically from the *Republikanische Union* (Republican Union). The trio are overcome with their own curiosity and board the rocket, the hatch open and gangplank lowered in anticipation, and are promptly abducted into space as the issue's title suggested.

Among the first things the newly formed Mosaik-Kollektiv did with the characters was to physically remove them from the royal courts and balls that raised the ire of their critics. The Digedags were not in the towns and villages, associating with the working proletariat, but found themselves among the intelligentsia, albeit an alien one, celebrated as the third prong of the East German Workers' and Farmers' State. Unlike the series preceding the *Weltraum-Serie*, launching the Digedags into space allowed *Mosaik* and, through the comic, the FDJ's educational regime to explore the science and technology of space travel and the vastness of space that was gaining traction and appeal in the late 1950s. The Soviet satellite Sputnik 1 launch, effectively setting off the Cold War era Space Race between the Soviet Union and the United States, was a little more than a year before the release of the *Weltraum-Serie's* first issue. The *Weltraum-Serie* provided the *Kollektiv* and the FDJ opportunity to inflect *Mosaik* with the educational, ideological thrust lacking in those earlier stories written by Hegen.

A central conceit of the *Mosaik* series was the Digedags seemingly magical movement through time, if not also through space. Though this concept allowed *Mosaik*'s creator the opportunity to play in the sandbox of historical periods, it also saw him play fast and loose with that history, especially working-class history, which was imperative to the SED and the East German state.[28] As such, *Mosaik* was unable to provide adequate depictions of socialist class struggle, at least in the FDJ's and Verlag Neues Leben's estimation, even though the Digedags travelled with the end goal of broadening the social and historical consciousness of those they met. And because movement between locations both temporal and geographic often occurred mid-issue until the early 1960s, the stories' focus centered on the Digedags' journey rather than the destination, supposedly drawing attention from the comic's socialist outlook. *Mosaik*'s temporal movement dislocated the Digedags from the typical passage of time and story continuity despite the comic's claims to tell an unending and unbroken narrative.[29] In transporting the Digedags through time, the comic adopted aspects of utopian science fiction popularized in the nineteenth century. Utopian fiction found renewed popularity under socialism, not only providing readers with fantastic narratives of the future but catering to the needs of Soviet-style communism demonstrating social advancement and technical and industrial progress that were supposedly possible only through communism. Under Joseph Stalin's rule in the Soviet Union, utopian fiction was characteristically set in the not-too-distant future, inspired by Russian works like Alexander Bogdanov's 1908 novel *Red Star*, giving the impression that the fiction's technological revolution was within reach because of the influence and machinations of communism.[30] Though *Mosaik* rejected the "close aim" fiction of Stalin's Russia, travelling across centuries by magical whirlwind between the *Orient-Südsee-Serie* and the *Römer-Serie* (issues 13–24, 1957–1958) to maintain their unbroken narrative thread, the Digedags were both spectators to their new location(s), unable or unwilling to affect change, and the story's protagonist upon whom change depended.

This dual status of the Digedags seems contradictory, though that is not the case. Borrowing elements of utopian fiction narratives, *Mosaik* posited the Digedags as being removed from the environs of their own stories. As a result, they became the flaneurs of that utopian fiction. Utopian fiction as a genre was often characterized by the protagonist being thrust forward in time through, relatively, inexplicable means. Once there, that protagonist would experience an idyllic future made possible through socialism, not unlike the adventure undertaken in Soviet author Innokenty Zhukov's 1924 *Voyage of the Red Star Pioneer Troop to Wonderland*; a form later adopted in the mid-1980s in East German cartoonist Erich Schmitt's *Ein Planet wird gesucht*. In this style of science fiction, the protagonist is often unwilling to act to avoid creating a temporal paradox or otherwise fundamentally altering the visited utopia.[31] In the case of the Digedags, however, the characters are spectators, wanderers, flaneurs, conveying to the reader the conditions of the society in which they find themselves, whether that be a South Sea island, the Middle East, the Roman Empire, or alien socialist utopia. Befriending characters local to the story-location and well informed in the workings of that society, the Digedags were provided information valuable to help the stories' people and societies. This plot device also conveyed important socialist educational content to the readers, which was then the point of East German comics as a product of the state. Nonetheless, the FDJ's publishing regime was critical of Mosaik creator Hannes Hegen's approach to the comic's historical content.[32]

And while the Weltraum-Serie focused on the light-hearted entertainment that defined the series to that point, not to suggest the FDJ's political agenda was entirely absent in those earlier issues, it was much more invested in providing readers with "textbook like" explanations of the science of space and space travel and thus of the modernity that arguably defined East German socialism. Moreover, the technology and perspectives employed by the aliens from Neos, who appeared human and were themselves fascinated by how alike Sinus and the Digedags were to them physically, the Digedags' goblin-like appearance notwithstanding, was similar to or extrapolated from that used in the GDR.[33] Part of this emerged from the dictates set forth in the utopian fiction of Stalin's Soviet Union. Stalinism equally influenced aspects of East German political and social culture as many of those in the SED leadership came from this Stalinist mold, including Party leader Walter Ulbricht. But Stalinist "close aim" utopian (science) fiction projected an air of possibility through Soviet-style communism. Emerging from the Socialist Realist style of artistic representation already the norm in the USSR, "close aim" science fiction was located in a near future recognizable to the reader, using technological innovations not far removed from those already available and in use in the Soviet Union, then later in the Soviet Bloc following World War II.[34] The idea demonstrated socialism's perceived superiority to capitalism, to show how technology improved society for all, and to impress upon the reader that the future far surpassed competition of Western capitalist-imperialism and was almost, if not already, here. At the same time, incorporating these aspects of "close aim" science fiction changed the shape of the Digedags' adventures, stripping away some, though by no means all, of the more fantastical elements preferred by Hegen to the omnipresence of socialist ideology.

Mosaik often touted itself as a single, unbroken narrative. And, until the conclusion of the *Weltraum-Serie* in 1962, this is arguably the case. However, movement from one story to the next and the Digedags' unexplained ability to move between time periods was reworked and, with the *Weltraum-Serie*, grounded in comic book logic and science. The adventure begins in what is suggested to be the nineteenth-century Ottoman Empire, though this remains unclear and disputed, and, after journeying by various means to pirate ships and islands in the South Seas, the Digedags are scooped up in a magical whirlwind and deposited in Ancient Rome. The *Weltraum-Serie* and the rocket encountered by the Digedags transformed the magical explanation for their movement into something plausible, certainly more so after Sputnik's success the previous year. And in the midst of the *Weltraum-Serie*'s publication and the Digedags exploration of the stars, three events unrelated to the comic, and arguably unrelated to East German children's literature generally, proved fundamental in shaping the content and perception of both *Mosaik von Hannes Hegen* and *Atze*.

At the SED's Fifth Party Congress in 1958, the development of the socialist personality was adopted as a core objective of East German education. Regarding the upbringing and education of children under socialism, it was imperative that children develop a perspective with comprehensive knowledge of economic and social conditions and express strong feelings toward the progress of humanity toward socialism and communism.[35] The socialist personality was dedicated to the construction of socialism, possessing the highest morality and socialist scientific worldview.[36] This notion was itself derived from a speech delivered and developed by Bolshevik Party leader Vladimir Ilyich Lenin at the Third Komsomol Congress in 1920, planting the basic idea for the education of a new communist generation.[37] At that same Congress, Anatoly Lunacharsky, the Bolshevik People's Commissar for Education, suggested "students must learn to make their lives collectively . . . to feel with the interests of the entire Soviet people." It was, in essence, necessary to organize children with "gestures" of solidarity, involving them in the working-class struggle through formal aspects of a socialist education system and also during moments left unorganized and uncontrolled by the state through publishing, newspapers, magazines, books, and comics for children.[38] After Erich Honecker ascended to the position of SED General Secretary, he reiterated the importance of the socialist personality, making it the Party's principal task at the Eighth SED Party Congress in 1971.[39]

But with the development of the socialist personality among children and youth already a matter of Party policy in the late 1950s, in April 1959 the Mitteldeutscher Verlag (Central German Publishing House) held an authors' conference in the electrochemical combine of Bitterfeld in the central East German district (*Bezirke*) of Halle, present-day Saxony-Anhalt.[40] In many ways, the course adopted at this conference mirrored developments in the Soviet Union's art scene of the early 1930s. Coming to be called the *Bitterfelder Weg* (Socialist Realism, from the Soviet example), it was adopted with the intention of its implementation as the leading style across the East German art community, including film, painting, sculpture, and, of course, literature. Stylistically, Socialist Realism collapsed the distance between the intelligentsia and proletariat, bringing art into the factories and the shop floors. Ideally, Socialist Realism clearly conveyed its subject matter to a lay audience. This was done without abstraction or expressionism as both forms were considered the artistic mannerisms of the bourgeoisie that kept High Culture inaccessible to the proletariat. Much of the content of Socialist Realist art described and celebrated the working class and their experience in socialist society which, in turn, maintained the ideological course of the SED and, nominally, the entire Soviet Bloc. This was of particular importance in children's media and entertainment, literature and film included, and in depictions of children's role as socialist citizen and their obligation to the state. Like those aspects of the utopian "close aim" fiction influencing the *Weltraum-Serie* the year before, Socialist Realism charted history in an ever upward societal trajectory, filled with moral optimism, celebrating the achievements of the present and the promise of the (socialist) future.[41]

And like the French Commission for the Oversight and Control of Publications intended for Children and Adolescents, West Germany's Law on the Distribution of Writings Harmful to Young People, and even England's Children's and Young Persons' Harmful Publications Act, the GDR's *Verordnung zum Schutz der Jugend* drew a distinction between bourgeois concepts of High and Low Culture, of which comic books and publications dependent upon pictures were considered lowbrow culture. The *Verordnung*, prior to the introduction of comics produced by the FDJ and its publishers, underscored comics' immorality and their lack of educational content to curb the spread of American capitalism. But even after the *Verordnung*'s implementation and the FDJ and the JP's relative success monitoring the reading material of East German children, the socialist alternative provided by *Mosaik von Hannes Hegen* and *Atze* was only nominally socialist. More often, these comics were derivative of the same Western publications against which they supposedly defined themselves. Before the end of the 1950s, comics were not held to the same standard as other areas of East German children's publishing as the FDJ developed a distinctive socialist *Kinderkultur* (children's culture).

Particularly after the implementation of the *Bitterfelder Weg* emphasized the importance of the socialist personality, the East German publishing regime sought to increase the visibility and status of children's literature throughout the Soviet Bloc and across the globe. That being the case, it was perhaps of greater importance that the value of this emerging children's literature be recognized by the SED state's most obvious and direct competitor in all things: the West German Federal Republic. It was thus unsurprising that the GDR was the first German state to seriously invest in children's literature as an art form with both the ability and obligation to mold East German children into the child-citizens required of state-socialism, educating and entertaining while providing children with intellectual challenge and stimulation. The developing children's literature was recognized for its ability to transmit ideological beliefs to the next generation, but also its commitment to "mirror national progress," acting in parallel with the state's Socialist Realist literature for adult readers. The emerging literature glorified themes of socialist heroism, turning to antifascism and antiwar as Cold War tensions with the Federal Republic and the United States increased and the West German state became the perceived inheritor of the Nazi legacy.[42] And though content for these children's books was controlled by the FDJ, Verlag Neues Leben, and the SED generally, active support for the production and authorship of content for children led to the development of a children's literature that was "officially committed to high artistic standards, humanism, internationalism, and a sense of class duty" difficult to come by elsewhere.[43] The *Bitterfelder Weg* blurred the distinction between what was considered to be High and Low Culture and constructed a proletarian literary culture as had arguably been the case in the Soviet Union following the adoption of Socialist Realism. As a result, the value assigned to the developing *Kinderkultur* ensured this working-class culture would be, with no sense of irony so far as children were concerned, High Culture.

As the SED state, not unlike the Federal Republic, considered itself a *Kulturstaat* and the inheritor of German literary and musical canons including the likes of Fontane, Goethe, Beethoven, and Mozart (defining German broadly enough to include Austria), not to mention those of

Russian and Soviet origin such as Tolstoy and Gorky given the Party's attachment to Moscow and Soviet-style communism, the FDJ insisted that East Germany's best and brightest artists and writers draw from these sources of *Kultur* to create a new, socialist literary canon directed toward youth "in the service of life, freedom, and progress."[44] The works produced in this new canon were, in many cases, masterstrokes of socialist literature. Problematically, the FDJ's goals with this new literature, shared by the writers hired to create this burgeoning *Kinderkultur*, were numerous. This new *Kinderkultur* was intended to create art that employed the themes and objectives of the East German youth group and educational regime to develop the new socialist personality among children and prepare them as citizens in the socialist state. At the same time, these artists sought to create literary art that could be enjoyed by children and adults alike. It was important that these new works stand on the shoulders of those earlier artistic giants so the new children's canon would be celebrated globally, and it was, cementing East Germany's role as a *Kulturstaat* and its perceived superiority in artistry on the world stage. Given the inevitable competition between East and West Germany, children's literature was a source of pride for the regime, especially because the Federal Republic had yet to make significant strides toward a *Kinderkultur* of its own.[45] The FDJ's insistence on children's literature as part of the new literary canon, produced works that were celebrated and technically masterful. They embraced bourgeois notions of High Culture but oftentimes were too advanced for their intended audience—the East German children for whom this *Kinderkultur* was supposedly developed in the first place.[46]

Despite the implementation of the *Bitterfelder Weg* allowing for the emergence of this *Kinderkultur*, regardless of the actual popularity of these works with children, and the imposition of the *Verordnung* four years earlier, Western comics and those produced in East Germany that drew their inspiration from the same were of more pressing concern for the SED and the FDJ at the end of the 1950s. These comics, *Mosaik von Hannes Hegen* in particular because *Atze's* relative influence was largely ignored until the middle of the following decade, posed a danger to the development of East Germany's *Kinderkultur*. The FDJ continued to perceive Western comics as counterrevolutionary. The violence these publications contained was blamed for the rise in youth crime and delinquency throughout the 1950s. Comics supposedly engendered militarism and imperialism among East German children and were weapons of Western governmental authority, poisoning youth against socialism.[47] Indeed, the 1957 DEFA children's film *Sheriff Teddy* by director Heiner Carow, based on the book by Benno Pludra, makes explicit this association between Western comics and criminality. The film's young protagonist, Kalle, receives Western comics from a delinquent older brother residing in West Berlin. Kalle's father, his teacher, and his friends refer to these publications as *Schmöker*, trashy books, subversive, and akin to a disease upon the body of East German socialist society.[48] While these arguments were grounded in socialist language and thought, the FDJ's approach to both Western comics and its own comics reflected the attitudes of larger discussions surrounding the supposed problematic nature of comic books in the 1940s and 1950s.

Beyond arguments against depictions of sex in comics during the postwar period, Fredric Wertham argued the violence and horror prevalent in American comics led to an increase in juvenile delinquency.[49] Wertham did not create facts in this instance, but the causal relationship between postwar delinquency and comics was grossly overstated. Every child in the immediate postwar period grew up reading comics such as *Action Comics*, *Tales from the Crypt*, and *Donald Duck*. This being the case, necessarily those accused of delinquency also read comics. The US campaign culminated in the creation of the Comics Code Authority (CCA) in 1954 as an industry self-regulatory body to prevent government-imposed laws and restrictions. Wertham's attacks ignored the prevalence of newspaper and magazine published comic strips like *Little Orphan Annie* and, regardless, the CCA wielded no authority over those strips. But the CCA neutered most comic book genres, superheroes included, killing off the crime and horror genres for decades to come. That being the case, Disney comics publisher Dell refused to participate and was thus left relatively unscathed.[50] While the conjecture of Wertham and contemporary moralistic crusaders in the United States permeated Western European thought, the European variety of the 1950s anti-comics campaign leaned on arguments of Americanization and US cultural imperialism. The implementation of laws and advisory bodies in England, France, and West Germany between the late 1940s and mid-1950s, with responsibilities like those of East Germany's *Verordnung*, approached questions of comics as a cultural force and their effects on youth development and national culture.[51] Similar arguments regarding the harmful effects of (American) comics to national culture emerged from Mexico and Latin America around the same time.[52]

Responding to the dangers posed by Western comics despite the enforcement of the 1955 *Verordnung* in late June 1959, Robert Lehmann, Chairman of the Thälmann Pioneers, made a request of the FDJ's Central Committee. Because *Mosaik* was aimed at a younger audience, Lehmann asked that the comic be handled by editors experienced with newspaper and magazine publications for children so as to influence and intensify the comic's socialist educational content. That said, Lehmann's letter read, "*Mosaik* as a magazine that appears mainly for children," indicating that, by the end of the 1950s at least, the comic's readership grew beyond its initial target audience.[53] Lehmann's suggestion, as it was approved by the FDJ, was to have the existing contract(s) between the FDJ's publisher Verlag Neues Leben, Johannes Hegenbarth, his wife Edith Hegenbarth, and Lothar Dräger as the leading members of the Mosaik-Kollektiv, cancelled at the end of the year (1959) and the comic's publication transferred to the JP publisher Verlag Junge Welt.[54] There, *Mosaik von Hannes Hegen* would find a home alongside other children's publications including *Frösi*, *Bummi*, and East Germany's second most popular comic, *Atze*. However, because *Mosaik* was now controlled by those with experience editing such publications and who subscribed to the *Bitterfelder Weg* from the previous year, the JP and the editors scrutinized the comic for which they were now responsible. Not only did they criticize *Mosaik*'s content, which was insufficient in its representation of socialist values despite a renewed focus on that ideology and education since the *Weltraum-Serie* in 1958, but they argued that the stories in *Mosaik* ran contrary to socialism and the *Kinderkultur* under development in other areas of East Germany's publishing and entertainment production.[55]

In this, *Mosaik*, and later *Atze*, was considered too Western, too American, for East German children. The comic threatened the development of the reader's socialist personality because of its relative freewheeling representation of history. In its effort to create an unbroken narrative, *Mosaik* suggested that time was something of a nonlinear space through which the Digedags travelled freely and without explanation. Until 1960 when Verlag Junge Welt became responsible for the comic's production, travel between the stories and the time periods in which those stories were set was often conducted via magic, a convenient though entirely out-of-place rocket ship, or other means to continue the narrative without long-winded or logical and scientific explanations of how, exactly, the Digedags moved so easily from the Ottoman Empire, to the Roman Empire, to a futuristic outer-space setting. Although the Digedags' travel between temporal and geographic spaces continued following the conclusion of the *Weltraum-Serie* in 1962, that which gave the comic the appearance of an unbroken narrative was removed. When Dig and Dag appear in the latter half of the *Erfinder-Serie* (Inventor Series), the first half of which featured the solo adventures of Digedag and appeared in alternating issues of *Mosaik* alongside the *Weltraum-Serie*, they are aboard a cargo ship arriving at a Spanish port in Peru during the summer of 1819. The return journey to Earth and how, exactly, the Digedags found themselves aboard this ship is ignored by the Mosaik-Kollektiv as the protagonists returned home, concluding the *Weltraum-Serie* in the final panel of the previous issue (Figure 1.2), via a two-seat rocket and the apparent favorable alignment of planets that made their voyage possible. Although the Digedags retained their apparent ability to travel through time, the act itself is largely ignored so the writers could focus on accurate historical depictions over convoluted or contrived explanations of Dig and Dag's arrival. New locations were introduced through text-boxes, setting the story to avoid reader confusion, and eliminating the perceived magic of movement in favor of (Marxist) historical accuracy.[56]

Despite the problems of the Digedags' movement to socialist ideology and the importance of accurate historical representation in Marxist and educational terms, this proved no less a problem for Verlag Junge Welt and the Thälmann Pioneers, serving as *Mosaik's* editorial board, than were the underpinnings of the comics medium itself. As part of the interplay between image and text that defines comics and differentiates them from the sum of their parts, North American and European comics often display text in narrative boxes and, more pronounced, in the dialogue balloons indicative of the medium. Problematically, the FDJ, the Thälmann Pioneers, and their respective children's publishers associated these dialogue balloons with the Americanization of the medium, and thus the *Schmutzliteratur* against which East German *Kinderkultur* bulwarked.

Comics were constantly accused of using poor grammar and the basest slang, not only in the GDR but in Western Europe and North America despite the use of comics as reading primers in the late nineteenth and early twentieth centuries.[57] Arguably, comics' association with the working class as a medium directed toward them, the interplay of word and image ensuring one's ability to comprehend comics' meaning(s) despite workers' uneven levels of literacy at the dawn of the twentieth century, hindered the medium's ability to penetrate middle-class notions of literature and High Art.[58] Comics were available at train stations and magazine vendors so workers could read them during their commute and dispose of them when finished. But regardless of these early associations with the working class, German socialists adopted bourgeois notions of High and Low Art and, in so doing, dismissed those same comics that they considered aimed at either children, the uneducated, or the uncultured.[59] The predominance of comic books in Germany and their ready availability since the end of World War II, conflated the comics medium with the occupying American soldiers in the minds of many Germans, not incorrectly.[60] In 1960, however, *Mosaik von Hannes Hegen* came under the editorial control of the Thälmann Pioneers, Verlag Junge Welt, and Hans Erhardt as Editor-in-Chief, further diminishing Hegen's sway over his own creation. These editorial bodies argued that not only did comics, *Mosaik* included, employ poor language that obstructed children's education and comprehension, the use of these dialogue balloons, long a staple of the medium, cluttered the illustrations and rendered many of them incomprehensible. By the time the final issue of the *Weltraum-Serie* was published in December 1962, and as *Mosaik* welcomed its new Editor-in-Chief, Wolfgang Altenburger, text was removed from the images completely. Instead, narration and dialogue appeared beneath the images, undermining the uniqueness of the comics medium compared to other forms of storytelling.

In his seminal 1985 textbook on the subject, *Comics & Sequential Art: Principles & Practices of the World's Most Popular Art Form*, legendary comics creator Will Eisner coined the term "sequential art" to describe the form and function of the images inherent to the comics medium.[61] Eight years later, Scott McCloud, imperfectly though no less significantly, expanded upon Eisner suggesting that comics are "juxtaposed images in a deliberate sequence to convey information and produce an aesthetic response in the viewer."[62] Though only Eisner points to the importance of dialogue balloons as a marker of time's passage within a comic narrative, both agree that the comics can be read completely without text. However, the Mosaik-Kollektiv and Verlag Junge Welt did not just move this text to the margins of the images, as it were, they inflated the amount of information conveyed in these text blocks. The narration included dialogue between the characters and explanations of the characters and their actions. By the end of the *Weltraum-Serie*, as the Digedags' companions bid them farewell and a safe return journey to Earth, the page is dominated by a text-wall encompassing nearly a third of the page.[63] The back cover is no better as a half page of text explains an image of prehistoric hunters on the European plains, largely in Southern France, Spain, and Czechoslovakia.[64] Descriptions of the action and dialogue neglected and negated the importance of the images as part of the storytelling in a comic narrative, especially of having Eisner's "sequential art" that could indeed be read without that text at all. Here, then, as the publishers and the FDJ attempted to devise a socialist-style comic that clearly conveyed the FDJ's educational man-

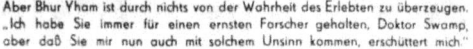

Figure 1.2. "In Grauer Zeit" (In the Stone Age) (December 1962): 23. Dig and Dag are sent back to Earth in a small rocket. From *Mosaik* by Hannes Hegen, Heft-Nr. 73, © Tessloff Verlag, Nürnberg, Germany.

dates within the development of East Germany's unique *Kinderkultur* and of the socialist personality, *Mosaik's* editors focused on the wrong aspects of the comic medium. East German comics were transformed into a kind of picture book where images were not integral story-telling devices but mere embellishments to the text printed below.

Although this deconstructed the uniqueness of the comic book medium and its interdependency of word and image, the transformation of East German comics spoke to longer traditions of the form in Germany. Wilhelm Busch's *Max and Moritz: A Story of Seven Boyish Pranks* (1865) is an illustrated story, not unlike a picture book, told in rhyming couplet verse. Much like Heinrich Hoffmann's *Struwwelpeter* (Shock-Headed Peter) published twenty years earlier, Busch's story used black humor and morbid satire to teach children the value of good behavior. *Max and Moritz* is often considered a forerunner to the modern comics medium given its propensity toward sequential images demonstrating aspects of the story, such as the visual appearance of the characters and their locales, not present in the accompanying text. The book is the direct influence of German-American comic artist Rudolph Dirks's popular comic strip *The Katzenjammer Kids*, first appearing in the *New York Journal* in 1897 following *New York World's* immediate success with *Down in Hogan's Alley* (colloquially referred to as *The Yellow Kid*) two years prior, arguably responsible for modern perceptions of the comic strip and its inclusion in newspaper publications. Though perhaps lesser known, *Max and Moritz* was also the basis of *Quick et Flupke, gamins de Bruxelles* (The Exploits of Quick and Flupke, 1930–1940) by Belgian cartoonist Hergé of *Les Aventures de Tintin* (The Adventures of Tintin) fame.[65]

Importantly, *Max and Moritz* spoke to the notions of German culture upon which the SED staked its claims as a *Kulturstaat* and its developing *Kinderkultur*. As noted, comics were often associated with the United States and the perceived Americanization of Europe, particularly in the Western zones of occupation, although this did not exclude the Soviet zone (also known in German as *die Ostzone* [Eastern Zone] or simply and derisively as *die Zone*). While the comic book itself was supposedly foreign to Germany and German culture, *Max and Moritz* as the German precursor to comics, and even books like *Struwwelpeter* for that matter, drew on a moral compass similar to the Grimm Fairy Tales.[66] And while reading material dependent upon pictures for meaning was considered inferior to the German literary canon, the works of the Brothers Grimm were notable within that canon. Of course, Grimm Fairy Tales, filled to bursting with royalty and magic, were somewhat difficult to reconcile with the working-class aesthetic of Socialist Realism and the insistence on collective solutions over individual exceptionalism (another reason why superhero comics as a genre failed to emerge in the GDR). Likewise, the Grimm tales were retold and retranslated so often prior to their publication they invariably picked up some traits of bourgeois life.[67] Nonetheless, fairy tales proved extremely popular in the GDR and provided material for hundreds of live action and animated children's films produced by both DEFA Babelsberg and DEFA Studio für Trickfilme Dresden (Animated Film Studio Dresden) with varying degrees of modification to suit the state's socialist climate.[68]

The new visual style for *Mosaik*, at least insofar as how text and dialogue were represented on the printed page, drew from *Max and Moritz* which itself borrowed thematically from the canonical works of the Brothers Grimm. This (dis)association between image and text provided comics published in the GDR with a sense of legitimacy given their indirect association with that canon. One simple change to its appearance and *Mosaik* no longer echoed Americanism and *Schmutzliteratur*. Instead, the image over text design of *Mosaik* drew from the visual storytelling of *Max and Moritz* and *Struwwelpeter* and, most important for SED claims to East German legitimacy and its legacy as a *Kulturstaat*, was indicative of an historically German form of children's literature and the sense of historic national identification and belonging with which it was associated. In doing this, John D. Benjamin suggests that the publisher and the FDJ set about the creation of a uniquely East German and socialist comics tradition independent of that in the West.[69] Problematically, though, this was mere window dressing. Beyond superficial changes to narrative text and dialogue that gave *Mosaik* the appearance of those nineteenth-century children's books, little else about East German comics changed until after Wolfgang Altenburger's appointment as Editor-in-Chief of *Atze* and *Mosaik*.

By 1961, the number of citizens fleeing the East German state (*Republikflucht*) reached critical levels. Since the end of World War II and the division of Germany into four occupation zones in August 1945, the SBZ was subject to increasing restrictions as the Soviet Military Administration in Germany implemented policy in conjunction with Walter Ulbricht's German Communist Party to Sovietize the *Ostzone*. This policy only accelerated after the merger of the KPD and the SPD, becoming the Socialist Unity Party in 1946, and the foundation of the German Democratic Republic three years later.[70] Throughout the late 1940s and 1950s, many Germans living in East Berlin and along Germany's inner-border regions worked in the West for significantly higher wages and consumer choice while taking up residence in the East, enjoying government subsidies on housing rentals, staple foodstuffs, and essential services. However, Germans increasingly chose to leave the GDR entirely for the perceived brighter future and the supposed abundance offered by this idealized "golden" West. This said nothing of those who fled the political persecution of the SED and their Soviet-trained secret police. In 1950, more than one hundred eighty thousand East German citizens moved to the West. Following the failed uprising in June 1953, fears of further border closure and police crackdowns drove this number well past three hundred thirty thousand. By the end of the 1950s, and despite the Soviets' official closure of the inner-German border in 1952, three and a half million East Germans fled to the West, most of these through the "escape hatch" provided by Berlin's anomalous status as a Western presence in the heart of the GDR. This number represented approximately 20 percent of East Germany's overall population. More important, those leaving for that better life in the FRG were the best and brightest East German youth, creating significant gaps in East Germany's labor force and the state's postwar recovery and socialist development.[71]

Beginning construction in the early morning hours of 13 August 1961, the Berlin Wall effectively plugged the gap in East Germany's border, largely though not entirely stemming the tide of East-West migration. The Wall fixed the East German population in place, allowing the FDJ a freer hand in the education and socialization of East German children.[72] Despite the 1955 *Verordnung zum Schutz der Jugend* and its ban on the possession and sale of Western children's periodicals in the territories of the GDR, the lack of any real and concrete border regulations in Berlin still allowed East German children to buy Western comics without harassment. Though this may be something of a generalization, the lack of border checks prior to the Berlin Wall's construction made accessible the consumption of West German and American culture by East Germans. Children purchasing banned comics in West German shops, taking them home to East Germany or East Berlin, is comparable to examples of youth crossing those same borders to watch Western films in nearby theaters or the appearance of a black market along Berlin's inner border for reasons of sector authorities and jurisdictions.[73] That said, given Berlin's special status in the emerging postwar division, the *Verordnung* was an imperfect means of staunching comics' perceived capitalist influence and their supposed harmful effects on the education of East German youth. Just as the Berlin Wall halted the *Republikflucht* threatening East German society, so too did it halt the cross-border cultural consumption that proved of equal threat.

Comics thus allowed the SED state the means to connect socialist education and schooling with the everyday lived experience of children. The Berlin Wall's existence suddenly, though imperfectly, provided for comics produced in the GDR to align with FDJ principles without the competition from Western influence. The accompanying ideological content of those Eastern comics allowed for socialization outside the classroom, relocating that socialization to the parental home which often proved a point of authority for children contrary to the Party line.[74] Moreover, membership within the Thälmann Pioneers was near universal and "inextricably intertwined" between education and socialization, organized around schooling and never separated from that educational imperative as many teachers were themselves youth group leaders.[75] As such, Pioneer work and activities focused on organizing the child's free time and holidays where children were "most likely to stray from the influence of the state," including home life, what children chose to read, and what reading material was available to them. This served to disallow a clearly defined separation between schooling, state-structured organizations like the JP, and the child's perceived free time.[76] Children and educators were encouraged to discuss the contents of the comics published by Verlag Junge Welt, both in class and in their JP meetings. Arguably, this provided the state with an indirect means of monitoring educators and JP leaders as children were equally encouraged to write to the publishers regarding their classroom and youth group activities.[77] This was not as much an issue for the Free German Youth as the state directed comics at nine to sixteen-year-old children, believing that children would outgrow those comics by the time they transitioned to the FDJ and to (young) adulthood.[78] Nonetheless, the FDJ, the Thälmann Pioneers, and the publisher made concerted efforts in the Berlin Wall's immediate shadow to bring together classroom educational experiences and the daily lives of the children they hoped to influence, largely through the development of East Germany's *Kinderkultur*. And here, comics were included as part of this new *Kultur*, beyond its transformative relationship with *Max and Moritz* and the Brothers Grimm, accessible to those children for whom the concepts and execution of East Germany's burgeoning children's literature proved too advanced. Of course, despite the existence of the Berlin Wall, comics were an imperfect ideological vehicle and continued to provide obstacles to the development of the socialist personality.

Following the Berlin Wall's construction and tightening connections between East German comics and the educational regime, *Mosaik* continued in a form that was not obviously ideological. Although the comic incorporated increasingly ideological elements with the advent of the *Weltraum-Serie*, a trend continuing as the story transitioned into the *Erfinder-Serie* in 1962, embracing mankind's scientific achievements and the ever upward social progress that was hallmark of the "close aim" utopian fiction from which *Mosaik* increasingly drew inspiration, it was equally given a relative permissiveness among children's publications. The *Bitterfelder Weg* insisted that Socialist Realism be the dominant mode of artistic expression in the GDR. Meanwhile, the SED Fifth Party Congress made the development of the socialist personality the core mandate of the FDJ's educational regime and likewise the central requirement of children's publications. Moreover, the Berlin Wall provided Verlag Junge Welt a captive audience for the comics they published. This should have led to a repressiveness surrounding *Mosaik*'s contents, their obvious connectedness to school subjects as the *Weltraum-Serie* most definitely was, and the appearance of a heavy-handed political-mindedness in the storytelling. However, as much security as the Berlin Wall provided by fixing the East German population, children included, the Berlin Wall was equally responsible for *Mosaik*'s arguable ability to stretch the bounds of acceptability in what was depicted in comics and *Kinderkultur* more broadly.

The Berlin Wall had little to no effect on *Mosaik*'s popularity. Indeed, until the fall of the Wall in November 1989 and the subsequent (re)unification of East and West the following October, *Mosaik*'s circulation only increased. What began with one hundred fifty thousand copies for its first issue, doubling two issues later, reached almost one million issues monthly by the mid-1980s.[79] But the Berlin Wall did affect East German youth, if not yet the children reading *Mosaik* and *Atze*. More than merely preventing East German citizens from defecting to the West, the Berlin Wall affected the ways teenagers and young adults consumed Western and West German culture. The previously open border allowed easy and unregulated movement of youth from East to West to attend a number of cultural events with perhaps movies being among the most popular and most important to easily spread Western culture.[80] As described elsewhere by Uta Poiger, the sudden shift in the patterns of youth, here meaning their movement, hangouts, the types of media, entertainment, information, and how youth consumed those cultural outputs, disillusioned an entire young generation against the SED and the East German state.[81] In 1963, after Party Secretary Walter Ulbricht failed to convince Erich Honecker, Ulbricht's protégé in charge of youth policy at the time, of the need to liberalize that policy, Ulbricht dissolved the Politburo's Youth Commission, reforming it with Party newcomer Kurt Turba at the helm.[82] The new policy direction that emerged from Ulbricht's own ideas about youth in the Berlin Wall's shadow, the new restrictions to their movement, and the newly formed Youth Commission was encapsulated by Ulbricht's address, "Youth of Today—Masters of Tomorrow. Trust and Responsibility for Youth," more commonly referred to as Ulbricht's Youth Communiqué.

The Communiqué was meant to mobilize youth in socialist society, to win back those disgruntled by the construction of the Berlin Wall and heal their disassociation from the Party and from their roles and responsibilities as GDR citizens. The address stressed the GDR society's need to modernize. The Party needed to mobilize youth to achieve this modernization, to successfully encourage youth to return to the tenets of socialism as the foundation of the East German state itself, to have those youth take up their positions in society in an active and consensual way. But to win back youth, the Party was required to grant youth an unprecedented, at the time, degree of freedom in society. This does not imply the same tacit relationship between citizen and state that existed under Honecker after 1971 with the relative toleration of the citizenship's privacy. Under Ulbricht, liberalization was intended to foster youth's genuine enthusiasm for state socialism and Soviet-style communism. The newfound freedom with which this was associated was arguably more than rhetoric on paper. But still, liberalization under Ulbricht's rule came with the caveat that such freedom required discretion.[83] Ulbricht's Communiqué inspired open expression among youth, from the relative openness and air of criticism in DEFA films of the early 1960s to the apparent acceptability of guitar bands, rock and roll, and beat culture.[84] And while these ideas and expressions were home-grown in the East, they originated in the West, undermining state sanctioned music and style, including the *Bitterfelder Weg's* Socialist Realism.

For comic book publications, the period of relaxation ushered in by the Youth Communiqué had little effect. The changes rendered to *Mosaik* during the *Weltraum-Serie* and the subsequent *Erfinder-Serie* continued. The walls of narrative text exiled beyond the illustrated panels and evocative of that nineteenth-century comic-style storytelling persisted. And though the stories retained the socialist slant introduced earlier, this was largely due to the influence of the Digedags themselves as the ambassadors of socialism throughout their adventures. Regardless of the intentions and motivations of the supporting cast they encountered, following changes made to the Digedags around the beginning of the *Weltraum-Serie*, the Digedags acted collectively, avoiding imperialist violence as an acceptable solution to problems in children's publications.[85] The locales and characters populating the comic's settings, though, slipped back into earlier patterns established in the *Orient-Südsee-Serie* and the *Römer-Serie*. In this, the Digedags associated not nearly as much with craftsmen in villages or farmers on the land with whom the readers were expected to identify as they did with the nobility, the Sultans, and Emperors, regardless of the perceived socialist intentions of the Digedags or the intentions of the Mosaik-Kollektiv responsible for writing and drawing their actions.

Beginning in May 1964, the Digedags found themselves in the Middle Ages, surrounded by European kings, queens, and their various attendants, alongside the eponymous knight of the *Ritter Runkel-Serie*. Meanwhile, Ulbricht was experiencing seemingly unrelated resistance from within his own party. The organization of meetings, specifically the Deutschlandtreffen later that summer as a space bringing together youth from both East and West to share ideas and culture, and the associated creation of rock radio stations, spearheaded by DT64 as part of Deutschlandtreffen and surviving right up to the end of the GDR, was part of Ulbricht's policy and inherent to his youth-oriented reforms. Moreover, they were tangentially connected to the reforms of Ulbricht's New Economic System (*Neues Ökonomisches System* or NÖS) which was implemented hand-in-hand with the Youth Communiqué in 1963.[86] Intended to correct economic stagnation through the decentralization of decision making at the factory level, the NÖS effectively implemented aspects of democratic capitalism contrary to socialist theory and practice. Youth were necessary for the continuation and perpetuation of these practices, of the East German state, and the economy more broadly. But support for the NÖS was not forthcoming from within the SED. Rather, this support came directly from Soviet Communist Party General Secretary Nikita Khrushchev. And as Khrushchev's own position in the USSR teetered and collapsed, supplanted by Leonid Brezhnev in October 1964, so too did Ulbricht's position within the SED.[87]

Led by Erich Honecker, criticisms against the SED-leader and his youth policy stemmed from the FDJ's belief that these reforms undermined its authority. To this point, FDJ policy understood youth only in terms of their obedience. Problems and criticisms coming directly from youth were virtually ignored as those in charge had little engagement with the youth they supposedly served. Nor did those in positions of authority within the FDJ have any legitimate interest in solving the problems facing youth under socialism. As such, youth policy enacted by the FDJ had little chance of effecting change at the ground level. And while Ulbricht's Communiqué was imperfect, it recognized that less than half of all East German youth over the age of fourteen were members of the FDJ. In Ulbricht's estimation, these youth needed to be won back to provide the future generations of leaders and workers necessary for socialism's prosperity.[88] As Ulbricht's position grew tenuous coinciding with Khrushchev's fall, by late 1965 the Youth Communiqué was repealed and, with it, many of the reforms already implemented. Ulbricht's ideas surrounding the modernization and reorganization of the FDJ failed and the youth group instead cemented its role as the "helper and fighting reserve" of the SED, lending the group an aura of ideological and organizational stability that it, perhaps, lacked in its early days. East German youth and their families concluded that the FDJ was a necessary evil for advancement within the state regardless of one's own beliefs and acceptance of socialist ideology. This failed to win youth to socialism as the FDJ closed itself entirely, not only to criticisms but to reform. And while the barriers to that reform were not entirely insurmountable before 1965, afterward it was "difficult and dangerous" as children and youth increasingly found themselves locked within a "frozen social structure."[89]

While the Youth Communiqué was in place, however, and youth were not entirely required to restrict self-expression to the privacy afforded the domestic space of the GDR's niche society, comics, and particularly *Mosaik von Hannes Hegen*, took on an air of belonging to an "ideological free zone" regardless of the truth to this perception.[90] Wolfgang Altenburger succeeded Hans Erhardt as *Mosaik*'s Editor-in-Chief at the dawn of 1963, attaining his degree in journalism the previous year from Karl Marx University in Leipzig for his thesis "The Special Tasks of Comics in the System of the East German Children's Press. An Investigation According to the Principles of the Unified Education and the Fourth Journalists Conference."[91] Despite the work of Hegen or of the Mosaik-Kollektiv, East German officials attributed *Mosaik*'s continued success to Altenburger.[92]

Hegen was against what he considered the patronizing ideological content he was forced to include in his comics and chafed against it, focusing instead on the adventure and fantasy of the Digedags' stories. To a degree, this was mitigated by the creation of the Mosaik-Kollektiv and, after 1960 as the publication was transferred to Verlag Junge Welt, the hiring of Erhardt as the comic's Editor-in-Chief. However, and despite Hegen's waning influence on the comic, relegating him to little more than an advisory position, that influence was still felt in the pages of *Mosaik*. The *Weltraum-Serie* foregrounded ideology to a greater extent than previously seen in the comic at a time when literature and children's culture were under fire from the regime for not adequately educating children in an appropriate socialist worldview. Despite the changes to the comic's physical presentation, the *Erfinder-Serie* and especially the *Ritter Runkel-Serie* returned *Mosaik* to the fantastical, swashbuckling stories of the *Orient-Südsee-Serie* and the *Römer-Serie* as the Youth Communiqué reduced the necessity for including those overbearing ideological concerns. As Altenburger boarded the publication with Erhardt's departure, he acted as mediator between Hegen and the publishing regime. In late 1965, FDJ Central Committee Secretary, Helmut Müller, called for the creation of positive socialist role models in cultural productions, children's publications and comic books included.[93] Shortly thereafter, the all-too-brief liberal interlude afforded by Ulbricht's Communiqué crumbled beneath the criticisms of Honecker and the FDJ. This renewed ideological fervor in most, if not all, aspects of East German entertainment and cultural policy, including the extensive ban against most films produced that year at the SED Eleventh Plenum in mid-December.[94] Altenburger, since taking up the job two years earlier and especially during the shockwaves of the final months of 1965, shielded *Mosaik* and Hegen as best he could from increased criticisms, deflecting the attention of the FDJ and Verlag Junge Welt.

As 1966 dawned, *Atze*, the first comic book created in the German Democratic Republic, was in disarray. Attention, both positive and negative, was showered on *Mosaik von Hannes Hegen* because of its popularity while *Atze* remained relatively unchanged and unfazed by the events in comic book publishing that helped shape Hegen's creation during its first decade. Even now, *Atze* exists in a fog in terms of GDR comics scholarship, eclipsed by the long shadow cast by *Mosaik*, the Digedags, and the Abrafaxe characters that replaced Hegen's own creations in 1976. The concurrent dismantling of Ulbricht's Youth Communiqué and its associated policies allowed the FDJ's increased calls for the inclusion of socialist education and ideology to be heard. This was especially true as the ideological education in children's popular culture was thought necessary for the successful development of the socialist personality among children and their own development into active citizens under socialism.[95] *Atze*, however, still lagged behind the development of its more popular contemporary, *Mosaik*.

Buoyed largely by the popularity of *Fix und Fax* created by Jürgen Kieser in 1958, which was itself arguably the result of similarities between these anthropomorphized mice and other characters in the "funny animal" genre of comics, *Atze* remained a fixture of Verlag Junge Welt's output. That said, as the Mosaik-Kollektiv formed around Hegen in order to accelerate *Mosaik*'s production schedule and paper allocations increased that comic's distribution, concurrent paper shortages meant *Atze* suffered delays and found it difficult, if not impossible, to appear at regular publication intervals.[96] By the mid-1960s, and as happened with *Mosaik* earlier in the decade, educators and the FDJ accused *Atze* of being "too flat," of not possessing sufficient ideological content to fulfill its function in developing the socialist personality of its readers.[97] At the

Figure 1.3. *Fix und Fax* 348, *Atze* 12 (1986). Fix and Fax are rescued from the ocean by a passing ship. Illustration by Jürgen Kieser © Familie Kunow.

same time, the idea of a comic and the elements that comprised comics as a medium continued to be problematic to the FDJ. Despite coming a decade after the first appearance of those original comics produced in the GDR, the word "comic" was itself still associated with the Western, specifically American, comics against which these East German children's publications positioned themselves.

At the 2 August 1966 meeting of the FDJ Central Committee, Altenburger proposed a new profile and direction for *Atze*.[98] Ulbricht's Youth

Communiqué and the associated liberalization of youth policy were already being repealed since December of the previous year. In the pages of *Mosaik*, however, the policy still affected content, demonstrating the comic book space as one supposedly free from the ideological implications of state policy, making that entertainment more palatable to the young readership, providing the illusion that socialist ideology was entirely absent from the comic book page.[99] Of course, this was not the case as will be discussed in subsequent chapters. But with the failure of Ulbricht's youth policy, Helmut Müller's desire for the inclusion of positive socialist role models rang as a call to arms for the FDJ on the rapidly evolving battlefield that was comics and comic book publishing in the SED state. As Editor-in-Chief of both *Mosaik* and *Atze*, Altenburger stepped between the two publications, temporarily drawing attention from the former and the accusations of bourgeois influence circling Hegen and the Mosaik-Kollektiv by highlighting the failings of the latter. Though the FDJ's issues with *Mosaik* would never be completely reconciled, and certainly not during Hegen's tenure on the book, Altenburger gave the comic the veneer of respectability in the FDJ's estimation when compared to the inconsistencies of style and substance afflicting *Atze*.[100] Going forward, *Atze* would carry the torch for socialism and socialist education. The new *Atze*, under Altenburger's direction, would provide East German children with the political-ideological education not apparent in *Mosaik*. The stories the comic contained would serve to familiarize those same children with the concepts of Marxist-Leninism and with the "revolutionary traditions of the German working class." In so doing, *Atze* would prove important in the development of notions of national citizenship among school-age children, mobilizing them in service of the SED state and socialism through the development of the socialist personality.[101]

Despite Altenburger's consideration that comics were potentially more reliable than television and film to deliver ideological education given the perceived permanence of the comic book form, his report still noted significant problems in *Atze*, problems that hindered the conveyance of the instructive material. Paper shortages caused long delays between issues that were, in turn, responsible for inconsistencies and inaccuracies in the stories and were blamed for the muddy messaging in the stories the comic contained.[102] Children were sometimes unable to access sequential issues, thus missing important aspects of the socialist, historical serials. Moreover, *Atze* had become a space of experimentation for changing trends in comic art and production, further complicating the ease with which the comic's message could be digested and internalized by its readership. Both Altenburger and the Thälmann Pioneer Central Committee found the comic's language murky, employing slang and intentional misspellings that hindered literacy and language use, a complaint not limited to the GDR but central to the anti-comics campaign in the United States.[103] As with *Mosaik* earlier in the decade, the Americanized word balloons through which the characters communicated with each other and the reader obscured the art, though they constructed the passage of time in an otherwise static medium.[104] This necessitated *Atze's* transformation to the image over text storybook style associated with those historic German proto-comics, *Max and Moritz* and *Struwwelpeter*, facilitating the socialist comic style argued by Benjamin, cited above, and to "amplify and explain the images." Likewise, Altenburger criticized the art as improperly depicting historical figures and heroes of the German workers' movement. These flaws obfuscated the comic's socialist character and made the "motivations of the characters involved . . . only partially apparent." Inconsistencies over the course of many installments of the serialized stories made comprehension of those stories difficult for young audiences.[105]

In Altenburger's estimation, *Atze* required a thorough overhaul if ever it was to live up to the FDJ's educational mandate and the example of quality set by *Mosaik von Hannes Hegen*. To this end, it was necessary to closely monitor the style and content of *Atze*, and to regulate that content with regard to the types of stories found within and how those stories related to the comic as a whole. When appropriate, Altenburger needed to reign in the creative impulses that clashed with his overall vision for the publication. That vision required writers' and artists' close adherence to historical accuracy, creating the representation of socialist heroes on the page and waking reader sympathies to the socialist cause. As children were exposed to socialist educational material in the pages of *Atze*, the representation of history encouraged them to choose the side of revolutionary socialism and further build the SED state. Cover images and the interior art of *Atze*, drawing earlier stylistic inspiration from both Disney and the West German *Fix und Foxi* by Rolf Kauka, now needed to "positively influence" children's aesthetic sensibilities and the Socialist Realist aesthetic appropriate to political stories. Moreover, the covers themselves typically related to the featured political story in each issue. Working with the JP leadership, educators, and the leaders of youth institutions, Altenburger and *Atze's* new editorial proposed that stories in *Atze* employ a multi-tiered solution. Serialized stories needed to address their political concept from a number of viewpoints and, as was the case in Socialist Realist literature, provide children an opportunity to gaze upon, internalize, and interact with socialist society at large. Having written his graduating thesis on the subject, Altenburger was of the belief that comics provided an "interpretation of fundamental philosophical problems." He felt the inclusion of this interpretation in comics allowed children to properly develop the socialist personality, finding ways to relate to the world around them and foster practicable political responsibility with immediate and direct application to their daily lives.[106]

Jürgen Kieser's *Fix und Fax* was something of an outlier in this new approach to *Atze*. Kieser himself worked on *Atze* since its beginnings, creating some of the comic's most recognizable characters including the eponymous protagonist and his sister despite their gradual disappearance from the book. Kieser also consistently produced *Fix und Fax* since the strip launched in 1958. And while themes befitting the FDJ's influence reverberated in the comic strip, the two mice, as well-traveled, helpful, and cooperative as they were and not entirely unlike the Digedags in this regard, were stylistically now at cross-purposes to *Atze's* new profile. The *Fix und Fax* strip proved itself more than capable of selling copies of *Atze* and for that reason could not simply be excised from the publication. Indeed, *Fix und Fax* was necessary for *Atze* to maintain the sales it previously enjoyed. But in the offices of Verlag Junge Welt, it was commonly understood that children wanting to read *Fix und Fax* needed to accept half an issue of socialist educational content, not to mention the strengthened ideological underpinnings affecting *Fix und Fax* itself following Altenburger's proposal.[107]

The *Fix und Fax* strip thus remained present in *Atze*. Its primacy within the publication continued unchanged, even though it appeared tucked in the back of the comic amidst ideological and educational features. Still, the characters periodically appeared on the cover, reminding children of their presence and the FDJ of their importance to *Atze*. Some of the more rigid structural changes suggested by Altenburger gave way to central features in addition to *Fix und Fax*. These included: *Pats Reiseabenteuer*, written by Altenburger himself and illustrated by Harry Schlegel; a letters page containing the most recent installment of the four-panel strip *Max und Maxi*, also by Schlegel; political cartoons; and editorials. These editorials lasted only until 1973, however, when they were replaced by additional pages for the featured political comic.[108] The serialized and political stories depicted socialist revolutionary heroes like V. I. Lenin in "der versiegelte Zug" (The Sealed Train, *Atze* Heft 1/89), East German relationships with the Soviet Union in "der Soldat von Treptow" (The Soldier of Treptow, *Atze* Heft 11/84) and other friendly nations such as Grenada in "Abschied mit Bitternis" (Bitter Farewell, *Atze* Heft 9/84), and antifascist resistance to Nazism in "Frühling im Oderbruch" (Spring at the Oderbruch, *Atze* Heft 6/75) and "Saschko, der Sohn der Kompanie" (Saschko, Son of the Company, *Atze* Heft 5/76).[109]

Just as frequently, these stories focused on the readership itself, depicting the lives children were expected to lead in relation to their responsibilities under state socialism. "Leuchtkugeln über den Karpfenteichen" (Flares over the Carp Pond), from *Atze's* July 1981 issue and illustrated by long-time contributor Günther Hain, is a story about unexploded munitions found in (East) Germany since the end of World War II and the importance of their safe removal. This is bookended, however, by the story of Thälmann Pioneers collecting recyclable metals. During this activity, the children accidently discover one of these shells in a neighbor's yard, decoratively painted as a lawn ornament. "Das Gespenst auf dem Fahrrad" (Spirit on the Bicycle, *Atze* Heft 12/86, Figure 1.4), meanwhile, tells of a day in the life of Thälmann Pioneers as they camp and climb trees, bird watch and study plants, play sports and joust at a medieval fair. In a self-referential nod, the artist Schlegel, depicts one of the story's protagonists sporting a hat similar to the one worn by Pat from the *Pats Reiseabenteuer* strip and has a flag emblazoned with the character's face waving from the back of his bike. This surreptitiously demonstrated the popularity of both the character and the strip by the mid-1980s. The FDJ expected the newly foregrounded propagandistic content, far more structured than previous, to direct children's energies in directions valuable to the continued construction of socialism in the East German state. The editorial regime anticipated that this would generate legitimate enthusiasm among the readership for the SED state and socialist institutions surrounding children on a daily basis and for the perceived heroism of the working class. Harnessing the accurate representation of historical forces in developing socialist society, coupled with comparative examples of imperialist aggression from the Western-capitalist world, Altenburger's report sought a clearly delineated sense of justice with which children could identify and upon which they could act.[110]

In much the same way that *Mosaik* was unshackled from conventions of the Western comic book medium earlier in the decade, *Atze* edged narration boxes and word balloons beyond the frame of the comic panel, adopting a style closer to an historic notion of (East) German *Kultur*. Even the word "comic" was burdened by negative associations with the United States and the American comic book industry. The term was thus vilified as the *Schmutzliteratur* the FDJ actively and eagerly avoided with its own comic book publications. As a compromise, the regime re-

Dann Kulturprogramm: Die Hederslebener stellten ihr Löffellied vor und erklärten uns die Rübenzuckerproduktion. Wir durften selbstgekochten Sirup probieren.

Ein Erlebnis war auch die Teeverkostung mit unterschiedlichen Geschmacksrichtungen.

Figure 1.4. "Das Gespenst auf dem Fahrrad" (Spirit on the Bicycle), *Atze* 12 (1986). Young Pioneer members learn about the production of sugar beets. Illustrations by Harry Schlegel © Martina and Günter Fuhlbrügge.

ferred to comics produced in the SED state as *Wort-Bildgeschichte* (quite literally, word-picture stories). While this was perhaps nowhere near as graceful a term as was "comics" itself, *Wort-Bildgeschichte* immediately recognized the interplay of text and image that defined the comics medium as a whole. Pictures were numbered and the accompanying text included descriptions of character action and dialogue, making the reading more akin to that of a book than of a comic per se. In describing the detail in each panel, readers were denied the voluntary participation required to fill the gutters, those white spaces between panels, with perceived "movement" and thus with meaning.[111] Artists created without concern for how the Americanized speech balloons obscured their illustrations. Writers employed their craft without the slang, misspellings, or compressed language needed to fit the confined spaces of those same balloons. Readers were effectively told how to read the images. In one fell swoop, Altenburger satisfied, for a time at least, the complaints of FDJ leaders and educators, disallowing interpretation of the comic's content contrary to the creators' intentions.[112] The renewed focus on the text over image presentation in the narrative marginalized comics' supposed inferiority, minimizing their dependency on pictures as storytelling devices required for meaning.[113] And as happened with *Mosaik*, this change effaced the apparent Americanness of the medium, conforming *Atze* to emerging norms of East German *Kultur*, children's literature, and educational practice.

Despite any new popularity *Atze* enjoyed after 1967, the comic still lagged behind *Mosaik* in real terms as a result of its inability or reluctance to conceal its ideology. *Atze's* biographies of socialist heroes (*Kämpfer der Revolution*) proved the least popular stories in the comic, trailing the popularity of *Fix und Fax* and *Pats Reiseabenteuer* by significant margins.[114] For this reason, *Mosaik*, not *Atze*, was selected as a test case for Western export in 1968. Whereas *Atze's* editorial regime took pains to sever ties with Western European and American comic book cultures, *Mosaik* remained, by and large, Westernized. The Mosaik-Kollektiv responded and adapted to criticisms against the comic during the anti-comics campaign in East Germany, maintaining the adventurous spirit first created by Hegen in the style of Barks' globetrotting Ducks in the pages of Disney's comics. That *Mosaik* was also able to naturally maintain a large audience, as opposed to the artificial numbers in Altenburger's report on *Atze* suggesting a circulation of two hundred thousand copies to ensure the comic's profitability, spoke to the general enthusiasm East German children had for these Western-style comics.

At the same time, *Mosaik* was as much an Eastern comic as *Atze* and possessed the same traditionally (East) German approach to comics storytelling. Narrative and dialogue were separated from the images. The characters typically avoided violence as a resolution, a long-time problem in American comics. *Mosaik* connected itself to East German ideas governing the development of *Kinderkultur* in children's literature and the new profile of *Atze*. This association does not necessarily imply the High Culture considered in German *Kultur* nor the notion of the GDR as *Kulturstaat*, but it firmly established *Mosaik's* own traditions located in the penny dreadful, German picture books, and popular and working-class culture generally. While the regime's educational content was most certainly present in *Mosaik*, it conveyed its bias subtly, demonstrating the ubiquity of the FDJ's benign power structures among these publications, convincing its readership of the heroism of the characters and the socialist worldview they represented. This was, however, a gratuitous gesture on the part of the FDJ. The 1955 Regulations and the construction of the Berlin Wall six years later gave Verlag Junge Welt a virtual monopoly over children's publishing in the SED state. That the FDJ, the JP, the publisher, and the editors of these periodicals invested themselves in the changes and improvements rendered to both *Mosaik* and *Atze* in the early 1960s demonstrated their collective belief in comics' ability to bring children into the fold of socialist society. More importantly, these changes were indicative of the

FDJ's faith that comics could successfully mobilize those same children in service of the SED state.

Examining ideology in these comics in the development of a unique East German comics form and the respective real popularity of those books, it is possible to suggest the extent to which ideology was acceptable to the readers. Even after the reprofiled *Atze* launched in 1967, *Mosaik* enjoyed significantly higher circulation and paper quotas. This suggests *Mosaik* regularly outsold its sister publication, attributable to the stories and the ways in which the ideology was presented. More likely, though, this reflected the way ideology was implemented and influenced how those stories were told. During discussions over the future of *Atze*, Verlag Junge Welt was convinced children would accept ideology in exchange for the comic strips that interested them, such as happened with *Fix und Fax*; a carrot offered to the readership by the publishing regime. A year later, in a report on *Mosaik's Amerika-Serie*, ideology was a prominent feature, but instead of stories on socialist heroes, role models, and East German and Soviet friendship, the Digedags were primarily about adventure and fun as they celebrated worker achievements and the socialist international in the American landscape. This idea was facilitated by *Mosaik's* appearance as an East German export beginning with the *Amerika-Serie* in 1968, discussed in Chapter Five. While *Mosaik* expressed itself in terms of the East German *Kulturstaat*, its presentation remained Western enough to prove palatable to the East German children longing for the escape and escapism offered by American comics but denied by the Berlin Wall. Though products of the same burgeoning *Kinderkultur* were fostered by the regime, East German comics rose above the children's literature that was quickly becoming incomprehensible to its audience. Incorporating ideology and packaging it in a form demanded by its audience, East German comics delivered educational content in a way and to a degree that children's literature more broadly, perhaps, did not.

Notes

An earlier version of this chapter appeared as Sean Eedy, "Reimagining GDR Comics: *Kultur*, Children's Literature, and the Socialist Personality," *Journal of Graphic Novels and Comics* 5, no. 3 (September 2014): 245–56.

1. Jobs, "Tarzan under Attack," 724.
2. Jens Kussmann, "'Nothing but Exclamation Points?' Comics in the Bavarian Academic High School," in *Novel Perspectives on German-Language Comic Studies*, ed. Lynn Marie Kutch (Lanham: Lexington Books, 2016), 68–69.

3. Reinhard Pfeiffer, *Von Hannes Hegen bis Erich Schmitt: Lexikon der Karikaturisten, Presse- und Comic-Zeichner der DDR* (Berlin: Schwarzkopf & Schwarzkopf Verlag, 1998), 271–72.
4. Dorothee Wierling, "Youth as Internal Enemy," 157.
5. BArch DY 24/1581. This and all similar references are from the Bundesarchiv (BArch) Berlin-Lichterfelde.
6. Bernd Nowak, "Erinnerung an Atze aus der 'Atze,'" Altes und Neues von Bernd Nowak, Dessau, retrieved 17 May 2018 from http://barrynoa.blogspot.ca/2014/08/erinnerung-atze-aus-der-atze.html.
7. BArch DY 24/1581, pag. 3.
8. Paul M. Malone, "A Periphery surrounded by centres: The German-Language comics market, transnational relationships, and graphic novels," *Journal of Graphic Novels and Comics* 11, no. 1 (2020): 16.
9. BArch DY 26/173, pag. 39.
10. Pfeiffer, *Von Hannes Hegen*, 128.
11. Catrin Gersdorf, "The Digedags Go West: Images of America in an East German Comic Strip," *Journal of American Culture* 19, no. 2 (Summer 1996): 36 and Brad Prager, Review of *Micky, Marx, und Manitu. Zeit und Kulturgeschichte im Spiegel eines DDR Comics 1955–1990. Mosaik als Fokus von Medienerlebnissen im NS und in der DDR* by Thomas Kramer, *German Quarterly* 76, no. 3 (Summer 2003): 364.
12. BArch DY 26/173, pag. 60.
13. BArch DY 26/173, pag. 61.
14. See Thomas Kramer, "Donald, Asterix und Abrafax," 41–66.
15. Fredrick Stroemberg, *Comic Art Propaganda: A Graphic History* (New York: St. Martin's Griffin, 2010), 69.
16. BArch DY 24/1581, pag. 3.
17. Guido Weißhahn, "Die Digedags im Mosaik," *DDR Comics*, retrieved 27 August 2013 from http://ddr.comics.de/digedags.htm.
18. Pfeiffer, *Von Hannes Hegen*, 127 and Joseph Witek, *Comic Books as History: The Narrative Art of Jack Jackson, Art Spiegelman, and Harvey Pekar* (Jackson: University Press of Mississippi, 1989), 110–11.
19. BArch DY 26/114, pag. 3–4.
20. Gerd Lettkemann and Michael F. Scholz, *"Schuldig ist schließlich jeder…der Comics besitzt, verbreitet oder nicht einziehen läßt" Comics in der DDR—Die Geschichte eines ungeliebten Mediums (1945/49–1990)* (Berlin: MOSAIK Steinchen für Steinchen Verlag GmbH, 1994), 38–39.
21. Scott McCloud, *Understanding Comics: The Invisible Art* (New York: Harper, 1993), 92.
22. Jovanovic and Koch, "Comics Debate in Germany," 104–5.
23. BArch DY 26/114, pag. 3–4.
24. BArch DY 24/1581, pag. 4–6.
25. BArch DC 9/1628, pag. 91. For more on the Digedags interactions with history and the socialist worldview, see Sean Eedy, "Back to the (Social-

ist) Future: History, Time Travel, and East German Education in *Mosaik von Hannes Hegen, 1958–1974*," in *Drawing the Past: Comics and the Historical Imagination*, ed. Michael Goodrum, David Hall, and Philip Smith (Jackson: University Press of Mississippi, forthcoming).
26. After sine and tangent, the third main trigonometric function is cosine.
27. Mosaik-Kollektiv, "Die Entführung ins All," *Mosaik von Hannes Hegen* 25 (Berlin: Verlag Neues Leben, 1957), 5.
28. BArch DY 26/173, pag. 61.
29. Eedy, "Future," forthcoming.
30. David Wittenberg, *Time Travel: The Popular Philosophy of Narrative* (New York: Fordham University Press, 2013), 30.
31. Matthew Jones and Joan Ormrod, "Introduction: Contexts and Concepts of Time in the Mass Media," in *Time Travel in Popular Media: Essays on Film, Television, Literature, and Video Games*, ed. Matthew Jones and Joan Ormrod (Jefferson, NC: McFarland & Co, 2015), 15.
32. Eedy, "Future," forthcoming.
33. Dolores L. Augustine, *Red Prometheus: Engineering and Dictatorship in East Germany, 1945–1990* (Cambridge, MA: MIT Press, 2007), 232.
34. Augustine, *Red Prometheus*, 232 and 244.
35. BArch DY 26/173, pag. 5.
36. Angela Brock, "Producing the 'Socialist Personality'? Socialisation, Education, and the Emergence of New Patterns of Behaviour," in *Power and Society in the GDR 1961–1979: The 'Normalisation of Rule'?*, ed. Mary Fulbrook (New York: Berghahn Books, 2009), 223.
37. The Komsomol, the All-Union Leninist Youth Communist League, was the Soviet Russian youth organization founded in 1918 and predecessor to the GDR's Freie Deutsche Jugend.
38. BArch DY 26/173, pag. 7.
39. Brock, "Producing the 'Socialist Personality'?" 224.
40. In 1952, the SED reorganized the East German provinces to centralize governance and redistribute land and resources. The fourteen *Bezirke* created by the SED as administrative territories were maintained until after German (re)unification in 1990 when the historic German Länder in the territories of the former German Democratic Republic were reconstituted by the nascent Berlin Republic.
41. Stephen Brockman, "The Eleventh Plenum and Film Criticism in East Germany," *German Life & Letters* 66, no. 4 (October 2013): 432–48.
42. Thomas Di Napoli, "Thirty Years of Children's Literature in the German Democratic Republic," *German Studies Review* 7, no. 2 (May 1984), 281–89.
43. J. D. Stahl, "Children's Literature and the Politics of the Nation State," *Children's Literature* 20 (1992): 197.
44. Alan L. Nothnagle, *Building the East German Myth: Historical Mythology and Youth Propaganda in the German Democratic Republic, 1945–1989* (Ann Arbor: University of Michigan Press, 1999), 51.

45. Di Napoli, "Thirty Years," 281–87.
46. Thomson-Wohlgemuth, "Official and Unofficial," 39.
47. Nothnagle, *East German Myth*, 54 and Ross, *Constructing Socialism*, 140.
48. For a broader discussion of the film *Sheriff Teddy* and the undermining role played by Western comics and culture against East German youth, FDJ education, and the SED state than I am able to provide here, see Sonja E. Klocke, "Teddy Boys in Ost und West: Eine generationenspezifische Metamorphose in Heiner Carows Sheriff Teddy (1957)," in *Von Pionierin und Piraten: Der DEFA-Kinderfilm in seinen kulturhistorischen, filmästhetischen und ideologischen Dimensionen*, ed. Bettina Kümmerling-Meibauer and Steffi Ebert (Heidelberg: Universitätsverlag), forthcoming.
49. Wright, *Comic Book Nation*, 96.
50. Jacqueline Danziger-Russell, *Girls and Their Comics: Finding a Female Voice in Comic Book Narrative* (Lanham: The Scarecrow Press, Inc., 2013), 17–18.
51. Jobs, "Tarzan under Attack," 688–89 and 696.
52. Anne Rubenstein, *Bad Language, Naked Ladies, & Other Threats to the Nation: A Political History of Comic Books in Mexico* (Durham, NC: Duke University Press, 1998), 100.
53. "daß die Zeitschrift 'Mosaik' als Zeitschrift, die hauptsächlich für Kinder erscheint."
54. BArch DY 24/5790.
55. BArch DY 26/114, pag. 4–7.
56. Eedy, "Future," forthcoming.
57. Chapman, *British Comics*, 11 and Charles Hatfield, "Comic Art, Children's Literature, and the New Comic Studies," *The Lion and the Unicorn* 30, no. 3 (September 2006): 363.
58. Sabin, *Comics, Comix & Graphic Novels*, 19.
59. Wright, *Comic Book Nation*, 90–91.
60. Wright, 31 and John A. Lent, "Introduction: The Comics Debate Internationally: Their Genesis, Issues, and Commonalities," in *Pulp Demons: International Dimensions of the Postwar Anti-Comics Campaign*, ed. John A. Lent (Cranbury: Associated University Presses, Inc., 1999), 21.
61. Will Eisner, *Comics and Sequential Art: Principles & Practice of the World's Most Popular Art Form* (Paramus: Poorhouse Press, 1985), 25, 40, and 141.
62. McCloud, *Understanding Comics*, 9.
63. Between the publication of "die Entführung ins All," in *Mosaik von Hannes Hegen* 25 in 1958 (Figure 2.3) and "In Grauer Zeit" in issue 73 in 1962 (Figure 1.2), Wolfgang Altenburger was appointed Editor-in-Chief of the publication. Among the changes he wrought was the elimination of word balloons in favor of the image over text format associated with children's picture books.
64. Mosaik-Kollektiv, "In Grauer Zeit," *Mosaik von Hannes Hegen* 73 (Berlin: Verlag Junge Welt, 1962), 23–24.
65. BArch DY 26/173, pag. 55.
66. Jovanovic and Koch, "Comics Debate in Germany," 98–99.

67. Qinna Shen, "Barometers of GDR Cultural Politics: Contextualizing the DEFA Grimm Adaptations," *Marvels & Tales* 25, no. 1 (2011): 71.
68. Benita Blessing, "DEFA Children's Films: Nor Just for Children," in *DEFA at the Crossroads of East German and International Film Culture*, ed. Marc Silberman and Henning Wrage (Berlin: Walter de Gruyter GmbH, 2014), 248–49 and Sean Eedy, "Animating the Socialist Personality: DEFA Fairy Tale *Trickfilme* in the Shadow of 1968," in *Celluloid Revolt: German Screen Cultures and the Long 1968*, ed. Christina Gerhardt and Marco Abel (Rochester: Camden House, 2019), 188–89.
69. John D. Benjamin, "Relocating the Text: *Mosaik* and the Invention of a German East German Comics Tradition," *The German Quarterly* 92, no. 2 (Spring 2019): 149.
70. The foundation of the East German state itself can largely be situated as a response to: the perceived threat posed by the West German Deutsche Mark (DM) in 1948, the failure of Soviet General Secretary Joseph Stalin's Berlin Blockade, and the subsequent formation of a nominally sovereign western Federal Republic under the auspices of US, British, and French authorities.
71. Hope M. Harrison, *Driving the Soviets up the Wall: Soviet-East German Relations 1953–1961* (Princeton, NJ: Princeton University Press, 2003), 145–50.
72. Wierling, "Youth as Internal Enemy," 162.
73. Poiger, *Jazz, Rock, and Rebels*, 84–85 and Gerd Lettkemann, "Comics in der DDR," in *Fortsetzung folgt: Comic Kultur in Deutschland*, ed. Andreas C. Knigge (Frankfurt: Verlag Ullstein GmbH, 1985), 321–22.
74. Brock, "Producing the Socialist Personality'?" 236–39.
75. Fulbrook, *People's State,* 116 and 136.
76. Saunders, *Honecker's Children*, 13–14.
77. BArch DY 24/237, pag. 3–10.
78. BArch DY 26/42, pag. 3, 11, and 22.
79. BArch DY 26/42.
80. Poiger, *Jazz, Rock, and Rebels*, 54.
81. Poiger, 209.
82. Monika Kaiser, "Reforming Socialism? The Changing of the Guard from Ulbricht to Honecker during the 1960s," in *Dictatorship as Experience: Towards a Socio-Cultural History of the GDR*, ed. Konrad H. Jarausch, trans. Eve Duffy (New York: Berghahn Books, 1999), 329.
83. Dorothee Wierling, "The Hitler Youth Generation in the GDR: Insecurities, Ambitions, and Dilemmas," in *Dictatorship as Experience: Towards a Socio-Cultural History of the GDR*, ed. Konrad H. Jarausch, trans. Eve Duffy (New York: Berghahn Books, 1999), 319 and Wierling, "Youth as Internal Enemy," 163.
84. Benita Blessing, "Defining Socialist Children's Films, Defining Socialist Childhoods," in *Re-Imagining DEFA*, ed. Seán Allan and Sebastian Heiduschke (New York: Berghahn Books, 2016), 256; Sebastian Heiduschke, *East German Cinema: DEFA and Film History* (New York: Palgrave, 2013), 59; and Shen, "Barometers," 71.

85. Lettkemann and Scholz, "Schuldig ist schließlich jeder," 37–38.
86. Alan McDougall, "The Liberal Interlude: SED Youth Policy and the Free German Youth (FDJ), 1963–65," *Debatte* 9, no. 2 (2001): 128–34.
87. Daniela Berghahn, *Hollywood Behind the Wall: The Cinema of East Germany* (Manchester: Manchester University Press, 2005), 143.
88. McDougall, "Liberal Interlude," 124–27.
89. McDougall, *Youth Politics*, 235–40.
90. Augustine, *Red Prometheus*, 230.
91. "Die besonderen Aufgabe der Bildzeitschrift im System der Kinderpresse der DDR. Eine Untersuchung nach den Prinzipien des einheitlichen Bildungssystems und der IV. Journalistenkonferenz." Numerous members of the Mosaik-Kollektiv also attended art school in Leipzig, receiving their degrees as part of the emerging *Leipziger Schule* (Leipzig School).
92. BStU Archiv der Zentralstelle MfS-HA XX Nr. 11285, pag. 13.
93. Lettkemann and Scholz, "Schuldig ist schließlich jeder," 40–44 and McDougall, "Liberal Interlude," 151.
94. Berghahn, *Hollywood*, 145–46.
95. McDougall, "Liberal Interlude," 154.
96. BArch DY 24/1581, pag. 4.
97. Lettkemann and Scholz, "Schuldig ist schließlich jeder," 49.
98. BArch DY 24/1581.
99. Augustine, *Red Prometheus*, 230.
100. Lettkemann and Scholz, "Schuldig ist schließlich jeder," 40.
101. BArch DY 24/1581, pag. 2.
102. BArch DY 24/1581, pag. 3.
103. BArch DY 24/1581, pag. 3, BArch DY 26/118, pag. 4, and Hatfield, "Comic Art," 363.
104. McCloud, *Understanding Comics*, 95. McCloud here suggests that time in comics is constructed through dialogue and the perceived length of time taken for a character to say his piece. Although the comic panel itself may illustrate a single moment frozen in time, character dialogue indicates that the image is, in fact, stretched out over several moments.
105. BArch DY 24/1581, pag. 3.
106. BArch DY 24/1581, pag.4.
107. Guido Weißhahn, "Atze." *DDR Comics*, retrieved 27 August 2013 from http://www.ddr-comics.de/atze.htm.
108. Weißhahn, "Atze."
109. For more on these stories and their depiction of antifascism, often at the expense of Jewish representation and the Holocaust, see Sean Eedy, "Four Colour Anti-Fascism: Postwar Narratives and the Obfuscation of the Holocaust in East German Comics," *Journal of Modern Jewish Studies* 17, no. 1 (2018): 24–35.
110. BArch DY 24/1581, pag. 6.
111. McCloud, *Understanding Comics*, 59–65.

112. Lettkemann and Scholz, *"Schuldig ist schließlich jeder,"* 38.
113. Führer and Ross, "Mass Media," 10.
114. Lettkemann and Scholz, *"Schuldig ist schließlich jeder,"* 50.

CHAPTER 2

State Power and the East German Zeitgeist

The SED state has been characterized as many things by the likes of politicians, historians, and especially by the population of the former German Democratic Republic itself both during the Cold War and since. In his role as Permanent Representative of the Federal Republic in the GDR, diplomat Günter Gaus characterized the SED state as a *Nischengesellschaft*. Lacking the liberty necessary for free political discourse in the public sphere, the East German population retreated into niches within society to find the freedom from authority denied them in their roles, obligations, and duties in daily life.[1] More often than not, these niches were found in the domestic space provided by the home or, equally popular, the country dachas where people literally retreated from the SED's and the Stasi's structures of control. The success and truth to this withdrawal from SED power notwithstanding, East Germans perceived these niches as being free from the state's machinations and used them as spaces in which they could be themselves and act freely without concern for the state.[2] Of course, the problem with this is the belief that the regime's reach ended at the threshold of the domestic space. There are literally kilometers of Stasi files detailing secret police surveillance, evidence of how that niche was a fabrication, a convenient lie believed by the GDR's population to allow the perception of freedom in a state and in a space in which there was none. And while the idea of the niche society willfully ignores the presence of the state within the domestic space, this does not make the perception of the freedom enjoyed within that space any less real to those living under SED rule.[3]

Elsewhere, and not incorrectly, Jürgen Kocka and, following him, Konrad H. Jarausch both characterized the GDR as a *durchherrschte Gesellschaft* (thoroughly ruled society). Simply put, this concept implies that the structures of the state and the Stasi penetrated every aspect of both public and private life. As everything without exception was a product of the state, every aspect of life acted also as a method and measure of state control. Of course, this includes the more obvious forms of control and repression such as the border regime, Stasi surveillance, harassment, arrests, and the lack of free and open elections. However, SED state control also included the more mundane aspects of East German life such as television and print media (which indeed may themselves be considered obvious forms of control through the propaganda on display), consumption, or the elaborate and bloated bureaucracy.[4] Max Weber and Mary Fulbrook take this concept of state power one step further, dissecting the notion of power itself. Neither take issue with the idea that SED power dominated most, if not all, aspects of life in the East German state, but they refine and define how these power structures operated in obvious and not so obvious ways. Taking Weber's stratification of power, Fulbrook reduces the conceptualization of SED power to the malign and the benign. This is to say that in order to penetrate all aspects of society as demonstrated by the model of the thoroughly ruled society, the SED regime employed the heavy-handed power structures of repression and the more subtle approach offered by entertainment and shopping.[5] Gaus's original characterization of the GDR as a niche society tends not to recognize this penetration of the domestic by the state. However, in coupling Kocka's thoroughly ruled society with Fulbrook's notion of the SED's deployment of benign power in service of the state, the idea of the domestic space, the private sphere, and of privacy itself in the GDR becomes both more complicated and more nuanced. It is here where we find the comic books and children's magazines published by Verlag Junge Welt including, but not limited to, *Mosaik von Hannes Hegen* and *Atze*.

In the previous chapter, I discussed the birth of comics in the German Democratic Republic, the problems associated with both *Mosaik* and *Atze* in their early years, through the editorial guidance offered those publications by Wolfgang Altenburger and the substantial changes he brought to the medium, bringing those comics in line with the larger socialist project. Throughout, the hands of the SED and the FDJ were more than apparent in steering those comics, particularly in terms of including the ideological content the regime felt necessary to develop children's socialist personality and perpetuate the socialist state itself. Elsewhere, Gaby Thomson-Wohlgemuth suggests that children's literature was imperative to deliver the regime's message to children.[6] Others, including the likes of Benita Blessing, Qinna Shen, and Marc Silberman have similarly suggested that children's media in a broad sense was charged, quite successfully, with this same task. At the same time, children's film, particularly adaptations of the fairy tales collected by the Brothers Grimm and of other classical literature, aided the GDR in its claims to modernity and as the inheritor of historic German culture.[7] And though comic books were intended solely for children and would be outgrown long before adulthood, a stigma still pervasive across the medium in modern Germany, the FDJ did its best to elevate comics produced in the GDR and legitimize their content, if not the medium as a whole.[8] That said, because comics were largely dismissed by parents and educators, though this was less true of the latter as the FDJ involved itself with comics' production, and they provided content entertaining to children, many of those children considered those comics free from the communist influence and institutionalized power organizing the majority of their time, such as the FDJ, the Thälmann Pioneer groups, or schools.[9] More appropriately, or more accurately, despite the inclusion of ideological and propagandistic content, children actively ignored that material in favor of the entertaining, though no less ideological, adventures of the Digedags, the Abrafaxe, *Fix und Fax*, or *Pats Reiseabenteuer*.[10] The latter of which contained intentional historical anachronisms developed to engage and interest children as part of a regular promotional contest.

Nonetheless, comics produced in the GDR exemplify this notion of the *durchherrschte Gesellschaft* in that they are indicative of the state's penetration of the most mundane daily activities as a means of controlling the population. Concurrently, it also speaks to Fulbrook's notion of benign power as the state exercises passive authority, requiring the interaction and acceptance of its intended audience to achieve the desired result. The above-mentioned assertion by Dolores Augustine in her monograph, *Red Prometheus: Engineering and Dictatorship in East Germany, 1945–1990*, that children perceived an absence of propagandistic content in these comics is testament to the benign nature of that content. As a result, comics stand at the nexus of state power and reader interest, an intersection between the two desires that were sometimes, if not always, at cross purposes. Above, I introduced the perception of a private space within the home or dacha regarding Gaus's *Nischengesellschaft*. Here, it is arguably the case that East Germans found comfort in the supposed privacy of that home regardless of the reality of SED ideological penetration or Stasi penetration of the domestic sphere.[11] While television also fulfilled the state's goal of projecting power into a space supposedly free of that power, comic books and comic publications for children accomplished this in a way rendered nearly, if not entirely, invisible to its intended audience.[12] As such, comics such as *Mosaik von Hannes Hegen* and *Atze*, not to mention the comic strips published in *Bummi*, *Frösi*, or *Junge Welt*, transgressed the boundaries of East German privacy, seeking to organize children's leisure time, arguably free of politics, by co-opting their interests and hobbies.

Although *Atze* was the first comic book produced in the German Democratic Republic and published by Verlag Junge Welt with characters created by Jürgen Kieser, this is not where comics in the GDR found their origins. Rather, the history of comics in the GDR began with the end of World War II and the arrival of the US occupation forces. During the war, a full quarter of every magazine shipped to GIs serving in Europe was a comic book. Thirty-five thousand issues of *Superman* alone were shipped to Europe each month. Comic books also, quite often, demonstrated shifting national priorities to showcase a seamless and inevitable triumph of the common man. During the Great Depression of the 1930s, this meant that superheroes most often fought corrupt politicians and greedy racketeers as the enemies of "loosely defined" American values of democracy, liberty, and freedom. With the rise of Adolf Hitler and the Nazi Party in Germany and the United States' eventual entry into the European war in 1941, evil and anti-Americanism transformed into militarism and oppression directed toward the Axis Powers and their sympathizers in the United States.[13] Once Germany was defeated and before the demarcation of the postwar division was firmly fixed in the minds of the occupiers and the occupied, children from what became the SBZ were exposed to these American comics brought into the country by the soldiers stationed there. For the Soviet Military Administration and the SED, not to mention the parents and educators throughout Germany (not only those in the eastern sector of the country), these comics were synonymous with American culture, or, more appropriately, the United States' perceived lack of culture and civility (*Unkultur*) and were demonstrative of the nation's immaturity, unsophistication, and the general harmfulness touted by Dr. Fredric Wertham's anti-comics campaign later in the decade.[14]

As comic books were wrongly considered to be a medium entirely foreign to Germany, American comics challenged German artistic merit and aesthetics and German education. Of course, comics were thought beneath any other form of literature due to their reliance on pictures to give their stories meaning. More important, perhaps, comics were considered a threat to Germanness and to the notions of German High Culture upon which the supposed foundations of the postwar states were laid. The perception of comics' harmful effects upon German children, to say nothing of German culture broadly speaking, went unchallenged. The violence and criminality apparent in American comics, whether this be the crime or horror genres openly attacked by Wertham and his followers in the United States or the superhero genre equally criticized for supposedly brazen homosexual and BDSM overtures, were considered a means unto themselves and were judged on ethical grounds as to their immorality in light of the immediate Nazi past. German critics were less interested in the possible violation of free speech when censoring comic book publications than they were with the inappropriateness of putting these comics, as products of US cultural imperialism, into the hands of children. Comics supposedly isolated the children that read them. As a result, these critics felt that, over the long term, these comic publications were counterproductive to the creation of a democratic and educated society.[15] Nonetheless, comics gained popularity in both halves of divided Germany as they did across the Western world, generally speaking. Though when they did, and much the same can be said of American comics across the European continent, it was Disney comics, particularly Mickey Mouse in those early days of the postwar period, that outsold the others and left superheroes and their supposed values of truth, justice, and the American way behind.[16]

Unsurprisingly, the SED's *Verordnung zum Schutz der Jugend* were implemented concurrently with the publication of *Atze* in April 1955. These regulations were indeed part of the anti-comics campaign as it manifested in the German East. They reflected similar actions and laws taken up in Western Europe. However, in the West, the campaign against comics and the moral panic associated with those comics and their deleterious effects on children were largely in decline after the mid-1950s due to communist parties' involvement in the movement.[17] Regardless, across Europe, the GDR included, laws and regulating bodies intended and attempted to remove American comics and US cultural influence from the shelves of booksellers and from the hands and minds of European children. In the GDR, the *Verordnung* made not only the sale but also the possession of Western comics illegal, insisting that parents could turn these publications over to the local Volkspolizei upon their discovery. And despite the popularity of Disney and the apparent innocuousness of those Disney comics, even Mickey Mouse and Donald Duck fell under the scrutiny of the East German socialist regime.

An FDJ report on the tasks of children's magazines and publications in a socialist society was drafted in the 1980s as justification for the approach taken by these publications in the preceding two decades, providing a brief history of children's publications in the GDR more broadly. This report established these comics and magazines within the longer history of children's publishing in Germany and connected children's literature and comics to the East German perception of itself as a *Kulturstaat*. In doing so, the FDJ criticized the comics medium as a tool of capitalist journalism for the mass, ideological influence of the child-readership. This not only critiqued American comics, though the report mentioned the superhero genre and the associated unnatural forces and experiences of those stories and how this genre glutted the industry following the introduction of Superman in 1938, but also those German comics appearing before World War I. German (proto-)comics of the nineteenth century including *Max und Moritz* and *Struwwelpeter* (and to a lesser extent, *The Katzenjammer Kids*, an American product by a German creator, inspired by those earlier endeavors into the medium) were praised, albeit faintly, for their humor, satire, and the clear demarcations of right and wrong wherein heroes emerged unscathed and evil received just punishment. But for those German comics appearing after the Great War, the East German regime vilified them as militarist, glorifying soldiers and warfare. The American comics of the inter- and postwar periods fared no better, as the FDJ justifiably considered these violent, racist, and anti-communist. Even the likes of Donald Duck, his Uncle Scrooge, and the more recent West German characters Fix and Foxi were thought to introduce readers to imperialist, bourgeois society wherein "so-called immutable values" (*mit sogenannten ewigen Werten*), largely associated with American capitalist values, were dominated by power and money.[18] This still left the FDJ and the GDR's state-owned publishers the problem of Disney's popularity in the early- to mid-1950s.

The East German youth groups attempted to rectify this problem, creating their own ideologically acceptable variation on the Disney spirit. This did not mean licensing Disney comics and tweaking, modifying, or rewriting these foreign stories and scripts to suit East German socialism and the ideological needs of the state. Although, the revision of Western and bourgeois children's fiction was often the case with DEFA screen adaptations of Grimm fairy tales and with foreign children's literature as the GDR developed its own brand of fiction dedicated to a youth audience.[19] Rather, the FDJ created their own characters that captured the essence of Disney comics and what made those comics popular among the children reading them. As such, following the issuance of the *Verordnung zum Schutz der Jugend* and the first few issues of *Atze*, the FDJ ordered Verlag Neues Leben to create a new comic book publication.[20] At the same time, Johannes Hegenbarth turned to Disney designs to create characters and refine his own style.[21] The Digedag characters he created attempted to foster readers' historical consciousness through their adventures through time and space. But, as we saw in the previous chapter, even this was considered inappropriate to the depiction of class struggle necessitated by the state.[22]

The *Weltraum-Serie* was arguably the most ideological story in *Mosaik* up to the point of its publication. Prior to this, the Digedags visited the South Seas and Rome, but their adventures largely mirrored those of the Disney characters they emulated. The South Sea adventure began with "Auf der Jagd nach dem Golde," the title of which does not retain much of the educational, socialist imperative meant to drive the publication, particularly after the *Verordnung* outlawed Western publications of a similar sort. It was, however, indicative of publications like "Donald Duck Finds Pirate Gold" (*Four Color* #9, 1942) and "Back to the Klondike" (*Uncle Scrooge* #2, 1953). Indeed, during their South Seas adventures, the Digedags encounter pirates ("Wer wagt—gewinnt," [Who Dares—Wins] *Mosaik von Hannes Hegen* #4) in only their third outing. At this point, *Mosaik* was published quarterly and the stories of the Digedags alternated with those of the "funny animal" genre. Indeed, in issue three of *Mosaik*, "die Bimmel-Bummelbahn," the Digedags are given the day off, sidelined to one of these animal stories. The Digedags emerged from this genre themselves, but the stories interspersed with those of the Digedags in *Mosaik* were more literal to the genre with anthropomorphized animal characters. And as discussed in the previous chapter, the early adventures of the Digedags intentionally mirrored those Disney adventures to rectify the problems of capitalist imperialist influence on the South Sea islands visited by Scrooge, Donald, and their nephews Huey, Dewey, and Louie. In doing so, however, *Mosaik* apes those Western comics a little too closely and is perhaps guilty of the same sins criticized by the socialist perspective of the FDJ.

Just as the Franco-Belgian comic *Tintin* or the American *Uncle Scrooge* portray Indigenous island peoples in a way demonstrative of racial if not racist undertones, the Digedags adventures in the South Seas similarly portray the islanders as "sweet dolls" (*"süße" Püppchen*).[23] The women in particular are attractive but not demonstrably intelligent. The island natives are primitive, in grass skirts, with bones worn through their noses or as jewelry. And compared to the Digedags, who themselves were never particularly tall, the island natives, with perhaps the exception of the rather obese tribal chief, are childlike and diminutive in both stature and technological advancement. This undermines the Digedags' efforts to liberate the islanders from imperialism and capitalist influence and greed. Instead, the Digedags are put on a path that pursues the adventures of Donald and Scrooge. And, like the capitalists of which the Digedags, the FDJ, and the East German socialist regime are critical, they characterize and mistreat the islanders in much the same way. The Digedags were responsible to "rescue child-like natives" from capitalists stealing local resources and associated (East) Germans with practical, hands-on technical ability and know-how. Moreover, there exists a general parallel between Eastern and Western racism as the characters in both Disney and *Mosaik* demonstrate frustration with those—the island natives—who refuse to modernize. This irritation illustrates a conflict between First and Third World cultural identity formations. As such, there is the fear that these developing cultures can cause potential harm to socialist society by undoing the gains, particularly those related to technological advancement at the heart of perceived socialist progress, of that society.[24] The earliest issues of *Mosaik von Hannes Hegen* were then indicative of the same type of cultural imperialism of which the FDJ accused Disney and Carl Barks's Duck comics, though suggestive of relative power relations under socialism and the perceived technological and ideological superiority of the East German socialist state.

Nonetheless, by the beginning of the *Weltraum-Serie*, *Mosaik* was considered insufficient to the task of developing East German socialism and the socialist personality toward the full realization of a communist state. The Digedags' ability to move through time foregrounded the educational and historical aspects of the stories. However, as the characters were unmoored from any single time or place and their temporal movement was dependent upon unexplained or unscientific forces, those aspects were thought to undermine potential development of the historical and political awareness of the children reading the comic. More specifically, as the Digedags were themselves considered guilty of imperialist tendencies, the FDJ thought it necessary to partner the Digedags with a character native to the time and place in which the story was located.[25] This provided a deeper understanding of the involved history and politics as the Digedags were foreigners to this and thus became surrogates for the children reading in the educational process. Perhaps more importantly, it provided opportunity for differentiation between Dig, Dag, and Digedag who were themselves interchangeable in the minds of the editors.[26]

But the *Weltraum-Serie* launched Dig and Dag into space at a time when the race to put a human being in orbit, a new Cold War battleground between the Soviet Union and the United States, was accelerating. The successful launch of the Soviet Sputnik 1 satellite in October

ie Gefahren im Weltraum

Viele Gefahren erwarten den Raumfahrer, wenn er seinen Planeten und die schützende Lufthülle verläßt.

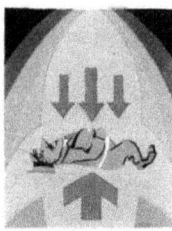 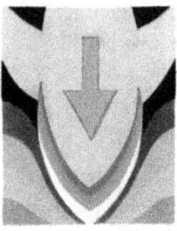 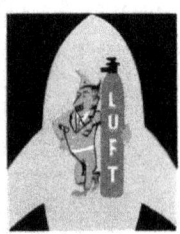

Auf dieser Tafel werden die Gefahren gezeigt, die allen Lebewesen im Weltall drohen. Noch forschen die Wissenschaftler nach wirksamen Schutzmaßnahmen, aber eines Tages wird der Raumfahrer ungefährdet von einem Planeten zum anderen fliegen können.

Innerhalb von 5 Minuten erreicht die Rakete eine Geschwindigkeit von 40000 km/st. Diese Beschleunigung vervielfacht das Gewicht des Piloten. Er kann sie nur liegend ertragen.

Beim Eintauchen in die Lufthülle reibt sich die Außenhaut der Rakete mit der Luft. Durch besondere Landemanöver verhindert man, daß sie wie eine Sternschnuppe verglüht.

Wenn der Raumfahrer die Atmosphäre verlassen will, muß er sich einen ausreichenden Luftvorrat mitnehmen, denn im Weltraum gibt es den lebensnotwendigen Sauerstoff nicht.

 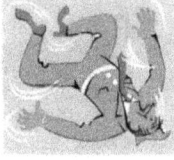  

Die Lufthülle lastet auf unserem Körper, der diesen Druck durch Gegendruck ausgleicht. Im luftleeren Raum würden wir ohne den schützenden Raumanzug beim Verlassen der Weltraumrakete zerplatzen.

In einem Raumschiff, das mit gleichbleibender Geschwindigkeit durch das All fliegt, ist jeder Körper schwerelos. Der Raumfahrer verliert die Körperbeherrschung und kann sich nicht mehr orientieren.

Die Schwerelosigkeit behindert auch die Nahrungsaufnahme. Ausgegossene Flüssigkeiten zum Beispiel schweben als kugelförmige Tropfen im Raum. Alle Getränke müssen daher gesaugt werden.

Während der langen Reise durch das All führen die Menschen ein ungewohntes Leben auf engstem Raum. Die erhöhte Nervenanspannung kann schließlich den sogenannten Weltraumkoller auslösen.

 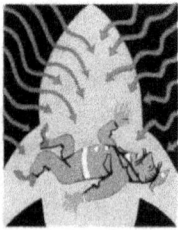  

Die Sonne sendet elektrisch geladene Teilchen aus. Diese Korpuskularstrahlen können die Wände des Schiffes durchdringen und den Weltraumpiloten gefährden.

Auch die kosmische Höhenstrahlung und die ultravioletten Sonnenstrahlen wirken äußerst schädlich auf den empfindlichen Organismus des Menschen.

Auf der Außenhaut der Rakete herrschen große Temperaturunterschiede. Auf der Sonnenseite enorme Hitze, auf der Schattenseite Weltraumkälte.

Meteoriten haben eine hohe Geschwindigkeit und damit eine große Durchschlagskraft. Sie können ein Raumschiff gefährlich beschädigen.

Figure 2.1 "Notlandung auf dem Mars" (Emergency Landing on Mars) (January 1959): 12. A page from the second episode of the *Weltraum-Serie* describes for children the effects of space travel on the human body and how people overcome those effects through technology. From *Mosaik by Hannes Hegen*, Heft-Nr 26, © Tessloff Verlag, Nürnberg, Germany.

1957 sparked fears in the United States that Western technology was being outpaced and outmatched by that of the Soviet Bloc. Across Germany, this launch and the subsequent launch of Sputnik 2 to celebrate the anniversary of the October Revolution (November by the Soviet Gregorian calendar adopted in 1914) a month later sparked immense pride among Germans, many of whom were convinced these successes could not have been achieved without German engineering secured at the end of World War II. Perhaps more importantly, the success of these launches cast a pall of doubt across the supposed superiority of Western capitalism given the Soviet Union's now proven ability to not only compete but surpass American technologies.[27] In the GDR more specifically, the two Sputnik satellites, beyond making a celebrity of the Russian dog Laika as the first cosmonaut, captured the German imaginary and the possibilities this signaled for East Germany and socialism more broadly. Here, a "cosmic culture" of sorts swept the East German landscape. East German architecture was dotted with mini-Sputniks, including a mural inside Café Moskau, cinemas were renamed to celebrate the events, and children's literature developed into a space where the cosmos could be explored in ways still denied to humans.[28] The *Weltraum-Serie* not only borrowed these tropes but also firmly entrenched itself in Soviet-inspired utopian fiction. With the comic's "textbook-like explanations" of technologies that were eerily similar to those employed by the GDR itself, the Digedags learn of the problems of life without gravity, of prolonged living arrangements in what is effectively an artificial environment, and the perils of space and the effects of a vacuum on the human body (Figure 2.1).[29] More important for the education of the comic-reading audience, perhaps, the Digedags find their new hosts locked in conflict with their rivals, reminiscent of the Earth-bound Cold War between the Soviet Union and the United States and their respective allies.

Here, the Digedags' hosts from the *Republikanische Union* of the planet Neos, embody the values of peaceful socialism and owe their name to the Union of Soviet Socialist Republics (USSR). Once the rocket abducting the Digedags docked with its mothership, the trio were welcomed aboard by the ship's captain, Peer Tyla, and introduced to some of the more prominent personnel including a lead-scientist, Bhur Yham. After these introductions and a quick visual tour of the spaceship conducted via splash page with a cutaway of the ship and its interior, indicating control centers, laboratories, and crew living spaces (Figure 2.2), Sinus explains to Dig and Dag the intricacies of outer space and the solar system as he understands them (Figure 2.3). Using an onion by way of example, Sinus employs the theories of Greco-Roman astronomer

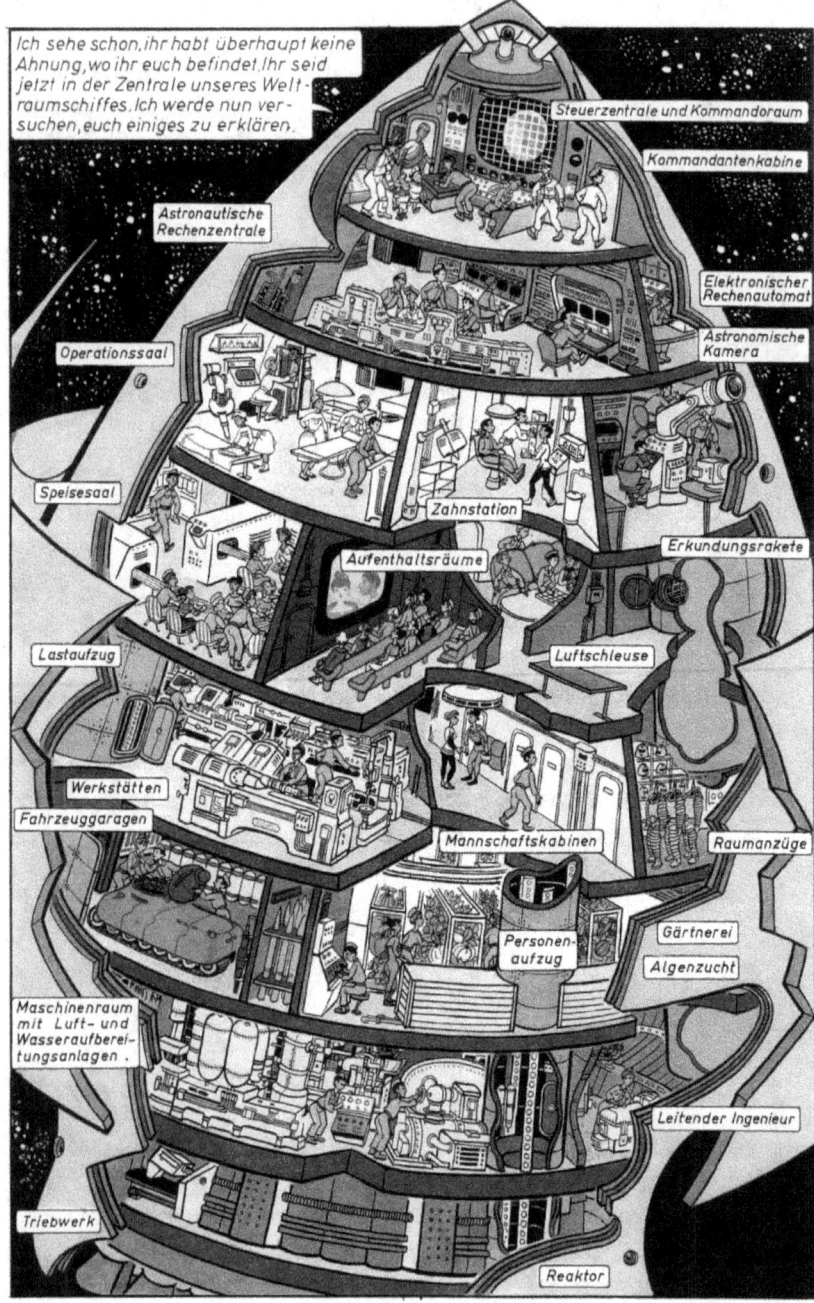

Figure 2.2. "Die Entführung ins All" (The Abduction into Space) (December 1958): 10. Neosian Union Spaceship diagram. From *Mosaik by Hannes Hegen*, Heft-Nr 25, © Tessloff Verlag, Nürnberg, Germany.

Ptolemy. He explains to the Digedags, and to *Mosaik*'s readers by extension, that space is composed of seven shells (*Schalen*) like the layers of the onion, with Earth at the center and the celestial bodies moving around it. This theory, however, directly opposes the modern, scientific knowledge possessed by the Neosians, and equally by the socialist modernity and worldview they represent. Yham steps in to correct Sinus's views; they have left Rome for the stars after all and no longer need do as the Romans do, explaining that if space was indeed like the onion as Ptolemy suggested, there would be holes blasted in these shells as the spaceship rocketed through them ("wenn es so wäre, müßte jetzt in sämtlichen Schalen ein großes Loch sein, denn wir sind doch da hindurchgeflogen"). Somewhat condescendingly, Yham says even children understand that the Earth revolves around the Sun and not the other way around as Sinus believes ("Außerdem irren Sie sich, wenn Sie glauben, daß die Sonne um die Erde kreist. Heute weiß bei uns jedes Kind, daß sich die Planeten stets um ihre Sonne bewegen").[30]

As Yham scrutinizes Sinus's approach to astronomy, he invokes a Darwinian notion of societal development apparent in the nineteenth-century utopian fiction from which the *Weltraum-Serie* drew inspiration. The future is an evolution of the present and of present-day technologies, marking an ever upward trajectory toward social and societal improvement, not entirely unlike Marxist theories of economic and social development.[31] The incorporation of familiar technologies allowed readers to envision a better tomorrow emerging from the socialist present, regardless of its actual or perceived superiority to Western, democratic contemporaries. Moreover, Yham's address is not intended for Sinus, though Sinus is taken aback by it, crying from the combination of his onion and the deconstruction of his Ptolemaic belief system, but for the children reading *Mosaik*. Yham is convinced that all (socialist) children were familiar with the most basic, and sometimes not so basic, scientific concepts and facts. Not only did this adhere to assumptions made by the SED leadership and FDJ educators that children should be interested and entertained by subjects like outer space and atomic energy that were indicative of a perceived socialist modernity, it also played to the popularity and interest surrounding space flight enjoyed in Sputnik's wake. East German educators connected material studied in the classroom and the entertainment consumed by children in *Mosaik*. As comics were a media perceived solely to provide entertainment and because their consumption was permissible in the time left unorganized by schooling, youth group meetings, and other social, though officially structured activities, comics' connection to socialist

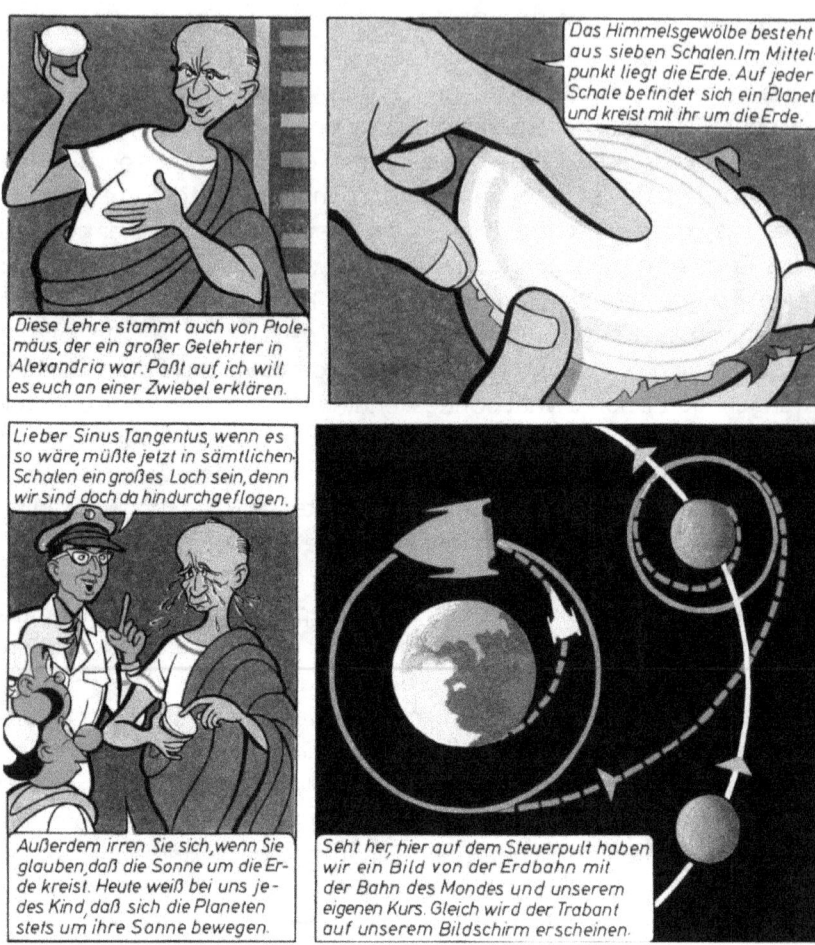

Figure 2.3. "Die Entführung ins All" (The Abduction into Space) (December 1958): 12. Sinus Tangentus explains space travel to the Digedags only to have his archaic ideas debunked by Neosian science. From *Mosaik by Hannes Hegen*, Heft-Nr 25, © Tessloff Verlag, Nürnberg, Germany.

ideology filled children's free time with notions of society, modernity, and the children's supposed role within those spaces as citizens of the SED state, demonstrable through the example set by the Digedags. In short, *Mosaik*, and comics more generally, promoted the state's ideological concerns and their perpetuation through seemingly innocuous forms of entertainment, employing the tropes of utopian fiction to demonstrate capitalist-imperialism's inhumanity while foregrounding socialism's own progressive superiority.[32]

This is apparent throughout the reader's introduction to the *Weltraum-Serie* and the society of the Neosian Republican Union. Bhur Yham, the reader's gateway character into the society represented on the page, appears to have Asian ancestry. Meanwhile, Peer Tyla seems to be apparently of Middle Eastern descent. Background characters are often, though not exclusively, Caucasian, demonstrating Neos to be a racially pluralistic society not unlike the idealized socialism. This suggests that difference between peoples in the *Weltraum-Serie* comes not from visible distinction of race, but from class, leaving issues of women's role in Neosian, and by extension socialist, society unaddressed. Although women are visible aboard the Union spaceship, as they also appear in various roles throughout the entire run of *Mosaik von Hannes Hegen*, they contribute very little.[33] In the first episode of the *Weltraum-Serie*, the most prominent female character does little more than serve as an object to be threatened by a spy from an "aggressive power" (*feindlichen Macht*), the imperialist *Großneonisches Reich* (Greater Neosian Empire). She is first introduced standing behind a table laden with beakers and samples of the lunar atmosphere. Of course, these are merely a plot device and are quickly broken upon the Digedags' arrival, requiring a trip to the moon's surface to obtain more. But despite the intimations of the character's scientific role on the Union ship, she is not actively doing anything of note with those beakers and samples prior to their destruction. In this first issue, her character does not even receive a name.[34]

Gender representation in the *Weltraum-Serie* and *Mosaik* at large notwithstanding, "*die Entführung ins All*" introduced ideological conflict to the pages of a comic which was, by and large in 1958, still intent on providing entertainment for children above socialist education. While Yham and the Digedags explore the moon's surface, Tyla is revealed as the Empire's spy. The depiction of an interstellar Cold War introduced into the comic here provided a veiled analogy for conditions experienced between East and West back on Earth. This gave the Mosaik-Kollektiv and the FDJ a platform upon which to make the socialist agenda accessible to children. Tyla as a spy for this foreign power taught vigilance, a theme repeated in children's publications such as *Frösi*, mouthpiece of the Thälmann Pioneers, and *Atze*.[35] Despite the inclusion of ideological concerns in the *Weltraum-Serie* and their importance for the FDJ and the East German publishing regime, by the time the story launched in 1958 and as demonstrated in the previous chapter, this was still the exception rather than the rule in children's publishing.

The Union's enemy, meanwhile, the *Großneonisches Reich*, is modelled after the capitalist-imperialist forces perpetually at odds with those "peaceful" socialist societies of the Soviet Bloc. Although "Reich" is the German word for "empire"' the name intentionally echoed Nazism, the Third Reich, and the destruction and death wrought by World War II and the Holocaust only a few years earlier, imperialist by its very nature within Soviet rhetoric. Despite Hegen's misgivings about the inclusion of propaganda guised as education in *Mosaik*, the *Weltraum-Serie* made space for the scientific education valued in the Soviet Bloc. Technological advancement was arguably a cornerstone of socialist ideology and the perceived march of progress perpetuated by a Marxist society.[36] Importantly, the *Weltraum-Serie* positions the Union, and by extension both the Digedags and the readers, on the side of angels, protecting developing civilizations from the Reich and preventing the Reich's exploitation of the highly valued mineral, Digedanium. In the series' first issue, the reader is alerted to Tyla's duplicity, having received orders to deliver the Union spacecraft into the Reich's hands. In this introduction, Tyla is conflicted with his obligation to the point of physical illness. Indeed, an innocent crewmember suggests Tyla suffers from *Raumkoller* (space sickness), which, as a matter of sorts, he does. In terms of the tropes of utopian fiction as a genre, Tyla falls ill from the influence of Western capitalism. This makes Tyla irrational and unable to act in the best interests of his crew or harmoniously with the "progressive power of revolutionary tradition."[37]

Though this may have been consciously unnoticed by the children reading the comic in the late 1950s, the significance of this was apparent to both the Party and the FDJ. As with the *Schwarza-Geschichten I* (Schwarza stories 1) comic by Bernd Günther appearing in *Atze* 10/1984 where Western saboteurs steal machine parts from a community in the SBZ being rebuilt after World War II, Tyla's deception and duplicity underscored the need for East German citizens to be vigilant and to defend their socialist homeland from their perceived ideological enemy.[38] Tyla's presence, not only aboard the Union spaceship but also as its captain, made clear that this danger could come from anywhere and from anyone in the supposedly ideal socialist society. Vigilance, particularly in recognizing and identifying the class enemy, became a theme common to children's literature and comics in the GDR. Moreover, the *Weltraum-Serie* taught children the difference and distinction between socialism and capitalist-imperialism. Of course, this education stemmed from the ideological perspective of East German and Soviet-style communism. This effectively set up the ducks from Carl Barks's and Disney's *Donald Duck* comics as ideological villains, even if those characters did not appear in the pages of *Mosaik* itself. The Digedags set themselves to the task of rectifying the problems created by Uncle Scrooge's perpetual quest to enrich himself and, in so doing, were helping the developing populations exploited by the Greater Neosian Reich. The aid the Digedags provided was extended to developing peoples beyond the confines of the *Weltraum-Serie*. And while comics were not official educational material in the GDR, the regime encouraged discussion of these publications with educators as part of a student's normal school routine, as suggested in the preceding chapter. This continued to be the case increasingly after the early 1960s when educators demanded more control over the kinds of stories told in comics.[39] That being the case, the increasing influence of educators and educational institutions over those comics pertained more to *Atze* than it did to *Mosaik*, at least until Hegen's departure from the latter publication in 1974.

Likewise, the *Amerika-Serie* provided *Mosaik*'s writers ample opportunity to demonstrate the differences between capitalism and socialism, while making clear the failings of the former. Beginning in 1969 in what was both the end of Hannes Hegen's tenure on the title and the arguable high point of the series, the *Amerika-Serie* was originally conceived to take place immediately following the US Civil War. The story itself ranged across the United States, intent to demonstrate the destructiveness of capitalist ideology and the continuing problems that war was supposed to solve. But of course, proving war as the solution to the problems created by capitalist-imperialism was an impossibility. In these days after the war's end, the Digedags would explore the reunified country (perhaps projecting a sense of wishful thinking, echoing Germany's own division at the time) with the newly built transcontinental railroad, completed in 1869, as a symbol of social modernity, celebrating the labor of the working class, and bemoaning the exploitation of those same workers. Just as important, the Digedags were to encounter African American characters, newly liberated from their bondage by the Emancipation Proclamation (1863), in order to explore the continuing problems experienced by the integration of African Americans into a predominantly white capitalist-imperialist American society and the lingering racism contained therein. In this original form, the *Amerika-Serie*, as it was proposed to the FDJ Central Committee, set the story in the aftermath of war. Doing so demonstrated the futility of such and that imperialist wars, which all wars are, did nothing to fix the problems of capitalist society beyond mere window-dressing.[40] This is to say that the societal problems responsible for capitalist wars remained while the bourgeoisie responsible for instigating those wars claimed solutions to social ills.

Instead of investigating the aftermath of the US Civil War, though, the *Amerika-Serie*, when it was finally released in the summer of 1969, was set in the last weeks and days immediately preceding the outbreak of that conflict. As with the series' initial proposal, children were impressed with the point of capitalism's responsibility for the social concerns plaguing the Western democracies, the United States in particular, and for any and all wars. As such, the purpose of the *Amerika-Serie* was very much like that of the Cold War dynamic found in the *Weltraum-Serie* and the relationship between the Republican Union and the Greater Neosian Reich. Throughout that earlier series, the Reich's imperialist aggression bore responsibility for tensions between the two states. With little explanation as to how they arrived there, the Digedags found themselves in New Orleans employed as newspaper reporters. This provided them opportunity and excuse to travel the country, reporting the conditions of American society to the children reading the comic as much as to their own newspaper, impressing their own brand of socialism, apparent since their earliest adventures travelling the South Seas, the Roman Empire, and outer space as they aided the exploited classes through teamwork and their "can do" spirit, while exposing the defects of the United States specifically and Western capitalist democracies more broadly.[41] The Digedags still took trains on their journey. And while this was still symbolic and celebratory of worker labor and engineering, no longer was this the transcontinental railroad linking the American nation. The African American characters encountered by the Digedags, particularly those in the southern United States, still suffered their bondage, foregrounding their exploitation without sacrificing the demonstrations of racism suggested in the original proposal. And throughout, the Digedags were pursued and harassed by Colonel Springfield, a tall, lanky man with white hair protruding from beneath his wide-brimmed hat and sporting a pointed white goatee, looking for all intents and purposes like the character of Uncle Sam, the embodiment of American ideals and idealism made famous by the World War I recruiting posters, illustrated by James Montgomery Flagg. Despite the heavy-handed socialist ideology in the formulation of the *Amerika-Serie*, *Mosaik* still owed a debt to American-style comics as the Digedags found themselves involved in treasure hunts as part of the California Gold Rush. However, this treasure was intended for the betterment of those around them rather than personal enrichment, unlike Uncle Scrooge's own adventures in the Klondike (*Uncle Scrooge* #2, 1953).

Part of this inclusion stemmed from the need to appeal to the East German children reading the comic; another part stemmed from *Mo-*

saik's expansion into Western markets to subvert Western capitalist ideologies through their own means.[42] As such, and as was indicative of *Mosaik* generally, the *Amerika-Serie* sought to appeal to children on either side of the Iron Curtain by embracing (Western) popular culture and injecting it with the socialist ideological and educational slant mandated by the FDJ and the East German educational regime. As the *Weltraum-Serie* looked to the stars and the fascination with space travel that engrossed both children and adults as the Space Race accelerated with the Sputnik satellites and the Vostok space vehicles in the late-1950s and early-1960s, the *Amerika-Serie* looked toward American-style Western stories popular among Germans in both the East and West.[43]

In Germany at large, long before defeat in World War II divided the country between occupying forces along ideological lines and even before the dawn of the twentieth century, Germans were fascinated by tales of American westward expansion. Friedrich Ratzel developed the concept of *Lebensraum* (living space in Eastern Europe), later employed by the Nazi Party during the Third Reich, and from whose work Frederick Jackson Turner developed his own frontier thesis, suggesting the link between national history and geography. Germans were thus fascinated with American expansion as it supposedly reflected their own perceived situation with Eastern Europe.[44] In other words, historically, Germans were drawn to notions of the American West and Manifest Destiny as they were indicative of Germany's own designs on Russia. These ideas were channeled by German author, Karl May, in his series of Western novels featuring the Apache Chief Winnetou and his white-European blood brother, Old Shatterhand, beginning in 1875. These novels, and part of the reason for their continued popularity in the East despite not receiving official endorsement from the SED regime, inverted the tropes of the American West story. In May's work, Winnetou and his tribe were heroic and noble warriors staring down American gunslingers and exploiters. Indeed, May heroicized Native Americans, imbuing them with characteristics that already resonated with most Germans.[45] These themes reappeared in the DEFA studio's productions beginning with *Die Söhne der großen Bärin* (Sons of the Great Bear) in 1966 in response to a wave of West German–Yugoslavian co-productions based on May's work. The Native American heroes here fought off American westward expansion, the inevitability of the railroad, and the encroachment of white Americans into their lands. As Winnetou and the Apache were in May's own works, the Native Americans in DEFA's Western films became socialist heroes, resisting the exploitation of the American bourgeoisie. The cultural popularity of American Westerns

Figure 2.4. *Fix und Fax* 116, *Atze* 9 (1967). Fix and Fax visit the moon in 1967, one year after the Soviet Luna Program landed an unmanned craft on the lunar surface. Illustration by Jürgen Kieser © Familie Kunow.

among Germans, more specifically the popularity of Native Americans as cultural artifact, led to the formation of Indian roleplay groups influenced by these stories of Native Americans and inspired the creation of more of these stories through their own visible presence in (East) German society.⁴⁶ Nor was this the only instance of Native Americans' cultural popularity and stories of the American West being harnessed by the regime through state-owned comic book publishers.

Thus far, much has been said of *Mosaik von Hannes Hegen* and with good reason. *Mosaik* was, without a doubt, the best-selling comic series in the GDR and was often able to subsume the state's ideological imperative to maintain its readership.⁴⁷ Although *Atze* was not without its own fanbase, that comic never sold the same number of copies monthly as *Mosaik* did, and it was more often targeted by the regime as the home for openly ideological stories intended to educate children in their expected roles in a socialist society.⁴⁸ *Atze*'s September 1958 issue was titled *Start in den Weltraum* (Launch into Space) and appeared on the racks at East German magazine vendors barely three months before the *Weltraum-Serie* began in *Mosaik*. And, as with that long-running story by the Mosaik-Kollektiv, this inclusion in the pages of *Atze* was part of the usurpation of popular culture in children's publications. Specifically in this instance, comics fixated on the burgeoning space-age culture and technologies surrounding the Sputnik launch, discussed elsewhere by Sonja Fritzsche, to fulfill the objectives of the FDJ and the SED state at large.⁴⁹ But the notion that the FDJ and their state-owned publishers adopted trends in popular culture to impress the needs of the regime upon children cannot and should not be thought limited to the comic books discussed to this point.

In March 1981, the children's magazine *Frösi* hosted the Frösi-treff, a "meet-up with *Frösi*." This gathering, held over two days at the *Theater im Palast der Republik* (TiP, Theater in the Palace of the Republic), the seat of the East German government, invited children to both watch and participate in a ninety-minute stage show that included music and dancing from the students of the *Haus der Jungen Talente Berlin* (House for Young Talents in Berlin), readings and recitations by famous East German children's authors, and a popular host, Gerhard Adolph. Adolph was better known as the typically track-suited television personality, Adi, from the popular Sunday morning sport-competition program *Mach mit, mach's nach, mach's besser* (Join in, do it, do it better). The weekend sports program educated school-age children and was largely successful in fostering enthusiasm around a variety of sports.

At the Frösi-treff, amidst the music, the inevitable political agenda, and the opportunity to interact with a number of people responsible for the more popular comic strips found in the pages of *Frösi*, such as *Käpt'n Lütt* by Horst Alisch and *Otto und Alwin* by Jürgen Günther, children were treated to an appearance by the Serbian actor, Gojko Mitić (Figure 2.5). Mitić was perhaps best known for his role in the popularization of the Red Western, or the *Ostern* (American-style spaghetti Westerns of Soviet Bloc origin), in the 1960s and 1970s. Appearing in *Die Söhne der großen Bärin*, Mitić became typecast as the heroic, Indigenous chief in numerous films produced by DEFA.[50] Mitić performed the songs "Lösch das Feuer" (Quench the Flame) and "Ein Mann kann viel erzählen" (A Man Can Tell Us Much), bantering with Adi between songs and again before departing the stage. And although Mitić's role in the Frösi-treff was relatively minor, his appearance was significant as the dramaturge and the production director costumed him in Native American garb from DEFA's own costume department.[51] As such, Mitić was not appearing as the actor come to greet his fans but as the character(s) that tapped the imaginations of those children, and perhaps also their parents, in the audience.

Mitić's costumed appearance shared thematic similarities to *Mosaik*'s *Amerika-Serie* comics released around the same time that Red Westerns were coming into their own in the GDR. The *Amerika-Serie* made the point of the educational aspects of the stories through the inversion of the good/evil dichotomy typically associated with stories of the American frontier. This included, but was not limited to, the comics' representation of Native Americans as an exploited yet heroic people with whom the Digedags cooperated to vanquish the perceived evils of the early American West and the bourgeoisie. Similarly, Mitić's roles, at least in terms of his performances in those Red Westerns, were consistently of Native Americans as tenacious, determined, and selfless heroes.[52] Both capitalized on the American-Western genre booming in the decades following World War II.[53] And although the comics' audience in 1981 was perhaps unfamiliar with the *Amerika-Serie* that concluded seven years earlier, the fascination with the American West and the frontier persisted in the East German imaginary through the continuation and popularity of the Red Western as a genre.[54] In both instances, though, the representation of Native Americans, and at the Frösi-treff through the appearance of Mitić in full costume, played to this inherent fascination, maintaining the interest of the children in the audience while making a political statement about the evils of Western imperialism.

Likewise, as Germany's first cosmonaut aboard the Soviet *Soyuz* 31 mission in 1978, Sigmund Jähn's name and image were invoked at the Frösi-treff. His visage, and thus the presence of space travel and exploration, was projected above the stage as Adi and the cartoonist Gerhard

Vontra quizzed members of the audience. The photo was published in *Frösi* for the anniversary of Jähn's flight, and Vontra asked some general questions regarding the cosmonaut's identity and the details of the photo and its publication.[55] As happened in *Mosaik* in the late 1950s with the *Weltraum-Serie* and discussed earlier in this chapter, the Frösi-treff drew on East Germany's participation and successes with the Soviet space program and the general enthusiasm youth held for the frontiers of space to transfix children in the audience. The appearance of Jähn summoned memories of his achievements and the possibilities he represented to the East German state as a whole. He was a symbol, not only of the possibilities of socialism in the continuation of those successes but of the utopian future promised by socialism more broadly. Paul Cooke suggests that the 2003 film directed by Wolfgang Becker, *Good Bye, Lenin!*, employed similar devices as "the importance of this utopian version of the state's ideology is symbolized throughout in the motif of space travel, and in particular the figure of Sigmund Jähn."[56] Quizzing the children demonstrated this, while tapping into their interests and the cultural zeitgeist. Through this use of the FDJ's benign power, the publisher and the creators of *Kinderzeitschriften* could educate without the need for overbearing propaganda campaigns. Though it should go without saying that those overt political speeches were still present at the Frösi-treff.

While this educational agenda must certainly be considered given the mission statement of East German comics since the reorientation of *Mosaik* and *Atze* in the early to mid-1960s, sometimes entertainment obfuscated educational moments as "the political meaning . . . is often carefully hidden under the entertaining fabric or clad in the garb of heroic adventures."[57] This does not suggest sinister motives on the part of the FDJ in the attempted formation of the socialist personality within East German youth. Rather, it was important to the regime and educators that comics take on a role valuable to society and to the development of children for no reason other than that they believed in the same ideological discussions that Hegen found so patronizing. Often, *Mosaik* was praised for its ability to entertain and, in doing so, to transmit the regime's historical education.[58] Proposals to bestow similar awards on *Atze* and Jürgen Kieser were met with resistance from the JP, necessitating the modifications to the comic's profile discussed in the previous chapter.[59] But this was not without precedent elsewhere. During the anti-comics campaigns in France, revolving around issues of national identity, concerned groups were convinced of the need to intervene in children's reading habits to provide a "solid education that

Figure 2.5. Gojko Mitić at the Frösi-treff, March 1981. BArch DC 207/686. Photographer unknown. Gojko Mitić appeared, singing on stage, in full Native American costume provided by the DEFA Studios wardrobe department. Used with permission of the Bundesarchiv-Berlin Lichterfelde, Germany.

would form citizens conscious of their duties."[60] At the same time, West Germans questioned the educational and ethical implications of American comics and their impact on children, comparing their violence and morality to the Grimm fairy tales, their appropriateness as children's entertainment called into question in light of Germany's recent experience with Nazism.[61] At the Frösi-treff in March 1981, entertainment was at the forefront of proceedings, bringing the audience into willing participation with the educational components and the perceived socialist personality.

But the appearance of both Mitić and Jähn were included and explored at the Frösi-treff for their pedagogical value. Indeed, with a twang attributable to the Red Westerns or even the American Western movies that inspired it, Mitić's song "Lösch das Feuer" is more evocative of the frontier and the American Old West than it was of the FDJ's ideological influence. Superficially about a man returning home, riding across the desert, Mitić's song seems influenced more by his own adopted persona and typecasting as a Native American than it was the obvious expression of socialism. And while the songs performed may not have spoken of socialism or encouraged the audience to think or act in a particularly socialist way, the appearance of Mitić in costume indicated this German fascination with the American Indigene and the zeitgeist surrounding such. Circuitously, Mitić's presence also invoked the FDJ's insistence upon an East German identification with the plight of Native Americans as the victims of imperialism and as antifascist fighters.[62]

Likewise, talk of Sigmund Jähn and the publication of his picture in *Frösi* recognized the educational value of a significant moment in East German history; a moment that was specifically connected to the GDR's scientific-technological revolution and linked to the development of East German heavy industry, computer technologies, and material goods.[63] Quizzing children on Jähn's accomplishments possessed no inherent entertainment value but reminded children of space exploration. It echoed the GDR's own involvement with those achievements in connection with the Soviet space program. Similarities can be drawn to the example of East German television. Quoting the SBZ regulations concerning the development of programming, Heather Gumbert writes that "in the television studios the first Propaganda-cadres of this 'airwave offensive' are being educated. Instead of 'steamroller tactics' [they] will henceforth attempt to fascinate the West German television audience with humor, sex, and jazz."[64] This approach was a decided effort to appeal to Western sensibilities, taking the perceived entertainment war on the offensive. Further, there are distinct similarities in this to the approach taken in comics and comic book culture, particularly with regard to the FDJ's use of zeitgeist as a political tool. Without overt reference to the state, these examples reiterated and reminded their audience of information learned in other environments and contexts such as the classroom. They underscored comics' unofficial linkages to socialist educational policy, drawing upon the perceived popularity of the Western and sci-fi genres within the popular imaginary.[65]

As a result, the Frösi-treff demonstrated official attitudes toward children and childhood permeating East German society since the mid-1960s and especially since Erich Honecker dethroned Walter Ulbricht from the SED Party leadership in 1971.[66] As the socialist personality infiltrated youth pedagogy from the Soviet Union and the FDJ dominated youth policy in the GDR, between the mid-1960s and the 1970s there was a shift from the scientific, materialist worldview to issues of citizenship and the development of a GDR consciousness.[67] Assuming the development of identity is a metaphoric conversation between youth and the powers in charge of youth policy, the interests of children influenced the development of policy as much as the policy was responsible for the formation of a childhood identity. In terms of the Frösi-treff, and the representation of ideology in the pages of *Mosaik* and *Atze* more generally, children's interests were as responsible for the shape of state ideology in its transmission and demonstration. The perceived lack of ideology on display at the Frösi-treff is attributable to the reader's perception of comics as space relatively free from state intervention and influence—a cultural product of the privacy found in the niche society. As the adventures in children's comic books unfold in the imagination, they were thus not considered subject to the machinations of the SED or the FDJ. This highlights the changing youth policy toward the development of GDR consciousness and the socialist personality, but also emphasizes those moments of ideology and solidarity as they appeared in a relative vacuum of such. This effectively bridged the space between the private and the public, addressing the negotiation between power and the masses.[68]

In a similar fashion, the unification of the classroom and the zeitgeist of popular culture echoed developments in West German educational reforms around the same time. Through the development of an education system independent of the authoritarianism of the earlier Nazi regime, many of these changes were implemented from the ground up and from within by educators, administrators, and, more importantly, the students themselves. In this, film and radio programming played an important role in the classroom development of West German pupils and became the basis of those students' political education, sparking debates on numerous topics to demonstrate the youths' own political awareness. The students themselves took the initiative organizing film screenings, trips to concentration camps, meetings, and "school-wide discussions of political problems."[69] Moreover, in a combined effort to ease tensions with East Germany, to provide a view of the West different than that suggested by the SED, and as part of West Germany's larger campaigns against "smut," a theme paralleled in the GDR's own comic culture and the perceived American influence in both Germanies, the Berliner Schülerparlament (Berlin Student Parliament) introduced Bill 399 in 1958 (coincidently, the same year Verlag Neues Leben began publication of the *Weltraum-Serie*) to discourage the number of "Wild West" films shown in theaters along the border.[70] This action suggests that West German students themselves employed popular culture, and in some cases discouraged that same popular culture, to mediate their own processes of *Vergangenheitsbewältigung* (coming to terms with the Nazi past). The supposed resistance to changing educational policy demonstrated by West German officials in the early postwar necessitated that those involved with the education system find their own way to negotiate reform, conducted through the critical public sphere.[71] This is similarly exemplified through the emergence of the *Außerparlamentarische Opposition* (extra-parliamentary opposition) as a youth-led public sphere to provide critical opposition absent in the Bundestag following the formation of the Grand Coalition under Chancellor Kurt Georg Kiesinger in 1966. Although the cultural zeitgeist and popular culture, including film and comics, played substantial roles in educational policy in both German states, the inclusion of these cultural trends in policy stemmed from different points of origin. The East German example itself emerged from the FDJ as having coercive, if arguably invisible, measures over children. However, by accident or intent, it was ultimately the students, the youth, and the children themselves that were able to effectively steer the direction of the cultural inclusions in education.

Nonetheless, the FDJ co-opted East German comics and comics culture to advance state-sanctioned ideological and educational imperatives, fostering the socialist personality among the child-readers of these publications. At the same time, the FDJ emphasized that this assimilation was neither malicious nor intended to detract from the entertainment value of those comics. *Mosaik* was subjected to criticisms regarding its perceived lack of educational content, at least insofar as a historical consciousness was concerned, as Hannes Hegen was irresponsible with historical accuracy when writing. The presence of the Berlin Wall as a supposedly impermeable barrier between East and West, at least until the normalization of trade relations following the German-German Basic Treaty in 1972, gave educators and youth groups the opportunity to affect the course and content of children's publications without the need to compete with the themes, tropes, and characters found in their western counterparts. However, in its newfound freedom to alter the course of those publications, Verlag Junge Welt and the FDJ retained much of what made these publications popular with children prior to 1961 in order to maintain that popularity as a vehicle for the state's educational agenda.

As happened with the Frösi-treff in 1981, the stories in *Mosaik* and *Atze* demonstrated significant steps by the FDJ to provide entertainment that spoke directly to the interests of the children whom the regime considered fans of these publications. Arguably the most widely researched and easily comparable area of East German popular culture is music and the perceived threat American "beat" music and culture posed to youth and the state. Despite the presence of the Berlin Wall and regulations regarding music considered acceptable to East German authorities, the Wall proved remarkably porous. This permeability allowed Western musical culture and influence through to the East as depicted in Leander Haußmann's 1999 film, *Sonnenallee*. Walter Ulbricht's 1963 Youth Communiqué and its accompanying reforms were, in part, attempts to bring children and youth back to the FDJ's fold and earn their support for socialism and the GDR generally. As such, the FDJ organized guitar band competitions and the "beat" radio station DT64 in time for the Deutschlandtreffen der Jugend (Germany's Youth Summit) in the mid-1960s. DT64 played Western and American rock 'n' roll and "beat" music under the condition that 60 percent of the station's content was produced in the Soviet Bloc. As youth were less interested in the music produced in the East, with some exceptions, than they were with that coming out of the West, DT64 manipulated this requirement, playing covers of Western songs by Eastern European artists and bands. Regardless, Western music, associated with American *Unkultur* broadly, as were comics also, was long considered contradictory to the ideological imperatives of the state and of the FDJ throughout the 1960s. With the weakening of Ulbricht's role as Party leader, both the SED and the FDJ took the initiative in youth policy, reversing many of the already implemented reforms. Western music remained popular, however, and to retain much of the good will generated toward youth in the 1960s, DT64 continued and thrived until the end of the East German state in 1990. This demonstrated what Patrick Major suggests was an effort to steer youth's rebellious adoption of Western culture into safer currents upon the realization that the SED regime could not overcome American influence and popular culture in the minds of youth.[72]

Space travel, the American West, exploration, and frontiers were recurring themes in East German children's entertainment. It is important to note that these themes were not limited to comics nor even exclusive to children's entertainment but included Red Westerns and Socialist Realist science fiction from Yugoslavia, Czechoslovakia, and the USSR, providing fertile ground for the creation and representation of superior forms of socialism and their utopian potential for society. Entertaining children was never mutually exclusive of education. Rather, the education and publishing regimes took important steps to educate in a manner that also entertained for the exact reason of maintaining the interest and attention of children. Maintaining that attention laid the groundwork for the socialist personality and historical consciousness necessitated by the FDJ. Comics, and comic book culture by extension, provided a malleable space wherein numerous genres over-lapped and ideas were represented without overt need for discussion stemming from the text–image relationship. In this, the state's moral and historical imperatives were subtly explored without drawing attention either to themselves or from comics' entertaining nature. The content of the comics and of the Frösi-treff was the ideology. Moreover, these themes and ideological imperatives constructed the space of comics as one that supported and maintained the acknowledged authority of institutions of governance.

Meanwhile, comics and comic book culture in the GDR transgressed the perceived separation between the public and the private domains, permeating the prized domestic niche. Children's enthusiasm for these publications meant they read them in their time away from classrooms and the officially organized daily events outside the home. Comics were taken and read in free time as they were not part of the sanctioned schooling and thus not considered part of the educational regime. Nor were these comics intended to replace approved East German textbooks. Comics were extra-curricular entertainment. That said, they still operated within the boundaries of state education. The comics' contents, the personalities and designs of their characters, their settings, and their stories spoke to the interests of youth even as the FDJ, the state-owned publishers, and the creators of those comics negotiated a niche for the publications within the regime's educational, ideological, and moral space.

Notes

1. Port, *Conflict and Stability*, 4.
2. Bart Beaty, *Unpopular Culture: Transforming the European Comic Book in the 1990s* (Toronto: University of Toronto Press, 2007), 121.
3. Saunders, *Honecker's Children*, 10.
4. Jarausch, "Care and Coercion," 52–54.
5. Fulbrook, *People's State*, 236.
6. Thomson-Wohlgemuth, *Translation*, 3–4.
7. Heiduschke, *East German Cinema*, 58.
8. Jovanovic and Koch, "Comics Debate in Germany," 108.
9. Augustine, *Red Prometheus*, 230.
10. BArch DY 24/23769.
11. Betts, *Within Walls*, 1–18, 119–47, and 173–92.
12. Heather Gumbert, *Envisioning Socialism: Television and the Cold War in the German Democratic Republic* (Ann Arbor: University of Michigan Press, 2014), 34 and 60.

13. Wright, *Comic Book Nation*, 31–42.
14. Wright, 31.
15. Jovanovic and Koch, "Comics Debate in Germany," 98–111.
16. Jovanovic and Koch, 100.
17. John A. Lent, "Comics Debate Internationally," 30.
18. BArch DY 26/173, pag. 190.
19. Qinna Shen, "Barometers," 70–74 and Thomson-Wohlgemuth, *Translation*, 225–30.
20. BArch DY 26/114, pag. 3
21. Pfeiffer, *Von Hannes Hegen*, 127 and Gersdorf, "Digedags Go West," 36.
22. Gersdorf, "Digedags Go West," 36.
23. BArch DY 26/173, pag. 197.
24. Augustine, *Red Prometheus*, 236–43.
25. BArch DY 26/173, pag. 62.
26. BArch DY 26/173, pag. 60.
27. Michael Geyer, "America in Germany: Power and the Pursuit of Americanization," in *The German-American Encounter: Conflict and Cooperation between Two Cultures, 1800–2000*, ed. Frank Trommler and Elliot Shore (New York: Berghahn Books, 2001), 128.
28. Sonja Fritzsche, "Dreams of 'Cosmic Culture' in *Der schweigende Stern* [The Silent Star, 1960]," in *Re-Imagining DEFA: East German Cinema in its National and International Contexts*, eds. Seán Allan and Sebastian Heiduschke (New York: Berghahn Books, 2016), 216.
29. Augustine, *Red Prometheus*, 232.
30. Mosaik-Kollektiv, "die Entführung ins All," 12.
31. Wittenburg, *Time Travel*, 30.
32. Darnton, *Censors*, 167–68.
33. Augustine, *Red Prometheus*, 230 and 243.
34. Mosaik-Kollektiv, "die Entführung ins All," 20–21.
35. For more on the depiction of spies in East German comics and *Kinderzeitschriften*, see Michael F. Scholz, "Images of Spies and Counterspies in East German Comics," in *Comics of the New Europe: Reflections and Intersections*, ed. Martha Kuhlman and José Alaniz (Leuven: Leuven University Press, 2020).
36. Eli Rubin, *Synthetic Socialism: Plastics & Dictatorship in the German Democratic Republic* (Chapel Hill: University of North Carolina Press, 2012), 32.
37. Darnton, *Censors*, 168.
38. *Schwarza-Geschichten I* begins as a story of antifascist resistance in a World War II concentration camp affiliated with Buchenwald, the subcamp KZ Außenlager Laura. This firmly entrenches the story in the context of the Holocaust. At the same time, this narrative effaces Jewish victims of the Holocaust choosing instead to foreground the war as an ideological struggle. The writers of this comic, as well as the FDJ and editors of *Atze* in which the strip was published, made this deliberate choice in an effort

to construct themes of East German socialist and antifascist identity. See, Eedy, "Four Colour Anti-Fascism," 24–35.
39. BArch DY 24/23769, pag. 1–4.
40. BArch DC 9/1628, "Kurzkonzeption der 'Mosaik'—Reihe," Berlin 10 October 1968, pag. 92–93.
41. Augustine, *Red Prometheus*, 232.
42. BArch DC 9/1628, "Betr.: Export," 12 May 1965, pag. 91 and Lettkemann and Scholz, *"Schuldig ist schließlich jeder,"* 44.
43. BArch DC 9/1628, "Kurzkonzeption," pag. 91. The editors of *Mosaik* clearly intended to set the *Amerika-Serie* in the United States described in the books of Mark Twain and Jack London and, in doing so, drew upon the popularity and familiarity of those American writers and their respective books when drafting plans for the continuation of *Mosaik von Hannes Hegen*. This is of particular importance as the *Amerika-Serie* were the first issues to be exported to the capitalist West. As such, both authors are mentioned, by name, in the proposal for the *Mosaik*'s *Amerika-Serie*.
44. H. Glenn Penny, *Kindred by Choice: Germans and American Indians since 1800* (Chapel Hill: University of North Carolina Press, 2013), 237.
45. Prager, Review of *Micky, Marx, und Manitu*, 364 and Darnton, *Censors*, 168.
46. Nancy Reagin, "Dances with Worlds: Karl May, 'Indian' Hobbyists, and German Fans of the American West since 1912," *Participations: Journal of Audience & Reception Studies* 13, no. 1 (May 2016): 567.
47. Lettkemann and Scholz, *"Schuldig ist schließlich jeder,"* 40–44.
48. Lettkemann and Scholz, 49.
49. Fritzsche, "Dreams of 'Cosmic Culture,'" 216.
50. F. B. Habel, "Biografie-Gojko Mitić—Schauspieler, Stuntman, Autor, Regisseur," Cinegraph-Lexikon zum deutschesprachigen Film, retrieved 14 January 2016 from http://www.cinegraph.de/lexikon/Mitic_Gojko/biografie.html.
51. BArch DC 207/686, "Zu klärende Probleme für die Frösi-Veranstaltung."
52. Habel, "Biografie-Gojko Mitić."
53. Films such as *Spur der Steine* (Traces of Stone, 1966), one of the unfortunate "Rabbit films" banned at the Eleventh Party Plenum, tapped into this imagery of the cowboy-Western movie to "occupy a place in the East German civic imaginary similar to that of Westerns in American self-understanding." It is not coincidental that this film was produced during the rise of the Red Westerns and the early developmental cycle of the *Amerika-Serie* as they all tapped into that same cultural milieu. See Joshua Feinstein, *The Triumph of the Ordinary: Depictions of Daily Life in the East German Cinema 1949–1989* (Chapel Hill: University of North Carolina Press, 2002), 185–86.
54. BArch DY 26/42, "Verlag Junge Welt, Bereich Produktion/Technik, Die Kinderzeitschrift 'Mosaik,' Berlin August 1983," pag. 1.
55. BArch DC 207/686, "Teilnehmer, Mitwerkende an der Veranstaltung FRÖSI-TREFF im Tip-Theater," pag. 2. Jähn was supposed to attend the event and Adi's script mentioned Jähn being seated in the audience; however, his

name and information are struck from the guest list perhaps suggesting a last-minute cancellation.
56. Paul Cooke, *Representing East Germany since Unification: From Colonization to Nostalgia* (Oxford: Berg, 2005), 132–33.
57. BArch DY 26/173, "Zu den allgemeinen Aufgaben der Kinderzeitungen und –zeitschriften einer sozialistischen Gesellschaft," pag. 5.
58. BArch DY 24/8674.
59. Lettkemann and Scholz, *"Schuldig ist schließlich jeder,"* 49.
60. Jobs, "Tarzan under Attack," 690.
61. Jovanovic and Koch, "Comics Debate in Germany," 98. Similarities may also be drawn to the American experience as education remained an imperative for critics of comics, including Wertham. As comics appealed to and largely targeted the working classes since the turn of the twentieth century, there existed a class-based bias surrounding comics and education linking comics with the unsophisticated and the poorly educated, see Wright, *Comic Book Nation*, 86–91. This, despite the use of comics as literacy tools: see, Shari Sabeti, "Reading Graphic Novels in School: Texts, Contexts and the Interpretive Work of Critical Reading," *Pedagogy, Culture & Society* 20, no. 2 (2012): 191. In East Germany, one of the FDJ's primary tasks was the socialist political education of youth that was inherently bound by notions of national identity and often created events purposefully to combine indoctrination and recreation, see Madarasz, *Conflict and Compromise*, 62–63 and Ross, *Constructing Socialism*, 73.
62. Reagin, "Dances with Worlds," 567.
63. Augustine, *Red Prometheus*, 230–32 and Rubin, *Synthetic Socialism*, 30–32 and 71.
64. Joseph Naftzinger, "Policy-Making in the German Democratic Republic: The Response to West German Trans-Border Broadcasting" (PhD diss., University of Maryland at College Park, 1994), cited in Gumbert, *Envisioning Socialism*, 34.
65. Nothnagle, *East German Myth*, 60–83. Nothnagle suggests the FDJ and Thälmann Pioneers specifically turned to representations of anti-fascist heroism in popular culture and fairy tales as children were considered too young to properly understand the "classics" of German *Kultur*. This worked hand-in-hand with larger FDJ practices to develop a dedicated *Kinderkultur* of high quality.
66. Benita Blessing suggests DEFA children's films employ stories of folk tales and fantasy, essentially tapping into the zeitgeist of childhood, as means of disseminating state ideology and education. This had the effect of bringing the classroom into film as the FDJ similarly brought comics into the classroom and made films as much for adults as for children, providing as much documentary as distraction. See Blessing, "DEFA Children's Films," 243–62.
67. Saunders, *Honecker's Children*, 10–15.

68. Mark Berninger, Jochen Ecke, and Gideon Haberkorn, "Introduction," in *Comics as a Nexus of Cultures: Essays on the Interplay of Media, Disciplines, and International Perspectives*, ed. Mark Berninger, Jochen Ecke, and Gideon Haberkorn (Jefferson: McFarland & Company, Inc., 2010), 3.
69. Brian M. Puaca, *Learning Democracy: Education Reform in West Germany, 1945–1965* (New York: Berghahn Books, 2009), 121–22.
70. Puaca, *Learning Democracy*, 142–43.
71. Puaca, 37–40. See also, Werner Bergmann, *Antisemitismus in öffentlichen Konflikten: Kollektives Lernen in der politischen Kultur der Bundesrepublik 1949–1989* (Frankfurt: Campus Verlag, 1997), particularly "II. Die Wiederkehr des Themas Antisemitismus 1958–1961," 187–278.
72. See Fulbrook, *People's State*, 130–35; Patrick Major, "'Smut and Trash': Germany's Culture Wars against Pulp Fiction," in *Mass Media, Culture, and Society in Twentieth-Century Germany*, ed. Karl Christian Führer and Corey Ross (Houndmills: Palgrave, 2006), 245–47; McDougall, "Liberal Interlude," *Debatte* 9, no. 2 (2001): 139–50; McLellan, *Love in the Time of Communism*, 24–26; Ross, *Constructing Socialism*, 139; and Wierling, "Youth as Internal Enemy," 162–66.

CHAPTER 3

Power, *Eigensinn*, and the Construction of Space through Comics

The previous chapters discussed East German comics and comic book culture as spaces employed by the SED regime in which to lay the foundations of a socialist education. Specifically, the changes made to *Atze* in the mid-1960s, the stories found in *Mosaik von Hannes Hegen* in the early 1960s and 1970s, and the Frösi-treff in 1981 were used to demonstrate what Mary Fulbrook conceptualizes as "benign power," typically unnoticed by the population. Here, I suggest this to be particularly so in terms of the thematic underpinnings of comics published by Verlag Junge Welt and their use by the FDJ in the construction of state socialism and the development of the socialist personality among its citizens. By employing these power structures in the comic books written and designed for consumption by children, as these books targeted those children too young for membership in the Free German Youth, state influence transgressed the perceived isolation of the private or domestic sphere.[1] However, for children to warrant bringing these comics into the home or otherwise engage with them in what would be construed as free time, comics needed to retain those aspects of Western comics that popularized titles such as *Mosaik von Hannes Hegen* prior to the construction of the Berlin Wall and maintain those levels of genuine popularity. In essence, the state's publishers needed to "win over" their readers, afterward. Tapping the cultural zeitgeist in the stories of those comics, the socialist regime largely rendered the educational nature of these comics invisible to the reader. Or, at the very least, the creators of those comics made efforts to present ideology in a way that was entertaining so as to distract readers from the comics' socialist agenda. Popular themes and subject matter gave child-readers an opportunity and the ability to overlook that ideology, regardless of the truth of those children's awareness of ideological influence. Co-opting the interests of children and catering to their interests to disguise education in entertainment, the FDJ blurred divisions between the public and private spheres, permeating the boundaries of what is often considered the niche, compartmentalized society of the German Democratic Republic.

As a result, Günter Gaus's notion of the niche society seems insufficient to capture the essence of the state and of the East German *Alltag*. The preceding chapter, and indeed this one as well, describes comics and comics culture in the GDR as products of the *durchherrschte Gesellschaft*. It is also necessary to understand these comics and the surrounding East German youth culture in terms of the concept of *Eigensinn*. As much as *Eigensinn* may be simply thought of as "doing things one's own way," it is equally the construction of space negotiated between state power and the population so that the population can live "normally" and arguably free of the state's influence, interference, and observation. And in this, concepts such as "normal" and "free" are based on the population's willful ignorance with regard to the acknowledged reach of the SED state and its institutions. This constructed space is tied to the process of identity formation, individual interests, and pursuits. While Gaus highlights the importance assigned to identity formation through the widely argued retreat into the private sphere, the "niche" fails to demonstrate the significance of interactions between the revered private sphere and the much more studied public sphere of the SED regime.[2] The conceptualization of *Eigensinn* suggests that identity in the GDR was a give-and-take relationship between the state and the population from which those in authority were desperate for popular legitimacy. *Eigensinn* connects the perceived divisions between dissent and conformity "by emphasizing how the pursuit of one's interests . . . is integrally related to social and political circumstances."[3] This interaction was essential to the formation of the loyalties demonstrated by children and youth in the SED state.[4]

This chapter moves beyond what appeared in the actual comics themselves and the, oftentimes, literal dialogue between the state-owned publisher Verlag Junge Welt and the children reading these comics and *Kinderzeitschriften*. The problem in writing a history of the German media, and this should by no means be considered a problem limited only to media in Germany, is that the perceived shortage of sources results in a relatively thin scholarship. This problem stems from the fact that these sources are often in the hands of private companies and publishers reluctant to open their archives to historians. In the case of (East) Germany, this is further problematized by German (re)unification in 1990, the privatization of East German firms, and the mishandling of that mission by the Treuhandanstalt (a trust agency set up for the task by the Ministerrat under Hans Modrow from a law passed by the East German Volkskammer). The history and connection of these publications to the former socialist regime have the potential to make their new owners unwilling to allow researchers access, even if these sources survived the process of privatization. As a result, the scholarship on the German press and genres of East German mass media, comics included, are subject to a reliance on sources produced by the state. This suggests that there exists a tendency toward drafting political histories of the German press.[5] While faced with these same limitations, I hope to overcome this obstacle in asking what these government-produced sources have to say about the children reading and influenced by these publications.

This chapter analyzes reports compiled with regard to letters written to *Atze* and *Frösi* and to the publisher more broadly over the course of 1972. These reports demonstrate that children sidelined the ideological impetus of the comics and magazines they read. In and of itself, this does not suggest that these children consciously attempted to rebel against the regime. That said, children favored what they perceived to be the apolitical material of those publications. Indeed, their willful ignorance of the state-sanctioned propaganda within those comics, as noted elsewhere by Dolores Augustine, in some ways align their actions with the sense of *Eigensinn* and of the culture of complaint conveyed by their parents. Moreover, children's actions potentially parallel how their parents' generation experienced notions of privacy and the private sphere in East German society. East German comics, and thus the FDJ's political influence, transgressed the perceived boundaries between the public and private as a combined result of their content and their popularity among youth. While children responded to the socialist content of these publications in their letters to the publishers and editors, these propagandistic aspects are often overlooked in favor of more obviously entertaining content. Of course, overt socialist content was not consciously ignored by the readership. There are strong indications that children engaged with this material along the lines of the FDJ's hopes and expectations, incorporating what they read into aspects of their state-sanctioned education in schools. However, children did not entirely understand these comics in the ways desired by the FDJ and often without conscious awareness of the power enacted over them. Within the space afforded by comics, children constructed their own understanding of what those comics meant and how they engaged and interacted with those meanings. State power was not wholly unrecognized, but comics were understood as part of the domestic sphere in which they were consumed. The spaces these comics constructed enabled points of interaction between the FDJ and children as each co-opted and reinterpreted the other's meaning and intent.

In 1986, West German journalist Theo Sommer wrote of the GDR, citing Günter Gaus, that: "the private sphere serves as a place of refuge where one can escape the reach of politics." In this way, Sommer understood and defined Gaus's conceptualization of the "niche society" as "the preferred space in which people there leave everything [. . .] behind . . . and spend time with family and friends" without giving thought to the state or acknowledging the state's intrusion into that space.[6] This suggests that, for the individual and their family, the state ceased to exist at the front door to the home. Of course, the perception of privacy ignores the reality as East German literature, news reporting, and television were constant reminders of the SED regime's benign presence in the daily lives of the population.[7] The domestic space was also indicative of the public's willful avoidance of the state's use of power to shape and control its citizens. This suggests something of a blind spot on the part of the state, unwilling to acknowledge those spaces "free" from its reach, and of the public, unwilling to acknowledge the state's intrusion into the domestic space. The "niche society" this created allowed GDR citizens the ability, within reason, to choose what aspects of the East German state, if any, were consumed by the individual.[8] The "niche" of privacy in the GDR was thus interpreted as a "semi-permeable refuge from public life and prescribed collective identity."[9] Within the home, citizens were relatively free, or considered themselves free, to inscribe themselves with their own constructions of identity in the absence of the state. At the same time, the regime's strength stemmed from the perceived invisibility of its own power. This permitted the state to cross the threshold of the private sphere unimpeded. Moreover, the home was a key instance of *Eigensinn* in that the perception of this privacy allowed the individual the construction of one's own self-identity and self-identification. This does not suggest individual dissent or resistance, but the opportunity to express desires and anxieties unrelated to the collective constructions of the state. In the compartmentalization of East German society and identity formations, the private space is never entirely separate from SED state power structures but run through by those constructions.[10]

Privacy and the home had no inherent or determined political meaning but depended upon the situation and individual, challenging the notion that it was simply a matter of repression and withdrawal from that repression in the GDR's "niche society."[11] Had the state chosen to politicize this retreat, to effectively characterize withdrawal as a political act, this would undoubtedly have created the East German population as a society of "heroic resistance fighters." Instead, functionaries avoided confrontation through the attempted satisfaction of workers' and, as is the case here, children's demands and interests.[12] Though speaking to East Germans' withdrawal from social and public life, the "niche" does not address why this withdrawal was necessary beyond the repressive measures enacted by the SED regime. Likewise, the "niche" does not recognize the permeability of privacy. The consumption of comics, in terms of *Eigensinn* constructed by tensions between state and individual and this retreat into the private, created a space in which children pursued their desires.

The perceived absence of authority gave comics the ability to "provoke" as anything imagined could be drawn, and drawings were simpler to digest and understand than words on the printed page.[13] The FDJ understood this as well. In a letter nominating the editors of *Mosaik* for a gold medal for outstanding achievements toward the socialist education in the 'Ernst Thälmann' Pioneer Organization (*Medaille für hervorragende Leistungen bei der sozialistischen Erziehung in der Pionierorganisation 'Ernst Thälmann'*), the FDJ suggested that comics developed the reader's imagination through their graphical style and colorful design in a way that both television and literature could not. Comics' power was specifically the result of the confluence of text and image inherent to the medium. Comics represented the socialist-humanist and educational objectives while providing an important counter to the imperialist *Schund– und Schmutzliteratur*.[14] Perhaps most important, the power of comics was found in the imaginations of their readers due to the perceived ease with which drawings were interpreted and given meaning and in the gutters the FDJ fought to control. Here, the FDJ and the creators of comics in the GDR thought messages given form in a comic book narrative had the tendency to shape the reality of the readership. Moreover, sharing themes across a group brought the individual into that group so that they identified with the larger group reality and symbolically converged with that group. To this end, the FDJ attempted to control the message in the comics they published and with the delivery of that message to bring child-readers into the larger grouping of socialist society.[15] In *Comic Books as History*, Joseph Witek argues that comic book reading requires discipline from the reader. In addition, the artistic controls with which the comic is imbued by its creator(s) shape how the reader perceives narrative structure. As such, the changes wrought to East German comic book productions in the 1960s not only affected and altered content on a rudimentary level but attempted to shape how that content was understood and how children interacted as a group and in society as a result of their reading experience.[16]

Among comic readership, the audience is a conscious collaborator in the creation of meaning between the text and image as the connection between the two is never made explicit. Rather, image and text exist as symbols given meaning by an audience that possesses an understanding of those symbols and how those symbols are intended to function together. This focuses the reader's attention through the universality of the symbols.[17] The gutters are spaces between comic panels in which nothing happens and "human imagination takes two separate images and transforms them into a single idea" in a conscious, consensual, and deliberate way.[18] The child-readers are active participants, making their own meaning of the socialist-educational, humanistic, and moral content present in their comics. For exactly this reason, comics were problematic in postwar North America and Western Europe as violence, sex, coarse and colloquial language, as well as other perceived threats to childhood development, supposedly occurred in the imaginations of the readers where it took the strongest root and did the most damage.[19] As such, comics transgressed the boundaries between the public and the imaginary. That is to say, comics' meaning was determined in the ultimate private space where the individual was considered alone within him or herself.[20]

When considering comics and the notion of *Eigensinn*, it is important to recognize this interaction and the level of that interaction between the audience, in this case the child-readers, and the FDJ.[21] Comics affected their audience in a way television could not as the consumption of television programming and content was a largely passive affair.[22] Comics provided a space more effective and conducive to the interaction of citizen and state. Children's engagement with these comics negotiated their perceived level of interaction with the regime and the state's penetration into the "niche" or private sphere of the domestic home.

In 1972, reports noted that most *Kinderzeitschriften*, including comics, typically received only a few hundred letters, some significantly fewer. The exception to this was *Atze* for its continuing stories of *Pats Reiseabenteuer* by Wolfgang Altenburger and Jürgen Kieser's *Fix und Fax*.[23] In January, the publisher Verlag Junge Welt received more than fourteen thousand letters of which nine thousand were written for *Fix und Fax* and another four thousand for *Pats Reiseabenteuer*. The following month, this number was flipped as *Pats Reiseabenteuer* drew in more than ten thousand of a total eleven thousand eight hundred letters. For the entire second half of the year, then, *Pats Reiseabenteuer* was noted as having received more than twenty-seven thousand letters from readers. This is not to suggest that Altenburger's comic strip became more popular than Keiser's. Rather, as the report notes elsewhere, the *Volkspolizei-Preisausschreiben* (People's Police competition) and the *Feuerwehr-Preisausschreiben* (Fire Department competition) each received more than nine thousand and thirteen thousand reader letters, respectively. The numbers for *Fix und Fax* from January 1972 were specifically for the *Fix und Fax-Preisausschreiben*. Another eighty-seven hundred letters were noted as received in April for the *Drushba-Preisausschreiben* (Friendship-competition).[24] To engage the child-readership not only with the comic-stories themselves but also with the regime and the social life of the society, the FDJ regularly employed competitions and sweepstakes in the publications of Verlag Junge Welt.

Pats Reiseabenteuer typically drew in a few thousand letters per month, vastly outpacing the average number of letters received for stories appearing in *Atze*. Written by Altenburger and illustrated by Harry Schlegel, *Pats Reiseabenteuer* followed the adventures of a wandering journeyman as he travelled throughout Germany during the latter half of the nineteenth century, meeting famous historical figures and getting into what the creators called "political turmoil." The feature regularly appeared in a four-color, two-page center spread in *Atze* from 1967 until 1991 when production of *Atze* ceased in the wake of German (re)unification.[25] Due to cost considerations, *Atze* was not printed using the four-color method entirely, but its sixteen pages were split between this and two-color printing. Without fail, *Fix und Fax* and *Pats Reiseabenteuer* were printed in four-color. Significantly, the political cover story was largely printed in only two-color (refer to Figure 1.4. as example) or shifted between the two print styles. This brought to the publisher, the editors, and the FDJ's awareness which aspects of the book were favored among children and which should receive the most attention. Therefore, at the end of each installment of *Pats Reiseabenteuer* was printed, often though not always, in red to stand out against the black text of the story: "What did not exist at the time? Write or draw it on a postcard and send it to *ATZE*." Three small prizes were offered for children sending in the correct answer. Some of these prizes were educational in nature while others were provided purely for entertainment

Figure 3.1. *Pats Reiseabenteuer* 240: "Das schönste Fest" (The Most Beautiful Celebration), *Atze* 12 (1986). Arguably, the "Was gab es damals noch nicht?" contest popularized the *Pat* comic strip among child-readers. Illustrations by Harry Schlegel © Martina and Günter Fuhlbrügge.

purposes. For example, the March 1984 issue offered Abrafaxe puzzles to winners. By contrast, the September 1984 issue offered globes and the December 1986 issue featured children's encyclopedia (*Kinderlexika*). Inside the back cover of each issue appeared an *Atze Post*, a letters column of sorts where, among the heavily edited reader letters and an editorial from *Atze*'s staff, winners' names were printed beside the correct answer from the issue two months prior under the heading *Pat-Auflösung* (Pat-Solution).

This contest kept children engaged with the material and maintained readers from month to month as the children submitting responses to the publication hoped to win. Asking children to identify aspects of these comics that did not fit the represented time period required that those children either possess or acquire knowledge of history and current events to fully understand the content of the comics. The *Pat-Auflösung* for the July 1984 and October 1986 issues, for example, respectively stated that neither latex paints nor hairdryers existed during Pat's time. Regardless of their perceived lack of context in *Pats Reiseabenteuer*, the presence of these objects, misplaced in time, spoke to the perceived "cult of technology" in the GDR. As with the inclusion of plastics, plastic products, and

Figure 3.2. *Max und Maxi* 75, *Atze* 12 (1986). Each issue of *Atze* closed with a letters page, including a short *Max und Maxi* comic strip by Harry Schlegel (pictured here), and the "Pat-Auflösung" announcing the winners of the "Was gab es damal noch nicht?" contest from two months prior. Illustrations by Harry Schlegel © Martina and Günter Fuhlbrügge.

advertising in *Mosaik*, this was part of a larger celebration of socialist achievement and the use of technology to create a utopian future.[26] At the same time, the contents in *Pats Reiseabenteuer* ensured that *Atze* was part of a larger educational agenda, subtly directing children's engagement with that material.

Despite the potential significance of these letters relating to contests run in both *Atze* and *Frösi* and the demonstration of the perceived success of the socialist educational program in East German comics and *Kinderzeitschriften*, these contest letters, and letters about *Pats Reiseabenteuer* and *Atze* more generally, received little attention in reports made to the FDJ. Elsewhere, Matthew Pustz suggests that American publishers used letter columns in the 1940s and 1950s, particularly with regard to EC comics, consolidating their audience in creating a sense of cooperation between reader and creator. Further, letter columns created a window into questions of readership and reader interaction and identification through the formation of a perceived meeting site. In this site, readers could address creators and other fans in a sense that speaks to Habermas's conceptualization of the public sphere and to the larger creation of fan culture and community not unlike Benedict Anderson's imagined communities.[27]

The authors of the reports recognized Pat's popularity, stating that by the mid-point of 1972 "Pat is consistently the most popular character in our magazine." The character is praised for "always urging the reader toward new perspectives." Rather than assessing why *Pats Reiseabenteuer* was popular in the first place, commentary on the feature suggested the inclusion of the activities of the Lenin Pioneers during the Great Patriotic War (World War II), of Western imperialist intervention in Vietnam, and the figure of Thomas Müntzer in potential future stories.[28] Indeed, many of these suggestions did not even fit the nineteenth-century setting of the comics, becoming themselves ironically reflective of the *Was gab es damal noch nicht* contests contained within the comic strip. This demonstrated some degree of ignorance toward the contents of the *Pats Reiseabenteuer* stories themselves and why those stories remained popular. The exception here was two excerpted letters in the report at the top of a series of excerpted letters. Both of these, and these were the only two specifically mentioning *Pats Reiseabenteuer* or the Pat character, were written by confessed long-time readers of the comic. Both children framed their love of the character and of the comics in terms of the socialist worldview and the perceived formation of the socialist personality. The first letter, from a female reader, suggested that Pat was her favorite "because he always thought of the poor and helped them." The second letter, meanwhile, came from a male reader who called Pat "exemplary of fighters who fought for freedom and justice in the previous century."[29] The authors of these letters understood the necessity of speaking the socialist language of the regime. In doing so, these children voiced their opinions and their love of the character and his adventures in a way that stood out among the thousands of letters received, garnering recognition from those compiling the reports. This is indicative of SED policy following Erich Honecker's ascendency in 1971, scaling back practices of indoctrination and requiring only that citizens demonstrate outward loyalty to the regime. These public demonstrations of Party loyalty were irrespective of practices within the home pertaining to the ersatz public sphere and of the *Eigensinn*. In turn, this allowed for the relative reduction of tensions between citizen and state.[30] That their letters were published in the report while many others were not belies the importance of "speaking socialism" as Sheila Fitzpatrick has noted elsewhere.[31] The letters that followed consisted of children writing of their experiences in school, with the Ernst Thälmann Pioneers or their Patenbrigades with little or no mention of *Atze*, its comics or characters.[32]

As with the letters specifically invoking *Pats Reiseabenteuer* as the point of discussion, these letters spoke to the regime by employing its own rhetoric. In this way, these letters gave the child audience voice. As these letters appeared largely uncritical of the regime, in any obvious sense, they framed problems in a way suggesting discourse with the FDJ to find solutions rather than firm opposition. The authors of the reports suggest that the children voiced confidence and trust in the comics, the characters, and the creators of *Atze* in addition to an awareness that the publication provided them a source of aid, advice, and suggestions to deal with the socialist world around them. Letters received from *Atze*'s readers and their use of socialist language within was then reflective of the East German practice of *Eingaben*. These petitions, officially endorsed by the state, provided for a limited public sphere, demonstrating the centrality of the private sphere as the point of interaction between the state and society.[33] The failures of the Honecker-led SED regime to fulfill the population's consumptive desires created conditions whereby citizens felt emboldened enough in their frustration to shed perceived anonymity to affect change through these *Eingaben*.[34] The letters written to *Atze* and compiled for these reports caught the attention of the publishing regime exactly because of the trust demonstrated in addressing the magazine. The children reading *Atze* approached the perceived problems of the classroom and their Pioneer groups in a conversational way that was not suggestive of failure on the part of the FDJ, the East

German state, or socialism more broadly. As a result, the publishing regime responded in a manner that sought to pursue and address the problems experienced by the child-readers. Promising to answer each letter individually, the report's authors suggest that for problems affecting the student-teacher relationship, it was important to involve parents and advisory bodies to help the Pioneers and strengthen these relationships.[35] This did not constitute an admission of failure from the FDJ, but, more accurately, described a desire to keep the children's expressed trust and demonstrate that said trust was deserved. Although in these examples, the children reading *Atze* may be simply expressing their devotion to the characters and comics they so loved, these child-readers appeared to understand their own letters and interactions with the publishers in ways similar to practices of complaint taken up by their parents. Children interpreted their comics as extensions and products of the private space in which they were consumed and treated them as such, as the ersatz public sphere they represented.

These letters, the comics, and their interactions within the private space, deconstructed an important sense of distance between citizen and state necessary to Gaus's "niche" society. Typically, these letters were not a laundry list of complaints against educators or Thälmann Pioneer group leaders. Letters appeared more conversational, not as though the children addressed schoolyard friends, but as though they shared experiences to parents or others in obvious positions of authority. These children spoke of what they learned in their classes or at their Pioneer meetings, including information and names the FDJ considered significant. For example, one letter mentions the struggles of the heroic peoples of Vietnam and the war against US imperialism as taught in school. Another discusses Angela Davis, a noted leader of the Communist Party USA, as part of the American protest movement against US military actions in Vietnam. Davis visited the German Democratic Republic the following year, 1973, to participate in the 10th World Festival of Youth and Students in East Berlin. Known as the "Red Woodstock," this festival was organized by the left-wing groups, the World Federation of Democratic Youth and the International Union of Students. A third letter, then, discussed recent youth group activities and named their involved Pioneer leader while a fourth child wrote about a visit from two representatives from the Patenbrigade to their classroom.[36]

The children do not openly complain about the content, activities, or practices of their classrooms or youth groups so far as the excerpts available demonstrate. It is clear, however, that the children reading *Atze* were comfortable discussing these aspects of their public lives with the editorial staff as representatives of the regime. Children established connections between comics, access to the regime, and their own sense of *Eigensinn*. The space that children thus created for themselves marks a distinction between the public and the private in that the private is not discussed in these excerpted letters. Of course, these letters are heavily edited by the authors of the reports and the portions included are only those considered important by the FDJ. But still, this engagement with comics brings the public into private life and the private sphere insofar as children necessarily transgressed the boundaries between public and private in their reading of comics and the production of their own, albeit limited and perhaps unintentional, use of *Eingaben*.[37]

That said, these letters regarding contests found in *Pats Reiseabenteuer*, or respondents to contests in other comics and features for that matter, held little real significance in these reports. This perception serves to explain why, in a section of the reports clearly demarcated to provide opinions about the book (*Meinungen zum Heft*), here meaning *Atze* and *Pats Reiseabenteuer* specifically, the reports' authors chose to focus on and excerpt those letters that mentioned the comic only in passing in order to favor letters regarding the educational and ideological agenda of the FDJ.[38] The assessment and extracts from letters from readers (*Einschätzung und Auszüge aus Leserschriften*) for the reports is dominated by concerns about preparations for the fiftieth anniversary of the Lenin Pioneers, solidarity with Vietnam, experiences in the classroom and youth group. This includes concerns regarding discipline and sponsorship relationships with the Patenbrigades, and the approaching International Children's Day.[39] In this way, the reports' authors and the FDJ leadership conflated the comics with issues of ideological significance to the regime as the child-readers themselves demonstrated, by accident or design, in the excerpted letters.[40] Indeed, the reports' authors were concerned with the contents of *Atze* only insofar as they served socialist educational agendas, chastising the publication for its perceived inability to produce the appropriate socialist personality amongst its readership.[41] This perhaps indicates that the letters regarding *Pats Reiseabenteuer* were more heavily edited than previously suggested and, indeed, were edited with the specific intent of demonstrating in an obvious fashion the regime's own associations between those comics and the state's ideological education. Despite this, the insistence still remains that the children writing those letters were able, at least in part, to adopt the language and positions of the regime, providing themselves voice in constructing their own limited *Eingaben* culture focused on these comics.

This was not, however, limited to the pages of *Atze*. Other reports on reader-letters received for *Trommel* and *Frösi* for the first half of 1972 bear striking similarities in both ideological objectives and reader response. Perhaps more important, these letters were categorized not only by their subjects as an indicator of the popularity of a particular feature but also by the readers' genders, locations, approximate age, including whether the authors were children or adults (parents, educators, or other interested parties), and whether these letters came from individuals or collectives such as a particular Thälmann Pioneer group, with additional categories for individual issues.[42] These magazines were not dedicated comic books as was *Atze*, but children's magazines closer to familiar North American publications like *Owl* (Owlkids Publishing, Toronto, 1976–present) and *The Electric Company* (Children's Television Workshop, New York, 1972–1987) that included comic strips such as *Mäxchen und Tüte* (in *Frösi*) in addition to other edutainment feature articles.[43] That these *Kinderzeitschriften* were not proper comics did not make them more obviously ideological than *Atze* or *Mosaik*. Indeed, following changes made to *Atze*'s content and format in 1966 under the direction of Altenburger, stories such as "The Sealed Train" (*Der versiegelte Zug*) and "The Soldier from Treptow" (*Der Soldat von Treptow*) made *Atze* every bit as ideologically driven as other aspects of FDJ policy.[44] But this pattern indicates that the notion of *Eigensinn*, demonstrated through the child-readers' limited *Eingaben*, intersected both the state's malign and benign diffusion of power.[45] It is to this interaction between public and private, the state's use of power in *Kinderzeitschriften*, and the child-reader's often unconscious resistance to state authority in the construction of identity and voiced preferences that this chapter now turns.

In the reports on *Frösi* and *Trommel* for the first six months of 1972, the authors clearly laid out the obligations of the Thälmann Pioneers and FDJ-ler and FDJ-lerinnen and, in turn, the responsibilities of these *Kinderzeitschriften*. As explained by the reports' authors, the publications were meant to fulfill the pioneers' duty for classroom engagement, suggesting that the pioneers who wrote to the editors typically demonstrated exemplary results in this area. However, this was not always the case as:

> It turns out that it is often impossible in the classroom to respond to each child and help their individual progress. Oftentimes grades are the most important thing, rather than the effort to awaken in each child the self-confidence that they are able to improve their performance. From the letters, it can be seen that the children themselves are often left with poor grades as they do not discuss what they must do and when in order to improve their performance. In many instances, praise and the sense of achievement did not work enough.[46]

As such, it was the responsibility of comics and *Kinderzeitschriften* not typically associated with the classroom to fill the educational void left by the system. As children struggled and educators were unable to help all of those students on an individual basis in the classroom as required by the state, the importance of the educational and ideological content of comics and magazines became central to the FDJ's educational policy platform.[47] A majority of the letters written to the publications that received replies addressed concerns regarding class trips and school work, including learning experiences, help with that learning, classroom discipline, and the completion of group projects (*Erfüllung der Gruppenplanes*). While the reports allowed room for letters written regarding the content of the comic and magazine publications themselves, this typically referred to the publications' ideological content such as the fiftieth anniversary of the Lenin Pioneers or pointed criticisms directed toward that content.[48]

These reports demonstrate a specific ideological skew directed by the authors of those reports and of the FDJ. Therein, the authors describe the importance of the educational objectives of these children's publications to make the appearance that readers engaged with those magazines through their letters. One reader requested the inclusion of quick and easy recipes, noting that her mother suffered from a repetitive motion injury (*Sehnenscheidentzündung*) and required help around the house. Another asked that the editors include, in every second or third published issue of *Frösi*, a map of different cities across the German Democratic Republic with pictures of highlighted attractions and natural resources in the area. Yet a third suggested the inclusion of trivia contests about cities and *Länder* (states or provinces) in *Mäxchen und Tüte*, a four-panel comic strip in *Frösi* that already taught readers about littering and bicycle safety, among other things.[49] This request connected *Mäxchen und Tüte* to the previous letter in its request for geographical education, thus explaining its inclusion in the report. At the same time, the suggestion of a contest connected the comic strip to the precedent set by *Pats Reiseabenteuer*, providing prizes that tested readers' historical knowledge. These requests, categorized as "wishes" (*Wünsche*) in the reports, were not critical of the publications' content, but suggested additional content serving the educational objectives of the FDJ and the overall formation of the socialist personality.[50] While these reader suggestions were compiled by the regime to demonstrate connections between the regime's planning and the readership's desires for what they read, these suggestions also imply that in some instances children made those connections themselves, arguably without the influence of the editorial regime.

These same reports indicate complaints made in those same reader letters. From time to time in issues of *Frösi*, the publishers included instructions for craft projects for the children to complete. These included pre-colored, designed, and decorated templates that the readers could cut out from the magazine, not unlike similar templates adorning the back cover of Western children's magazines or cereal boxes. The template receiving the brunt of complaints in these reports was for a box printed on sheets, perforated to presumably aid children with removing them from the publication in order to cut along predetermined seams without the need for scissors. Throughout the letters, children complained of holes being too small and pieces of the design jutting at odd angles once the box was constructed so that the completed craft was unattractive and not at all what was promised in the instructions. The letters do not make broad, political complaints against the FDJ or the regime.[51] Instead, these letters focused on deficiencies in the execution of the plan as opposed to the potential failures of the plan, and thus the failures of the construction of socialism and the socialist SED state itself, not unlike practices elsewhere in popular culture.

Heather Gumbert points to *Eingaben* in relation to East German television and viewer interest and interaction with the programming. Although her monograph opens with an example of an individual writing in with a proposal for a vigilante-style action show more suited to West German or American television, perhaps indicating where the viewer's interests lay and in which direction his television receiver was pointed, this is followed later in the book with numerous examples of *Eingaben* and the culture of complaint discussed here. Importantly, Gumbert indicates complaints made regarding the following: the Deutsche Fernsehfunk's (DFF) inability to transmit live creating a temporal chasm between when a soccer (*Fußball*) match was played and when the television audience could actually watch that match at home, rescheduling the Black Channel so child-viewers could watch as it was popular with their demographic, and political complaints made against a televised play despite the same radio play being so well received by the regime. None of these examples leveled complaints against the DFF or criticized the SED regime itself. What was brought to the attention of officials here was the audience's perceived right to that televised entertainment and the population's ability to engage with the regime through the medium of television. As such, a broader argument can be made regarding the ways in which East Germans understood and consumed entertainment and how this is influenced by supposed freedoms enjoyed across the East-West divide. Moreover, the perceived culture of complaint emerging in East German comic culture was not limited to that medium, but spread throughout popular culture generally and suggested how entertainment informed the citizen's own engagement with the regime.[52] Likewise, Esther von Richthofen warns that *Eingaben* should be treated carefully as they are constructed to fulfill a specific agenda by the author. As such, *Eingaben* are not indicative of the true thoughts and feelings of their authors but demonstrate "what people had come to expect from the SED."[53] Likewise, this includes what children expected from comics, magazines, and their associated entertainment.

This continued the culture of *Eingaben* as the children involved here engaged with these comic books and *Kinderzeitschriften* to develop their own interests and in their own ways.[54] The letters and petitions in these reports, termed "critical notes regarding the perforated template" (*kritische Hinweise zur Lochschablone*) by the reports' authors, expressed disappointment in the promises of the publication and with the provided craft activity as much as they appear critical of the deficiencies of the template provided.[55] As much as this suggests children criticized the forms of entertainment provided to them when they did not fulfill their stated purpose or function, by extension and unconscious though it may be, these readers criticized the FDJ in terms of its own consumerized politics.[56] This underscored the significance of the East German niche society, often associated with the privacy offered by the domestic sphere, as a space allowing for the interaction of citizen and state. Although arguable as to whether the culture of complaint generated through the *Eingaben* allowed East Germans an actual "voice," those letters permitted different and various means by which children created their own sense of space. In that private space, the child-readers provided the state with the degree of participation necessary for the perpetuation and acceptance of the FDJ and SED structures of power.[57]

These letters addressed exactly the educational beliefs that educators and the FDJ concerned themselves with since the early 1960s. While these templates were intended for entertainment purposes, their instructions also suggested they be used to craft a box for Teacher's Day, as recounted by the author of one of those letters. The author lamented that, due to the template's problems, "I cannot craft a nice box for Teacher's Day. That is too bad." Another wrote that "the perforated sheet for the hole decoration was a little too small. My classmates also complained. *Frösi* is the best regardless."[58] While these voiced the complaints of the child-readers, those complaints were not explicitly directed at the regime or the FDJ. Rather, these complaints were framed in terms of the child-readers' intention, but inability, to engage with the educational-ideological content provided in the pages of *Frösi* and *Trommel* and on its own terms, not to mention similar content provided in either *Atze* or *Mosaik*. Complaints leveled against the deficiencies of this craft project were discussed for the direct connection being made by the publishers themselves between the *Kinderzeitschriften*, the craft project, and the classroom. These letters established the effectiveness of the educational nature of the *Kinderzeitschriften* and the child-reader's desire to participate in the classroom or with the educational content of those publications, and with the regime more broadly speaking, on a level beyond the rudimentary student–teacher relationship.

Of course, the act of letter-writing does not suggest an actual desire to engage with the FDJ or with the regime, only the perception of such. The culture of *Eingaben* provided a substitute for a legitimate public sphere, located within the domestic niche, around which citizens voiced complaints to the SED regime in a limited way that was acceptable within the regime's framework of Konrad Jarausch's "welfare dictatorship." Built upon the notion of the GDR as both a *durchherrschte Gesellschaft* and a "modern dictatorship" as a means to explain the contradictory forces working in the organization of the East German state, the "welfare dictatorship" characterizes the SED regime as patriarchal politics that "demonstrated [their] concern for a powerless population," buttressed by Stasi surveillance and bureaucracy.[59] This suggests that the GDR and the SED regime were dependent upon social policies, including education, "social services, material policy, and artistic cultivation," to foster popular support that was fundamental to Honecker's "unity of economic and social policy."[60] This support was largely conditional upon the state's ability to fulfill the population's material needs, creating what Jarausch terms "reluctant loyalty."[61] While this "reluctant loyalty" does not precipitate the East German population's retreat into the niche or domestic sphere, it was an acceptable and not entirely unwelcomed by-product of those outward demonstrations of loyalty mandated by the SED leadership after 1971.

This process of "reluctant loyalty" made the domestic home a space of increased personal freedom while creating a confluence of "alternative identity formation" and state anxiety and surveillance.[62] In terms of the comics and *Kinderzeitschriften* discussed here, the child-readers used their own variation of the *Eingaben* petitions to affect their situation(s) based on the perceived deficiencies of the material goods provided them. They consciously decided to engage with publishers on their own terms, understanding that the crafts project was made available to them as part of their classroom engagement and thus part of their educational regiment. Issuing complaints over the failings of this project suggests the children reading these publications recognized those deficiencies as failure of the material promises issued by the GDR as a "welfare dictatorship." As such, these children expressed their problems with the regime, via the publication, in terms of their disappointment. While the children still demonstrated their "reluctant loyalty," professing that *Frösi*, and the regime by extension, was still great, their letters spoke to the regime's inability to deliver the material goods required for the continuation of their support of the FDJ and its educational campaign. In a slightly different context, Katherine Pence suggests that *Eingaben* were not only for the population to make their needs and desires known but they were also employed as indicators of loyalty. Women often established connections between those desires and the relative health of the state. There exists, in this, a correlation between the perceived happiness of the individual citizen and their willingness to participate and engage with the regime.[63]

However, the culture of complaint fostered by the *Eingaben* is in no way representative of the majority of letters received.[64] As complaints made against Verlag Junge Welt regarding these publications were relatively few, this may arguably be indicative of genuine support for the *Kinderzeitschriften* by those child-readers. Although children demonstrated that they understood the domestic space in terms of the ersatz public sphere that was itself associated with the *Nischengesellschaft*, and did so in ways similar to the undertakings of their parents, this lack of complaint perhaps suggests that children's understanding of complaint and their own roles within socialist society were still developing. It also suggests that the culture of complaint developing among these children and located within the domestic niche was itself influenced and informed by observing both their parents and their parents' interactions with the state. A detailed breakdown for the month of August 1972 indicates that, of the more than forty-seven thousand letters received, only sixty were categorized as criticism, wishes, or praise. As a result, the child-reader's engagement with the FDJ's publications cannot be understood solely in terms of the "reluctant loyalty" located in the significance of the domestic. More often, it was the case that children used these publications, and here we may arguably include the likes of *Atze* and *Mosaik*, as spaces in which to voice their individual interests. In this way, these children's magazines act as extensions of the domestic space in which the child-readers themselves engaged with the publications in a variety of ways. As was the case with *Atze* and *Pats Reiseabenteuer*, most of the letters received responded to the *Drushba-Quiz* (12,934) or else were directed to pen pals either within or outside of the East German state (*Briefspartner—Ausland—DDR* 13,152; *DDR—Ausland* 8,287). Other notable topics included what the reports' authors categorized as "Art Connoisseurs" (*Kunstkenner*) (3,117); the *SL-System* (*Schnell Lade* or speed loading, a cassette film camera made by the *ORWO* company in Wolfen, GDR based on a *Agfa Karat* design with 2,753 letters); and *Mini-Max* (a comics supplement to *Frösi* starring the *Mäxchen* character; 1,620). Other letters are spread across a number of other subjects ranging from Pioneer work (803) and work for the FDJ (7) to holidays (234) and sport (25), with numbers typically ranging between a few dozen and a few hundred, though never in sufficient quantities to challenge those leading categories.[65] With such a wide range of categories spread across a great number of reader-letters, the reports' figures suggest that children recognized this space of letters as more than a site of complaint. They recognized this space as one in which they were free, within understandable limits, to express thoughts and desires normally reserved for the domestic space.[66] At the very least, these letters provided a site of interaction that was, in and of itself, without political meaning but served as an accepted substitute for an ersatz public sphere.

This perceived extension of the domestic space or niche is evidenced through the ways in which these child-readers chose to engage with the *Kinderzeitschriften*, the publishers, or the regime. While a decided minority wrote in with criticisms of the publication's supposed deficiencies with its craft template for a Teacher's Day box, many others wrote of subjects that were either not typically associated with the content of *Frösi* or else were beyond the scope of topics deemed ideologically relevant by the FDJ. The authors of the reports themselves considered this an unusual month for reader letters, attributing not only the high volume generally but also the abundance of letters regarding holidays in particular to the increased free time afforded children by the school summer break. And although the reports' authors chose to focus on the claims to good or bad grades made in these letters, further associating the *Kinderzeitschriften* with the perceived success of its educational mandate, they considered these letters and the children who wrote them to be very engaged in their accounts (*beschäftigt sie auch sehr das Zeugnis*), honest and open (*ehrlich und offen*).[67]

Further, it must be mentioned that those child-readers engaging with the "wishes" wrote to the publications as though writing to and making requests of friends. One child-reader wrote in, asking: "In addition, could you arrange a small exchange-corner in *Frösi*?" Another child-reader, mentioned earlier, asked, "can you not include contests about cities and states in the adventures of *Mäxchen* and *Tüte*?"[68] In these examples, and indeed in all the excerpted letters where the child-readers make requests of the publishers, the children address the *Kinderzeitschriften*, their creative and editorial staffs, and by extension the FDJ, using the informal "*du*." Although it is difficult to draw too many conclusions from this usage given the relatively small number of letters published in the reports, this tends to suggest that children understood the editorial regime in terms of the publications themselves. Comics and the *Kinderzeitschriften* were thus considered part of the private sphere in which they were consumed rather than of the "welfare dictatorship" that produced them. When children wrote to these publications, they did so with the notion that the editorial regime was on their side and in such a way that allowed those children to discuss not only those subjects of particular interest to the FDJ but also those topics that may otherwise remain behind closed doors.

This does not, however, suggest that children treated these publications the same or that they responded to them in the same ways. Generally speaking, it is considered that those children who engaged with the editorial regime through these letters did so in ways that blurred distinctions between public and private, political and domestic. As a rule, this group is also dominantly female. Of the excerpted letters provided in these reports in any category, only the one requesting the formation of an exchange corner, noted above, was written by a boy. While this is insufficient in itself to make assertions regarding the gender of these young letter-writers, the reports' authors note that East German girls typically wrote to the publications in numbers greater than boys for the years 1972 and 1973. In June 1972, of the 467 submissions received regarding the question of *Frösi*'s "picture of the month," those sent in by girls (326) accounted for more than twice as many as those received from boys (141). Likewise, letters regarding the question "where is your workspace" numbered forty submissions from girls while boys accounted for only nineteen.[69] In the second quarter of 1973 across all categories of letters received, those letters written by female-readers numbered more than fourteen hundred. Boys, on the other hand, accounted for a paltry four hundred forty-nine by comparison.[70] Of course, these numbers may not hold since the debut of *ABC-Zeitung* in 1947, *Frösi* in 1953, or the launch of *Atze* and *Mosaik* in 1955. That is not suggested here. In the period under discussion, the early to mid-1970s, girls engaged with the editorial regimes of these publications more often and in a larger variety of ways than did boys.

Overall, these numbers do little to explain why girls were more inclined to write letters to these publications. This cannot be attributed solely to concerns regarding chores in the home or cooking, although these subjects were apparent. Nor was this suggestive that girls were somehow more interested in the publications than boys. *Mosaik* was itself a very male-oriented publication having little interaction between the genders and when men and women did interact, women were by no means in positions of authority.[71] However, gender difference is crucial to notions of privacy and of the domestic sphere in which the niche society tended to operate. Women were typically responsible for most of the *Eingaben* written to the regime and more often dominated campaigns for improvement in the social, cultural, educational, and organizational lives of their regions.[72] These *Kinderzeitschriften* were brought into and, more often than not, consumed within the domestic space. As such, they were arguably considered part of that private sphere and conflated the ideas of the public and of the private through the reader-letters themselves. Women's experience with the domestic created a female consciousness that resisted the regime through private challenges made in the domestic sphere.[73] This consciousness manifested in the *Eingaben* as a private challenge to the regime couched in the regime's own rhetoric of gender equality and female emancipation, not unlike those letters written to Verlag Junge Welt.

Although the SED regime, and the regimes of every state across the Soviet Bloc for that matter, made claims pertaining to the equality enjoyed between men and women under socialism, the reality was that women were more likely to work outside the home in addition to upholding traditional gender norms related to women's role in the domestic space. As Mary Fulbrook argues, work, political engagement, and other areas typically associated with the sphere occupied by men were tacked on to the existing and "traditional" roles of women. This double burden was often reinforced by East German men who perpetuated those gender roles. Of course, it would be a gross generalization to suggest that to be the case without exception across the whole of East German society. However, the uneven distribution of housework and child-care proved the rule more often than not.[74] V. I. Lenin recognized this problem shortly after the October Revolution in Russia, unsuccessfully attempting to organize communal kitchens, laundries, child-care, and other facilities and services to alleviate the exploitative burden put on women in terms of their labor in the home.[75] As women often had more experience and more disillusionment when it came to the realities of shopping, consumer items, child-care, job opportunities, or even of those equal rights much touted by the regime, the culture of complaint arising within the home was itself often, though not exclusively, a feminized site of contact with the regime.[76] Moreover, Hilary Chute argues comics themselves to be a feminized space. The perceived feminization of the comics medium emerged from its association with the lowbrow culture that was not at all indicative of the East German state. At the same time, comics blended genres through their integration of image and text. This blending or "blurring," as Chute notes, emasculates each of those distinct genres. In effect, the whole is less than the sum of its parts and as a result associated here with the feminine.[77] With the relationships established by readers in their letters and in the practices of reading these comic books and other publications intended for children, and the regime's own efforts to penetrate the domestic with these publications, these reader-letters created the ideal space for young girls to engage with state-sanctioned aspects of their "private" lives, like the educational and Pioneer activities that occupied their everyday lives, through the domestic sphere and in ways endorsed by the FDJ.

At the same time, the FDJ and the publishers of these *Kinderzeitschriften* responded to these letters in roughly equal proportions to the genders of the letter writers themselves although in nowhere near the same volume. In August 1972, of the more than forty-seven thousand letters received, only 504 received direct responses from the editors of *Frösi*. Of these, 365 responses were addressed to girls with another 133 to boys. These numbers are relatively proportionate to the approximate numbers in which letters were received. Overall, they addressed the more pressing concerns of the regime, the FDJ, and the publishers in terms of the content of their comics and *Kinderzeitschriften*. That is, these responses were grouped into only four thematic categories: Pioneer work (187), FDJ work (19), school (67), and opinions regarding *Frösi* both as a whole and as individual issues (242).[78] In terms of reader gender divisions and the regime's decision to respond in roughly proportionate numbers, an argument can be made regarding women's perceived niche within the private sphere and the regime's own desire to blur its distinction from the public and the political. Women employed the domestic space as resistance in ways inaccessible to men or else in ways men themselves did not pursue. However, these reports do not support or refute such assessments of publisher motivations when responding as they did. Neither do these reports suggest that girls read *Frösi* in greater numbers than boys nor that the regime felt it necessary to target girls more directly in their ideological campaigning. Simply, these publications were associated with the private space and, as such, girls interacted with them in ways boys did not, arguably a result of girls' and women's perceived roles within the domestic space associated with East German niche society.

But the FDJ's motivations and those of the publishers coincided with the larger machinations of the regime. In the early to mid-1960s, the FDJ entertained new concepts and formats for *Mosaik* and *Atze* to address the concerns of the regime and of educators over the perceived insubstantial content of these publications. Children's magazines such as *Frösi*, *Trommel*, and *ABC-Zeitung* which were not comics per se, but included comic strips in addition to other content, were not as problematic to the FDJ as were the Western-influenced comics largely due to their diversity of content.

We also must not forget the weekly youth publication, *Neues Leben* (New Life), published by the Central Committee of the FDJ in which Erich Honecker served as both founder and chairman when the publication first launched in 1946 and then again when it was relaunched in 1955. Honecker's role in the FDJ in addition to his direct influence over youth policy, and with regard to publications intended for youth, suggest the extent to which Honecker valued youth participation and the importance of youth indoctrination into the socialist system. Of course, this does not explain Honecker's hesitation toward his mentor's Youth Communiqué and tolerance of Western influence in the early 1960s. Nor does it explain Honecker's adoption of some of those same influences following his rise to power and the promises he made during the SED Eighth Party Congress in 1971 over the fulfillment of consumer desires: Honecker's "unity of economic and social policy." In this instance, however, it is important to note Honecker's influence over these youth publications, his long-standing interests in steering the energies of East German youth, and the tolerance coupled with increased surveillance that characterized the "thaw" associated with the early period of Honecker's term in office.[79]

Nonetheless, the motivations and transitions within the ranks of those children's publications may, in part, be attributed to Margot Honecker's appointment as Minister of Education in 1963, around the same time *Mosaik* and *Atze* underwent their drastic transformations of form and function, and her hardline belief that educational work should foster an emotional bond between youth and the state in support of SED policy.[80] More properly, though, this approach to children's interaction with the publications may be understood with Erich Honecker's assumption of SED authority from Walter Ulbricht in 1971. East German youth policy only stabilized after the implementation of the Act on the Integrated Socialist Education System of 25 February 1965, two years after Margot Honecker's appointment. However, it was at the SED Eighth Party Congress, in the immediate wake of Erich Honecker becoming SED General Secretary, where Honecker declared efforts to forge the socialist personality among East German youth as the primary task and duty of the SED state. At this moment, children's publications were inundated with images of the unfaltering antifascist hero, led by a sanitized version of the popular socialist hero, Ernst Thälmann, or "Teddy" as he was known.[81] As it was conceived here, the socialist personality encompassed "socialist awareness" over the focus on community and social order that characterized the concept during the 1950s and 1960s when *Mosaik* and *Atze* were turned toward a clarified educational strategy under the direction of Wolfgang Altenburger.[82] The significance of the socialist personality continued through the transition of power from Ulbricht to Honecker, but this continuity was in name alone as youth policy under the Honecker-led SED embraced the outward demonstration of socialist awareness at the expense of a greater foundation or building-up of socialist society as a whole.

Efforts to draw children and youth toward the socialist project during the Honecker era were characterized less by honest attempts to win youth loyalty than they were by pragmatic efforts to win loyalty through material goods.[83] This was, in turn, accompanied by an increase in surveillance, not only among the dissidents or youth sub- and countercultures but among children as well. Children understood these comics and *Kinderzeitschriften* in terms of their constructions of self and created a space perceived to be an extension of the domestic niche and supposedly free of the regime's influence. At the same time, their letters, and specifically the reports about those letters, marked a shift in the perception surrounding these publications and the supposed division between the public and the private, the political and the domestic. These reports appeared immediately after the implementation of policies enacted in the wake of the SED's Eighth Party Congress. As these compiled large amounts of data on the child-readership via their letters, they represent potentially pervasive and intrusive forms of surveillance that tread softly between benign and malign forms of power.

The publications themselves were typically demonstrative of the regime's benign power, promoting the FDJ's ideological and educational concerns in ways that went largely unnoticed by readers. *Mosaik*'s *Amerika-Serie* provides a prime example of this overlooked use of ideology through the use of the comics medium and the adventures of the Digedags travelling across the United States. Even the frequent inclusions of the Volksarmee (People's Army) in these publications went unremarked by most readers and did nothing to change attitudes among youth when it came time for compulsory service.[84] This obfuscation of the regime's intent allowed comics and *Kinderzeitschriften* access to the domesticity and privacy afforded by the niche society even as children recreated those publications as spaces of identity and engaged with these publications for their own interests and desires, perceptibly rendering the content of these magazines harmless. That said, the reports' authors compiled information regarding readers' genders, ages, school districts, and home addresses. Not only this, but the purpose of these reports was to describe for the FDJ leadership, in an easily digestible form, the thoughts and feelings of the readership toward those publications to determine the overall effectiveness of the ideology printed within their pages.[85] In writing letters to the publications and engaging with those publications in ways asserting their own sense of *Eigensinn* or otherwise providing children space to voice their desires within what was assumed to be the private sphere, the child-readers gave the FDJ the tools required for their own surveillance. Writing letters, mimicking the culture of complaint fostered by their parents, these children provided the regime information well beyond their likes and dislikes as they related to the comics and the characters about which they read. As such, these comics and *Kinderzeitschriften* acted as constructions of the state to invisibly enable and enact SED rule.

In terms of the private space inhabited by the child-readers, these publications moved between the forces of benign and malign power demonstrated by the regime. For our purposes, malign power was the "repressive, coercive and manipulative means of exerting power." This form of power included the vast state bureaucracy, the omnipresent Stasi, and their implementation of carrots and sticks used to keep the East German population in line, if not as active participants within the state.[86] Typically, these reports were not drafted with the obvious intent of repression or of surveillance, but to examine aspects of the publications to which children responded on an emotional level to further promote the goals of the regime. Nor is there evidence enough to support the supposition that these reports were malicious and actively used as a means of surveillance, despite children having provided the tools for such in their letters to those publications including their ages, genders, classroom experiences, and, in some instances, information related to their home lives. That being the case, the idea of deploying state-sanctioned malign power through these reports to coerce or manipulate child-readers into adhering to specific ideological tenets or educational objects seems not only unlikely but unnecessary.

However, the editors of *Frösi* drafted 504 responses to letters received in August 1972. Categorizing these responses, the FDJ and *Frösi*'s publishing regime channeled the dialogue and interaction with those child-readers in a direction beneficial to the *Kinderzeitschriften* and to the goals of the creators, publishers, and educators involved. Arguably, the editorial regime had no intent beyond a profound belief in the socialist project and the formation of the socialist personality among those child-readers. Wolfgang Altenburger was himself an ideal and loyal party member, believing in and supporting the ideological and educational work of these comics and *Kinderzeitschriften* during his tenure as Editor-in-Chief of *Atze* and *Mosaik*.[87] Rather, in following the directives before them, the editorial staff of these publications focused on areas of interest and discussion that fostered this sense of the socialist personality in all its nebulous forms. It was important that these conversations were conducted through children's interest in and interactions with those publications. Engagement with ideological aspects of the FDJ's youth policy was endorsed in the pages of *Frösi*, *Trommel*, *Atze*, and the other *Kinderzeitschriften* and comics published in the GDR, though it was difficult to measure the level by which these messages were received and internalized. Responding directly to those children who willingly engaged with the political components of the publications allowed the FDJ access to the private, the domestic sphere, and the mental space in which the readership understood their comics and magazines. These children allowed the regime access to the niche society that was supposedly free from the intrusions of the state, as did their parents through the act of writing *Eingaben*. While this interaction bore aspects of the regime's malign power, those strong-arm ideological forces were largely subsumed by interactions with the child-readers already engaging with the socialist educational content in their own ways of understanding, in their own spaces, and on their own terms.

Comics and *Kinderzeitschriften* were never subject to any single meaning by either their publishers or the children reading them. Though this information was filtered through the publications' editorial regime and the authors of the reports, the reports themselves demonstrate a variety of interpretations to the publications. These publications occupied a liminal space between the desires of those parties involved, not only in their creation but also in their consumption. As a result, comics and *Kinderzeitschriften* moved between and were understood in terms of both the public and the private sphere, often at the same time. These publications were created as part of the public sphere occupied by the state. At least since the early 1960s, they addressed the FDJ's educational and ideological needs through the reorganization and streamlining of content and the ways by which that content was delivered, particularly with regard to comics noted in earlier chapters. However, due to the nature of these publications and the ways the child-readership interacted with them, they were also part of the private sphere of the domestic home and the niche society. Largely these publications were read during moments that went unregulated by authority figures. Although the comics and magazines addressed concerns dealt with in schools and at youth groups meetings, the methods of consumption associated these publications with leisure, privacy, and domesticity more than they did with the official FDJ institutions with which they interacted.

This largely feminized the space of comics and the space associated with the writing of letters to those children's publications. As with the notion of the *Eingaben* themselves, due to the social constructions of the state, the reality of gender divisions, and the masculinization and feminization of roles and spaces within East German society despite official rhetoric to the contrary, privacy and the domestic space were typically associated with women. Of course, this does not suggest that girls were the only ones reading and interacting with these publications. Many boys also wrote to the editors and many more than that also read *Kinderzeitschriften* and the masculinized space within the stories of *Mosaik*. However, in these reports compiled for 1972 and 1973, children's publications were accepted as part of the domestic and girls appeared to interact with them to a greater degree than did boys. As a result of this interaction between the child-readers, the FDJ, and the comics publications, *Kinderzeitschriften* became a feminized space of childhood and childhood interaction due to the domestic space with which they were associated. These publications were transported into the feminized domestic space, co-opting them for the purposes of consumption and engagement. The perceived linkages between these comics and magazines and the private space as a site of engagement through the practice of *Eingaben* gave children the ability to separate those publications from the masculine spaces and constructions of paternal state authority.

Although the FDJ and its publishers attempted to use the space created through letters as a means of engaging readers, directing how those readers interpreted and interacted with the content, the publishing regime interacted with the readership in terms of the *Alltag* as much as with the publications' ideological and educational content. Letters addressing the contests in *Pats Reiseabenteuer* or requesting recipes in *Frösi* suggested that readers internalized the purposes of the contents of those magazines and what was required of the socialist personality even though this was not openly discussed. This required the FDJ to respond to these letters in ways that, often, did not suggest the SED state's repressive tendencies that were more readily demonstrated outside the domestic space. The regime's reaction thus allowed the private space to develop as a perceived niche within East German society. These publications encouraged child-readers to give voice to their interests and desires, to develop their own limited sense of *Eigensinn* as a negotiation between the needs of the regime and those of the readers themselves, finding expression within this domestic space.

Notes

1. BArch DY 26/42, "Verlag Junge Welt Bereich Produktion/Technik, Berlin August 1983," pag. 1.
2. Saunders, *Honecker's Children*, 10–15.
3. Corey Ross, *The East German Dictatorship: Problems and Perspectives in the Interpretation of the GDR* (London: Arnold, 2002), 124 cited in Saunders, *Honecker's Children*, 228.
4. Saunders, *Honecker's Children*, 228.
5. Führer and Ross, "Mass Media," 15.
6. "A Liberal Western Journalist Praises the Progress of the GDR (1986)," German History in Documents and Images, retrieved 1 February 2016 from http://germanhistorydocs.ghi-dc.org/docpage.cfm?docpage_id=44.
7. See Jürgen Kocka, "Eine durchherrschte Gesellschaft," in *Sozialgeschichte der DDR*, ed. Harmut Kaelbe, Jürgen Kocka, and Hartmut Zwahr (Stuttgart: Klett-Cotta, 1994), 547–53 and Alf Lüdtke, "'Helden der Arbeit'—Mühen beim Arbeiten. Zur mißmutigen Loyalität von Industriearbeitern in der DDR," in *Sozialgeschichte der DDR*, ed. Harmut Kaelbe, Jürgen Kocka, and Hartmut Zwahr (Stuttgart: Klett-Cotta, 1994), 188–213. Both authors here suggest that the *durchherrschte Gesellschaft* functions through the perceived conflation of state and society. This was not always the case, however, and the notion of this conflation was sometimes stronger and more omnipresent than the reality.
8. See also, Annette F. Timm, *The Politics of Fertility in Twentieth-Century Berlin* (Cambridge: Cambridge University Press, 2010).
9. Paul Betts, "Building Socialism at Home: The Case of East German Interiors," in *Socialist Modern: East German Everyday Culture and Politics*, ed. Katherine Pence and Paul Betts (Ann Arbor: University of Michigan Press, 2008), 114.

10. Betts, *Within Walls*, 13–14.
11. Betts, 14–15.
12. Port, *Conflict and Stability*, 275–81.
13. Anne Rubenstein, *Bad Language*, 7.
14. BArch DY 24/8674, "Vorschlag zur Auszeichnung der Redaktion der Zeitschrift 'Mosaik'," pag. 1–2.
15. Jonathon David Tankel and Keith Murphy, "Collecting Comic Books: A Study of the Fan and Curatorial Consumption," in *Theorizing Fandom: Fans, Subculture, and Identity*, ed. Cheryl Harris and Alison Alexander (Cresskill: Hampton Press, Inc., 1998), 62–63.
16. Witek, *Comic Books as History*, 7–9.
17. McCloud, *Understanding Comics*, 30–31.
18. McCloud, 66 and 68.
19. Jobs, "Tarzan Under Attack," 692.
20. Martin Barker suggests that no encounter with media is passive as the audience will actively choose what is consumed. That said, the act of watching television requires less from its audience as that audience cannot affect or influence the narrative or its meaning. As such, Shari Sabeti, drawing from Barker, contends that comics foster a symbiotic relationship with their readership. See Martin Barker, *Comics: Ideology, Power and the Critics* (Manchester: Manchester University Press, 1989), 11 and 244; and Shari Sabeti, "The Irony of 'Cool Club': The Place of Comic Book Reading in Schools," *Journal of Graphic Novels and Comics* 2, no. 2 (December 2011): 144.
21. For more on the relationship between state and subject and how it is negotiated through the notion of the *Eigensinn*, see Thomas Lindenberger, "SED-Herrschaft als soziale Praxis—Herrschaft und 'Eigen-Sinn': Problemstellung und Begriffe," in *Staatsicherheit und Gesellschaft. Studien zum Herrschaftsalltag in der DDR*, ed. Jens Gieseke (Göttingen: Vandenhoeck & Ruprecht, 2007), 23–47.
22. McCloud, *Understanding Comics*, 68–69; BArch DY 24/1581, "Konzeption für das neue Profil der Bilderzeitschrift 'Atze'," pag. 3.
23. BArch DY 24/23769.
24. BArch DY 24/23769. The word for friendship here derives from the Russian as the competition itself spoke to the notion of the East German-Soviet relationship in the postwar.
25. BArch DY 26/42 and Guido Weißhahn, "Pats Reiseabenteuer," *DDR Comics*, retrieved 7 February 2016 from http://ddr-comics.de/pat.htm. Four-color refers to the early process of coloring comics whereby cyan, magenta, yellow, and black were used to create the complete spectrum of color in comics.
26. Rubin, *Synthetic Socialism*, 32–33 and 118.
27. For further, see Benedict Anderson, *Imagined Communities: Reflections on the Origin and Spread of Nationalism* (London: Verso, 1983); Pustz, *Comic Book Culture*, xi–xiii and 155–57; Jessamyn Neuhaus, "How Wonder Woman

Helped My Students 'Join the Conversation'": Comic Books as Teaching Tools in a History Methodology Course," in *Comic Books and American Cultural History*, ed. Matthew J. Pustz (New York: Continuum, 2012), 15–17.
28. Thomas Müntzer was a reformer during the Protestant Reformation and rebel leader during the Peasant's War in Thuringia (1524–25). Twentieth-century Marxists consider Müntzer an early leader of bourgeois revolution against feudalism toward a classless society, see Manfred Bensing, "Thomas Müntzer," *Encyclopedia Britannica*, retrieved 9 February 2016 from http://www.britannica.com/biography/Thomas-Muntzer.
29. BArch DY 24/23769, Jan–June 1972, pag. 7–9.
30. Under Honecker's leadership the SED supposedly opened itself to public criticisms in order to give the impression of freedom within the state, as was partially necessitated by ongoing negotiations toward the German-German Basic Treaty (1972). However, this was coupled with an unprecedented enlargement of the Stasi and of the state's observational regime. See Grieder, *German Democratic Republic*, 10–14 and Saunders, *Honecker's Children*, 50–104.
31. Fitzpatrick, *Everyday Stalinism*, 166.
32. BArch DY 24/23769, Jan–June 1972, pag. 7–9. Patenbrigades were children's collectives sponsored by factory, agriculture, or other worker organizations, sometimes even the Nationale Volksarmee (National People's Army), with the intention to give children work related experience as part of the regime's educational mandate, see Fulbrook, *People's State*, 121–22 and 225–27.
33. Betts, *Within Walls*, 174.
34. McCulloch, "Sword and Shield," 75.
35. "Bei schwierigen Problemen, die das Lehrer-Schüler-Verhältnis betreffen, wird immer versucht, den Pionieren zu helfen, ein gutes Verhältnis zu ihren Lehrern und Erziehern herzustellen, die Eltern einzubeziehen und auch die Autorität der Gruppenrät zu stärken," see BArch DY 24/23769, Jan–June 1972, pag. 9.
36. See BArch DY 24/23769, Jan–June 1972, 6–10 and Martin Sanders, "10th World Festival of Youth and Students, East Berlin, 1973," University of Warwick Library, Media Resource Centre, retrieved 10 February 2016 from https://www2.warwick.ac.uk/services/library/mrc/explorefurther/filmvideo/worldfestival/.
37. For the centrality of consumption in both the public and private spaces and then the differentiation between the two, see Jarausch and Geyer, *Shattered Past*, 274–97. For more on the *Eigensinn* as negotiating the space and difference between public and private spaces, see Palmowski, "Between Conformity and Eigen-Sinn," 494–502. Also see Thomas Lindenberger, "Alltagsgeschichte," 298–325.
38. BArch DY 24/23769, Jan–June 1972, pag. 7.
39. BArch DY 24/23769, 2.

40. Although the reports for the second half of 1972 fail to provide a clear assessment of the contents of the report and a breakdown of the findings of letters written in to the publisher, these reports find similar focus as the reportage of January–June 1972 on issues concerning solidarity with Vietnam, Patenbrigades, and Pioneer meetings and stories in *Atze* that polemicize the socialist morality of West German television. see BArch DY 24/23769, 2–6. Also see Gumbert, *Envisioning Socialism*, 153–54. Gumbert also speaks here of the "Rabbit films" banned at the Eleventh Plenum in 1965 as representative of a morality that was decidedly un-socialist in spirit.
41. BArch DY 24/23769, July–Dec 1972, pag. 6.
42. BArch DY 24/23769, "Trommel Statistik," pag. 3–4 and "Analyse Bild des Monats," pag. 1.
43. Joseph Witek contends that readers of typically gag-based comic strips do not bare the same stigmas as readers of general comic books as those strips target both children and adults with their humor. At the same time, comic strips are not assumed to have the same psychological impact as comic books and, as a result, do not suffer the same criticisms. Although, this also means that more of the academic literature is geared toward those strips, see Witek, *Comic Books as History*, 5–9. However, due to this perception of the comic strip as the "funnies," as it were, social significance is often dismissed within these strips. That said, both comic strips and books rank higher on the cultural hierarchy in countries such as France, Belgium, Italy, and Japan, than in either the United States or Germany. Matthew P. McAllister, Edward H. Sewell, Jr., and Ian Gordon, "Introducing Comics and Ideology," in *Comics & Ideology*, ed. Matthew P. McAllister, Edward H. Sewell, Jr., and Ian Gordon (New York: Peter Lang, 2001), 3–5. In *Envisioning Socialism*, Heather Gumbert discusses how the Deutsche Fernsehfunk balanced entertainment and education necessary to East German television programming in the 1950s, particularly following the 1953 Uprising in the GDR. These efforts were again redoubled following the Hungarian Uprising in 1956. See Gumbert, *Envisioning Socialism*, 60–80. Joshua Feinstein makes similar connections in relation to DEFA films, including the "Rabbit Films," suggesting that the "problem was education and was inseparable from the conceptualization of state authority itself," particularly in the wake of the Eleventh Plenum. See Feinstein, *Triumph of the Ordinary*, 71–73, 80, and 171–73. As such, and given this perceived inseparability of education and the state, particularly after the mandate of Socialist Realism in the arts following the *Bitterfelder Weg* in 1959, it is unsurprising that comics and *Kinderzeitschriften* followed this model of edutainment as the same largely permeated East German popular culture in one form or another. For more on ideology and comics specifically and GDR popular culture generally, see Thomas Kramer, *Micky, Marx und Manitu: Zeit- und Kulturgeschichte im Spiegel eines DDR-Comics 1955–1990: "Mosaik" als*

Fokus von Medienlebnissen im NS und in der DDR (Berlin: Weidler Buchverlag, 2002).
44. *Atze* 12/88 and 11/84.
45. Fulbrook, *People's State*, 235–49.
46. BArch DY 24/23769, *Halbjahresanalyse der Redaktion "Frösi,"* pag. 1–2.
47. This was not the only instance where education was a policy taken up by governments, educators, publishers, and the church as a means to influence children and youth, especially in the immediate postwar period and during the height of Cold War tensions between the United States and the Soviet Bloc. See Heike Elisabeth Jüngst, *Information Comics: Knowledge Transfer in a Popular Format* (Frankfurt: Peter Lang, 2010); Alexander Maxwell, "East Europeans in the Cold War Comic *This Godless Communism*," in *Comic Books and the Cold War, 1946–1962: Essays on Graphic Treatment of Communism, the Code and Social Concerns*, ed. Chris York and Rafiel York (Jefferson: McFarland & Company, Inc., 2012), 190–203; Mark McKinney, *The Colonial Heritage of French Comics* (Liverpool: Liverpool University Press, 2011); Stroemberg, *Comic Art Propaganda*; and Allen L. Woll, "The Comic Book in a Socialist Society: Allende's Chile, 1970–1973," *Journal of Popular Culture* 9, no. 4 (Spring 1976): 1039–45.
48. BArch DY 24/23769, "Trommel," pag. 4–5.
49. BArch DY 24/23769, *Analyse der Redaktion "Frösi,"* pag. 18. It should be noted that the German term, *Länder*, means both states within the Republic and countries. Although edited, the context of the letter places *Länder* in relation to cities, suggesting the former translation and as such this is the form used here. While an understanding of the word to mean countries does not specifically fly in the face of the education and ideology put forward by the FDJ, it potentially suggests an intellectual border crossing and an interest in travel as made clear in comics such as *Mosaik* and *Pats Reiseabenteuer*. Though it is not believed to be the case here, there does exist the possibility that this may, in fact, be representative of an internal *Republikflucht* demonstrated elsewhere in the watching of Western television as part of the retreat into the domestic space associated with niche society, see Betts, *Within Walls*, 144 and 214–15. Betts also suggests that television was instrumental is teaching children the importance of the private sphere.
50. BArch DY 24/23769, *Analyse der Redaktion "Frösi,"* pag. 17.
51. BArch DY 24/23769, 19.
52. Gumbert, *Envisioning Socialism*, 52, 196 n12, and 123.
53. Esther von Richthofen, "Communication and Compromise: The Prerequisites for Cultural Participation," in *Power and Society in the GDR 1961–1979: The 'Normalisation of Rule'?*, ed. Mary Fulbrook (New York: Berghahn Books, 2009), 144–54; Felix Mühlberg, "Konformismus oder Eigensinn? Eingaben als Quelle zur Erforschung der Alltagsgeschichte der DDR," *Mitteilungen aus der kulturwissenschaftlichen Forschung* (February 1996): 331–45; and Ina Merkel and Felix Mühlberg, "Eingaben und Öffentlichkeit," in *Wir sind doch*

nicht die Meckerecke der Nation! Briefe an das Fernsehen der DDR, 2nd ed., ed. Ina Merkel (Berlin: Schwarzkopf & Schwarzkopf, 2000), 15. See also, Alf Lüdtke, ed., *Akten, Eingaben, Schaufenster: Die DDR und ihre Texte. Erkundungen zu Herrschaft und Alltag* (Berlin: Akademie Verlag, 1997), particularly these chapters: Katherine Pence, "Schaufenster der sozialistischen Konsums: Texte der ostdeutschen 'Consumer Culture,'" 91–118; Uta G. Poiger, "Amerikanischer Jazz und (ost)deutsche Respektabilität," 119–36; Thomas Kramer, "Die DDR der fünfziger Jahre im Comic Mosaik: Einschienenbahn, Agenten, Chemieprogramm," 167–88; Dorothee Wierling, "Der Staat, die Jugend und der Westen. Texte und Konflikten der 1960er Jahre," 223–40; and Ina Merkel, "'. . . in Hoyerswerda leben jedenfalls keine so kleinen viereckigen Menschen.' Breife an das Fernsehen der DDR," 279–310.
54. Saunders, *Honecker's Children*, 10.
55. BArch DY 24/23769, *Analyse der Redaktion "Frösi,"* pag. 19.
56. John Bornemann, *After the Wall: East Meets West in the New Berlin* (New York: Basic Books, 1991), 80.
57. Gary Bruce, *The Firm: The Inside Story of the Stasi* (Oxford: Oxford University Press, 2010), 183.
58. BArch DY 24/23769, *Analyse der Redaktion "Frösi,"* pag. 19.
59. Jarausch, "Care and Coercion," 60.
60. Jarausch, 60–61.
61. Jarausch, 62.
62. Betts, "Building Socialism," 114. Sheila Fitzpatrick has made much of similar ideas in the context of Stalinist Russia, suggesting that "the normal posture of a Soviet citizen was passive conformity and outward obedience," see Fitzpatrick, *Everyday Stalinism*, 222.
63. Katherine Pence, "Women on the Verge: Consumers between Private Desires and Public Crisis," in *Socialist Modern: East German Everyday Culture and Politics*, ed. Katherine Pence and Paul Betts (Ann Arbor: University of Michigan Press, 2008), 296–300.
64. Elsewhere, Jonathon Grix indicates that, for East German elections, the use of *Eingaben* as a release valve for popular discontent was used with growing frequency and resultant threats of nonparticipation constituted the majority of those letters, see Grix, "Non-Conformist Behavior," 75. Judd Stitziel meanwhile suggests that the practice of complaint was prolific and often directed toward manufacturers, trade organizations, and the editorial boards of magazines and newspapers including comics and *Kinderzeitschriften*. Beginning in the 1960s, the television show *Prisma* requested these *Eingaben* and often responded to them on air. Judd Stitziel, "Shopping, Sewing, Networking, Complaining: Consumer Culture and the Relationship between State and Society in the GDR," in *Socialist Modern: East German Everyday Culture and Politics*, ed. Katherine Pence and Paul Betts (Ann Arbor: University of Michigan Press, 2008), 265. In the context of children, Mike Dennis and Jonathon Grix suggest that children were enthusi-

astic to participate in this complaint culture and went to great lengths to do so when there was a legitimate concern, see Mike Dennis and Jonathon Grix, *Sport under Communism: Behind the East German "Miracle"* (Houndmills: Palgrave, 2012), 75–76.
65. BArch DY 24/23769, *Redaktion "Frösi" Analyse August 1972*, pag. 2.
66. Roger Sabin makes similar suggestions regarding the significance of fan letters and letter columns in comics of the 1960s and 1970s in Great Britain and the United States, stating that these served to generate a sense of belonging among the child-readership thus increasing loyalty toward certain publications, see Sabin, *Comics, Comix & Graphic Novels*, 33.
67. BArch DY 24/23769, *Redaktion "Frösi" Analyse August 1972*, pag. 5.
68. BArch DY 24/23769, 18.
69. BArch DY 24/23769, *Redaktion "Frösi" Analyse Juni 1972, Analyse "Bild des Monats,"* pag. 1 and *Analyse "Wo ist dein Arbeitsplatz."* Here, Arbeitsplatz is translated to mean "workspace" as opposed to "work place." Given that the answers provided in these letters are from children and encompass answers such as desk [*Schreibtisch*] and living room [*Wohnzimmer*], contextually this seemed most appropriate.
70. BArch DY 24/23769, *Redaktion "Fröhlich sein und singen" Analyse der Leserpost im II. Quartal*, pag. 4.
71. Augustine, *Red Prometheus*, 230.
72. Betts, *Within Walls*, 15–16. This plays an important role in the Wolfgang Becker film, *Good Bye, Lenin!* (2003). Christine (Kathrin Sass) is a loyal Party member and Pioneer leader who also engages in the writing of complaint petitions on behalf of her neighbors, Wolfgang Becker, dir., *Good Bye, Lenin!*, DVD (Berlin: X-Filme Creative Pool, 2003).
73. Harsch, *Revenge of the Domestic*, 7–8.
74. Fulbrook, *People's State*, 163–66.
75. Ronald Grigor Suny, *The Soviet Experiment: Russia, the USSR, and the Successor States*, 2nd ed. (New York: Oxford University Press, 2011), 204.
76. Fulbrook, *People's State*, 170–72.
77. Hilary L. Chute, *Graphic Women: Life Narrative & Contemporary Comics* (New York: Columbia University Press, 2010), 10.
78. BArch DY 24/23769, *Redaktion "Frösi" Analyse August 1972*, pag. 3–5. The authors of the report account for the discrepancy in the numbers, suggesting that some reader-letters address more than one of the four categories and thus count twice in the report.
79. See Fulbrook, *People's State*, 131; McDougall, "Liberal Interlude," 124 and 155; and Nothnagle, *East German Myth*, 48–51.
80. Madarasz, *Conflict and Compromise*, 66.
81. Brock, "Producing the 'Socialist Personality'?" 227.
82. Brock, 223–27.
83. McDougall, "Liberal Interlude," 155.
84. Brock, "Producing the 'Socialist Personality'?" 234.

85. BArch DY 24/23769, *Halbjahranalyse der Redaktion "Frösi" über die Leserpost*, pag. 1–5; *Redaktion ATZE/Mosaik Leserpostanalyse für das 2. Halbjahr 1972*, pag. 1–7; *Redaktion "Frösi" Analyse August 1972*, 1–6; *Statistik der Leserpost im II. Quartal 1973*, pag. 1–6.
86. Fulbrook, *People's State*, 236. For further examples of this in the context of GDR comics, specifically the presence and reader response to the inclusions of plastics and technologies in *Mosaik*, see respectively Rubin, *Synthetic Socialism* and Augustine, *Red Prometheus*.
87. BStU, MfS, AIM, Nr. 9409/69. This is part of the reason why Altenburger was thought to be an ideal candidate for recruitment as one of the Stasi's informants (*inoffizielle Mitarbeiter* or IM) in May 1960. Altenburger also had family living in the Federal Republic of Germany and this, it was thought, made both Altenburger and his wife, Christina, perfect for gathering information from and about the West. However, there is a period of inactivity in Altenburger's file of nearly five years (September 1964–April 1969), during which time he was apparently not contacted by the Stasi. During this time and by the admission of the Altenburgers' handler, the Altenburgers reconsidered their relationship with the Stasi, though the records provide no insight as to what triggered these second thoughts. While the Altenburgers apparently provided information regarding coworkers at Verlag Junge Welt, the handler reported their genuine reluctance to provide information regarding much else or to provide much information of value. At the beginning of July 1969, the Altenburgers' handler recommended severing ties with Wolfgang and Christina Altenburger.

CHAPTER 4

Escape, Escapism, and the Cultural Imperialism of Comic Book Travel in *Mosaik* and *Atze*

As we have seen in earlier chapters, comic books in the German Democratic Republic were always about travel insofar as travel was necessary to transport the main cast into exotic locations. Once there, the characters, whether they were the Digedags, Fix and Fax, or Pat, were given the time and opportunity to demonstrate the differences between the protagonists and the perceived antagonists of the stories and, by extension, between socialism and capitalism. Hannes Hegen developed the Digedags' adventures to emulate formulas found in Disney comics, following the tropes and story-beats of the *Donald Duck* and *Uncle Scrooge* stories by Carl Barks whose name is now synonymous with those characters and much of their mythology.[1] Moreover, Verlag Neues Leben accepted Hegen's proposal for the comic following an FDJ directive to create a counterpart of Mickey Mouse.[2] And while *Mosaik* and the Digedags followed the lead of Uncle Scrooge, or more precisely followed the iconography of Scrooge's grandnephews, this prescription gave the publication and comics in the German Democratic Republic the impetus and endorsement to allow their characters the freedom of movement denied the population at large. With no small degree of irony, this made comic books in East Germany as much travelers as the characters and adventures depicted in their pages. Travel was literally and metaphorically necessary to mobilize the values of the state and the combined educational and ideological agendas of the FDJ's publishing regime toward the formation of the socialist personality. As much as the Digedags emulated the Western characters after which they were created, travel was ultimately employed as a means of spreading a socialist worldview to both the Western and the Developing Worlds as they existed on the printed page.

Following the construction of the Berlin Wall in August 1961 and the transformation in the pages of and among the editorial and creative teams for both *Mosaik* and *Atze*, travel in comics took on new dimensions of significance for the FDJ and the child-readership. Despite the 1955 *Verordnung zum Schutz der Jugend* and the initial publications of *Atze* and *Mosaik* to regulate the infiltration of Western publications for children in the fledgling German Democratic Republic, the inner-German border remained permeable to most aspects of Western youth culture, comic books included. The SED and the FDJ considered the American influence in West German culture to be barbarous to German youth, destroying German culture and making youth prone to fascism and fascist tendencies.[3] Arguments between adolescents and the authorities in both Germanies ballooned into debates over moral, cultural, and political authority. Cultural consumption in both East and West Germany became central platforms for their respective authorities.[4] In the East, certainly, comics emerged as extensions of the state itself, representative of SED power structures while perpetuating and maintaining the regime's institutional structures. It was not until after the construction of the Berlin Wall and the mistaken perception of its impenetrability that those authorities in the GDR were able to master the cultural consumption of youth given the perceived drought of Western publications for children and comics that followed. However, this mastery was never complete and itself proved something of an illusion.

At the same time that the Berlin Wall arguably staunched the cultural import from West to East, the Wall quite literally halted the movement of bodies across the inner-German border, limiting travel of GDR citizens to those states friendly to both the GDR and their Soviet allies. Prior to 1961, East Germany suffered a refugee crisis and brain drain that ebbed and flowed from the end of World War II until the summer of 1961.[5] Massive numbers fled from East to West in the early postwar years. In Berlin, the relative ease with which the population could cross from one sector of the divided city to another saw many residents working in the West for higher wages, benefits, and consumer choices while still living in the East to enjoy subsidized housing and staple foodstuffs.[6] Following the tightening of the inner-German border in 1946 and again in 1952 to stem this tide of migration, Berlin remained an escape hatch in the otherwise, though arguably, secure socialist German state.[7] When the Wall was built by the SED regime at the insistence of Party Secretary Walter

Ulbricht and with the approval of the Soviet Politburo, East Germany effectively sealed itself from the West in terms of the population's physical movement and that of cultural products. Of course, the Berlin Wall was not entirely impenetrable. Western culture slipped through cracks in the Wall via West German television and radio, western visitors to the East, and parcels sent by western relatives.[8] And though this perceived imprisonment of East Germans did not completely stop those people from travelling, the Berlin Wall brought an end to the unimpeded physical movement across the inner-German and inner-Berlin borders for both the population and desired consumer goods.[9]

The Berlin Wall provided the FDJ the opportunity to reconceptualize and reimagine comics as a more fundamental aspect and extension of the child-readers' educational and formative experience as a GDR citizen. This transformation, however, did not directly or noticeably impact the comic-characters' ability to travel or transgress inner-German, international, or even temporal borders and boundaries. Instead, the Wall and the newfound inclusion of ideological and educational purpose in these *Kinderzeitschriften* encouraged the perceived mobility of those characters. The Digedags, and later the Abrafaxe, in *Mosaik* and Pat from *Pats Reiseabenteuer* were socialist emissaries transporting ideology and political awareness wherever they went. Their travels and adventures condoned and encouraged the spread of socialism as the responsibility and obligation of those travelers. In effect, these characters took up the role and activities vacated by the Soviet-led Communist International (Comintern), dissolved in 1943, toward educating the worldwide proletariat through less violent though still revolutionary means. The socialism conceptualized in these comics and carried abroad by their protagonists was composed as much of education and ideology as it was of idealism as these characters effaced the political and social repressions of the Stasi and the SED regime, whitewashing Soviet-style communism. This presented an image of socialism demonstrative of the state's officially sanctioned antifascism, anti-imperialism, and pacifism. These aspects found more traction after the dawn of the 1960s and the East German peculiarities of the larger anti-comics campaigns. Characters reacted against perceived class-based oppression, regardless of the identity constructions of race or religious difference, lending aid when such aid was required. Socialism was understood as a spatial and temporal universal, improving the quality of private and political life throughout history, not only in the lives of the oppressed but also in those of the oppressors once educated about the errors of their imperialist or fascist tendencies.

Travel not only demonstrated what socialism could be, attempting to make it more appealing than the lived reality of shortages and unfulfilled promises, it also made the Berlin Wall itself invisible. This does not suggest that the Wall or German division were rendered impermanent but revealed the permeability of the Berlin Wall and the artificial nature of Cold War division through both intention and accident. For the FDJ, travel in children's comics demonstrated the potentials of socialism in ways acceptable for and accepted by the East German child-readership. The travel of these comic characters offered children the occasion for "inner emigration" within the sanctity of the domestic niche society. As such, these comics envisioned a world without perceived Cold War divisions and through the associations made between those comics and the private sphere in which those comics were consumed. The travel depicted in Verlag Junge Welt's most popular children's publications created expectations among the readership through the demonstration of socialism's potential, rather than its reality, that the regime could never fulfill. While the FDJ fostered the socialist personality amongst readers, attempting to create genuine support for East German socialism, these comics provided escape, both literal and figurative, luring children away from the lived experience of socialism even as it attempted to draw them close. Moreover, travel in East German comics demonstrated a freedom of movement that was neither counterintuitive nor a threat to the existence and perpetuation of state-socialism.

Likewise, Heather Gumbert suggests that the Sandman character, from the children's program *Unser Sandmännchen* (Our Little Sandman, 1959–1989), "whisked children away on exotic adventures . . . like travelling to the moon. But he was just as comfortable in—and familiarized children with—territory closer to home in the GDR." Arguably, the Sandman was emblematic of the children themselves who often crossed the border to "buy comics and 'trash' literature, or to check out the latest American film at the cinema."[10] Moreover, the makers of the program were sometimes given stern warnings from the regime for some of the program's content. During an African excursion, the Sandman drove "a west-European car" and enjoyed "a cold beer to help him cope with the heat." Depictions such as these made the Sandman less than the ideal socialist role model. That said, the character was arguably more representative of the East German wanderlust as a result. Nor did this affect the popularity of the character or of the program. In this way, both the Sandman and the Digedags were indicative of the frustrated inclination toward travel manifesting itself in popular culture.[11]

The Digedags were meanwhile locked into their roles as explorers and adventurers due to their relationship with the Disney comics by Barks. While the FDJ characterized the Digedags as drawing their motivation from the improvement and advancement of those around them with intelligence, wit, and guile, it was impossible to do so without also critiquing their attachment to the traditional and "clichéd" figures and ideas that were detrimental to the Digedags' socialist purpose. The Digedags were character "types" in the estimation of the FDJ and, as such, character development was inconceivable (*die Entwicklung von Charakteren ist nicht denkbar*) and the characters, themselves, were interchangeable. This supposed problem prompted the FDJ to draw unintentional comparisons with the Western comics and tropes that originally inspired the Digedags. The same report that criticized the Digedags also suggested that Uncle Scrooge, mentioned by name, was a monopoly capitalist living only for love of profit. Similarly, Donald Duck was unlucky and remained in the stories only to understand his position within the family. The FDJ discussed the characters in regard to their perceived "types," regardless of Barks's characterizations, by way of explaining the Digedags' own inability to evolve as personalities and, arguably, their inability to develop the required socialist personalities. As such, the FDJ recognized the Digedags' connection not only to the Disney comics but also to larger comic book tropes. Over the course of *Mosaik von Hannes Hegen's* first twenty-five issues, the FDJ understood the stories those comics contained as a series of masked balls, pirates, and treasure hunts while history and language, and presumably also the socialist ideological and educational impetus, were played fast and loose for the sake of a punch line.[12]

The acknowledgement of *Mosaik*'s Western roots, particularly in terms of Barks's *Donald Duck* and *Uncle Scrooge* comics following the titular characters' transition toward the globe-trotting adventurers, also demonstrated a confluence of unease and acceptance of the Digedags' collective role in the comics. Some problems originated from the FDJ and the publishing regime's criticisms of the comics medium generally. Here, though, the regime's concerns with the characters stemmed from their apparent lack of individuality as the FDJ reported that the trio were not only identical (*identisch*), but a single entity spread across three similar bodies (*eine Gebilde in gedrittelter Form*). While an argument could be made conflating the Digedags with the perceived and idealized East German collective, the FDJ itself drew different conclusions, indicating the characters' similarities as reason against their potential growth and thus their inability to learn from a situation. The stagnation of the

Figure 4.1. "Das Turnier zu Venedig" (The Tournament in Venice) (May 1964): 15. The Knight Runkel von Rübenstein with Dig and Dag. From *Mosaik by Hannes Hegen*, Heft-Nr 90, © Tessloff Verlag, Nürnberg, Germany.

Digedags' personalities affected their ability to be heroes within their own stories, in the FDJ's estimation, necessitating their accompaniment by other characters native to the situation and who were fully formed individuals themselves, not associated with the perceived sameness of the Digedag characters. This lack of individuality and the need for the other character as hero within the situation was necessitated by the comics' focus on travel as a theme and as an educational storytelling device.[13] Because of both their homogeneity as a trio and their obvious difference from those around them, the Digedags were perpetual outsiders to every situation they encountered. They thus required that the hero character, their companion, was embedded in the surroundings of the story to articulate that situation for the Digedags. The Digedags' foreignness required explanation of the situation, the history, and the character relations for the reading audience as the Digedags acted as proxy for the child-reader. This also made travel a mandate in *Mosaik von Hannes Hegen*, creating opportunity for the state-sanctioned educational content.

The most famous example of this type of character native to his surroundings is the Knight Runkel von Rübenstein, appearing in the eponymous *Ritter Runkel-Serie* (*Mosaik von Hannes Hegen* issues 90–151). Drawing inspiration from "classic East German travel literature," Runkel himself is a combination crusader and Don Quixote when he encoun-

Figure 4.2. "Die Grosse Herausforderung" (The Great Challenge) (August 1969): 9. Colonel Springfield, heedless of his step, slides in a puddle of mop water and loses his balance. From *Mosaik by Hannes Hegen*, Heft-Nr 153, © Tessloff Verlag, Nürnberg, Germany.

ters Dig and Dag. As these latter are themselves searching for their friend Digedag, in the midst of their own quest of sorts, travel through the Middle Ages is essential to the progression of the overall story, but also as a means of transitioning from one arc to the next. Runkel's quest, one for gold that again draws comparison to the *Uncle Scrooge* comics, takes the characters to Italy, Dalmatia, Byzantium, and finally to China. Along the way, Dig and Dag find traces of their missing comrade (the second volume is titled "On the Trail of Digedag") and Runkel accompanies them down the Euphrates River to the Persian Gulf before returning to Germany and his beloved.[14] Likewise, in the *Amerika-Serie* that followed, Colonel Springfield is a retired military man accompanying the widow Victoria Jefferson across the United States when they encounter the Digedags. With his long goatee and striped pants, resembling Uncle Sam, Springfield is indicative of the American landscape across which he travels. As he is both able to get up after being injured (Figure 4.2) and somewhat disillusioned with the military itself, Catrin Gersdorf suggests that Springfield "moved on a narrow line between affirmation and subversion" of socialism, deconstructing the thesis of capitalism's collapse.[15]

The title of the first story featuring the Digedags (issues 1–4), "Auf der Jagd nach dem Golde," was reminiscent of the Barks's Duck comics that inspired it, including, "Donald Duck Finds Pirate Gold" and the Uncle Scrooge comic "Back to the Klondike."[16] This was not by accident. Due to the permeability of the German-German border in the mid-1950s and the relative openness of Berlin until the summer of 1961, these Western comics were readily available to East German children.[17] Creating the Digedags as treasure hunters ideologically opposed to the monopoly-capitalist Uncle Scrooge and his grandnephews allowed Hegen and the Mosaik-Kollektiv to have their characters effectively correct the exploitation left in the wake of Uncle Scrooge's own adventures. The Digedags were treasure hunters only insofar as they exploited the genre to upend its meaning, as is the entire purpose of the "funny animal" genre. While the FDJ was critical of the lack of individuality between Dig, Dag, and Digedag, this was partially to provide point-of-view characters for the child-readers themselves.[18] Even the publication's title, *Mosaik*, does not suggest the Digedags to be the primary focus of the stories but part of a larger tapestry. As outsiders to the character relations and to the history as depicted, the Digedags provided a lens through which the child-readers defined themselves rather than being defined by preconceived notions of childhood.

The characters, as they were conceived, built travel into the foundations of *Mosaik von Hannes Hegen* in that those characters were meant to explore a world, or worlds in the case of the *Weltraum-Serie*, entirely new and foreign to them. Reinhard Pfeiffer's work makes similar suggestions, pointing to the "funny animal" genre upon which the Digedags were based, even though they are not animals themselves, as a means by which the characters explored their world.[19] This does not necessarily imply the physical exploration of the world, but certainly does not preclude the possibility. And although the FDJ did not consider this an appropriate depiction of the socialist class struggle, the Digedags travelled through time and geographic space to develop the historical consciousness of those they met.[20] But as the Western comics the Digedags emulated frequently employed travel without political issue, it was necessary for the Digedags to do the same, particularly under this guise of the antithesis of Disney's Uncle Scrooge. The first dozen issues, collected in the three volume *Wie alles begann* (How It All Began) and containing the stories "Auf der Jagd nach dem Golde," "die Rassende Seemühle" (The Frantic Fan-Boat, issues 5–8), and "Aufruhr im Dschungel" (Uproar in the Jungle, issues 9–12), saw the Digedags in the Middle East, attacked by pirates, and lost on a jungle island as part of the *Orient-Südsee-Serie*.[21] Here, the Digedags conceptually followed Barks's Ducks, rectifying problems left by capitalist influence in the previously mentioned "Donald Duck Finds Pirate Gold" and the Uncle Scrooge story "Race to the South Seas" (*March of Comics* #41, 1949). In the first of these stories, Donald and his nephews race perpetual Disney villain, Black Pete, to a lost treasure. In the latter story, Uncle Scrooge is stranded on an island where the natives wait on him as servants while Scrooge runs his businesses. The financial order in these Disney comics demonstrated Duckburg, the city in which Barks's characters lived and, by extension, the society occupied by the reader as one without solidarity due to an economically imposed hierarchy. Society in these comics was almost entirely defined by competition and magnified by those adventures in which Donald, Scrooge, and the nephews travelled abroad to economically depressed regions. Not only did the FDJ perceive these comics as spreading American ideology, but that their creators were "active agents" of the same.[22] As the socialist by-product of those Disney comics, then, the Digedags and Hannes Hegen both spread socialism despite the FDJ's reservations over how that message was packaged, delivered, and received. Travel and the notion of movement allowed the Digedags to compare and compete with Barks's Ducks in the marketplace and in the imaginations of East German youth.

In the pages and panels of *Mosaik*, travel was instrumental due to the construction of the Digedag characters themselves as much as it borrowed from those tropes employed in Disney comics and the perception of "adventure" comics stories. Disney was, first and foremost, a carrier, if not *the* carrier, of American cultural imperialist ideology. Although Barks used the perceived American obsession with money as a means of relating how it "deceived and destroyed" people, this ultimately led both the characters and the readers toward an inability to progress in order to maintain the status quo of the world inhabited by the Ducks.[23] The readers were thought to be trapped in a perpetual state of childishness as the comics, and Disney products more generally, masked open imperialism and an equally childlike representation of Third World peoples with comedy to distract readers.[24] The Digedags were locked into this process of cultural imperialism emerging from a Western tradition of spreading so-called eternal values that were determined by power and money through means the FDJ considered brutal, racist, and anti-communist.[25] *Mosaik* was a perceived bulwark against this influence of Americanization, relaying humorous, interesting circumstances (*humorvolle, interessante Gegebenheiten*) in graphic narratives suitable for the socialist awareness and arousal of the poor and oppressed (*die Armen und Unterdrückten*).[26] Travel provided the Digedags opportunity to mimic the imperialism of capitalist society and of the Digedags' own Disney progenitors. The Digedags also spread the socialist worldview in a way similar to how those Disney stories were interpreted by the FDJ. Problematically, these echoes represented Indigenous and Third World peoples in the same light as those Disney stories. Populations were infantilized and in need of the socialist influence brought by the Digedags, whether to encourage socialist spirit or to spread the supposed superiority of technology.[27] Using travel and adventures in a fashion similar to those undertaken by Barks's Duck characters, the Digedags subverted the perceived cultural imperialism already familiar to child-readers through the accessibility of Disney comics prior to the border closure in 1961.[28]

At the same time, the Digedags' inability to change, as a point of FDJ criticism, suggested an endorsement of the perceived status quo. *Mosaik* and the roots of its creation validates the Western cultural imperialism at play in Disney comics and narratives.[29] However, the perceived defense of the supposed imperialist status quo allows *Mosaik* to subvert the narrative's expectations as well as the underlying narrative of socialist superiority.[30] By the FDJ's own admission, the Digedags were types of characters rather than characters in and of themselves and as such were impervious to change within their own stories. Despite this, the Digedags were agents of change in the status quo of their comic book world. In terms of the American superhero narrative, the stories create the illusion of change to the character and to the world around them, though the superhero character, like the Digedags, remains a fixed point to maintain the telling of stories over the long term. Effectively, the Western superhero is itself a "type" and thus while effecting change, does not change itself. Or, if and when change does occur for the sake of a story, the status quo is reasserted by the conclusion of that story. While this device establishes the notion of change necessary to storytelling, the illusory nature of that change ensures the accessibility of those stories to new readers and familiarity to long-time fans.[31] Much the same can be made of Barks's Duck characters as Uncle Scrooge does not spend or lose wealth, unless such happens in the context of a story in which case everything is restored by the end. Instead, Scrooge is in a perpetual loop of acquiring money and sitting on or swimming through his vaulted fortune. In a twist to the formula upon which the Digedags are based, Dig, Dag, and Digedag use travel to quite literally change the world in which they exist in a fundamental way without the apparent reversion of the perceived status quo. They are accompanied through their adventures by characters that can, in fact, change as dictated by the rules of storytelling and before that world can fall into a state where the Digedags are required to help yet again, and perhaps effect the same change a second time, they are whisked off to a new setting with a new cast of secondary characters.[32] While this is arguably the closest to change the Digedags themselves are able to come, it also suggests the permanence of the changes wrought over the previous issues and adventures and the perceived permanence of the construction of socialism itself.

By late 1975, this travel and the constant change of locale from story to story was a staple of the adventures in *Mosaik* and, despite the FDJ's apprehensions over the problematic representation of history and the struggle of the working class, was characterized as precipitating the joyful experience of reading an issue of *Mosaik*.[33] These aspects of the comics were continued after Hegen's departure from the publication when the Digedags were replaced by the Abrafaxe (Abrax, Brabax, and Califax) in January 1976. Indeed, much was maintained in the transition from Hegen's version of *Mosaik* such as the tropes employed in the visual language of the comic and the identification of the characters themselves.[34] So much, in fact, was held-over in the visualization and depiction of the Abrafaxe characters, created by Hegen's co-writer Lothar Dräger and Mosaik-Kollektiv cartoonist Lona Rietschel, that Hegen and the publisher spent the remainder of the GDR's lifespan in litigation over potential copyright infringement and the use of the *Mosaik* name. As far as the FDJ was concerned, these new characters continued the Digedags' traditions of "socialist attitudes and behaviors, partisanship, love for the working people, sense of justice, solidarity, but also diligence, courage, resourcefulness, humor, and optimism to broaden and expand their readership" in new ways.[35] However, the FDJ never clearly defined how this was the case or exactly what these "new ways" were. Typically, the publishing regime considered these new comics more historically, culturally, and educationally valuable than their predecessors as a result of the Abrafaxe's inclusion and the new settings that formed the foundation for the series' new direction.[36] It was always the intention of *Kinderzeitschriften* in the GDR to publicize the objectives of the Thälmann Pioneers and spread the socialist ideals and values of the FDJ and the SED regime. *Mosaik* used travel specifically to stimulate children's interests and imagination in history and culture and engender respect for the accomplishments of other peoples (*anderer Völker*).[37] The dual objectives of demonstrating the proliferation of socialist ideals and the "elicitation of children's feelings for the exploited and oppressed proletariat in various stages in the development of human society," particularly how this occurs in states beyond the closed borders of the GDR, could only be conveyed to child-readers through the humorous travels and mobility found in *Mosaik*.[38]

Jan Fleischhauer suggests that Karl May created adventure fiction, located in the German fascination with travel literature, as a means to "dream his way out of the narrow confines of his real life" through a combination of genius and triviality. This capitalized upon a desire to see and experience distant places that was as appealing in May's time as in the present.[39] Moreover, Tim Bergfelder suggests that May's America is one of allegory that does not so much dwell on the notion of the frontier as it does "present an enclosed utopian Arcadia" diverging from the American Western through its frequent use of white cowboys, engineers, and oil barons as villains. May's Wild West was one of fantasy, grounded in the cultural trappings that the author and his readers shared.[40] *Mosaik*, during and after Hegen's time on the book, operated in much the same fashion. Both the Digedags and the Abrafaxe fulfilled youths' desire to see that which was new and foreign to them, providing them the vicarious ability to transcend their own lives through a combination of historical "triviality" and high adventure. As such, and beyond the linkages regarding Western comic book tropes and traditions, *Mosaik* was an instrument of East Germany's developing *Kinderkultur* and can thus be situated within a larger and longer tradition of German adventure and travel literature.

In this way, the Abrafaxe, as happened with the Digedags before them, were cultural ambassadors of the German Democratic Republic, and not only of the GDR but of Soviet-style state-socialism broadly. They visited seventeenth-century Dalmatia and freed slaves from the nearby Ottoman Empire (issues 1–12/1976 and 1–5/1977) with their first companion, Harlequin (*Harlekin*), before going to Venice in "die italienische Komödie" (The Italian Comedy, issue 9/1977), part of the *Adria-Serie* (Adriatic-Series, also known as the *Harlekin-Serie*, January

1976–December 1977). By the end of the 1970s, the Abrafaxe were involved in the War of Spanish Succession, visiting eighteenth-century Austria and Hungary. Both before and after the transition from the Digedags to the Abrafaxe, the characters rescued "child-like" natives from capitalists looking to exploit natural resources, including labor, from those natives. They imported nuclear power as a constructive tool of socialism rather than the perceived destructive force that it was under capitalist imperialism. However, and because of their status as East German ambassadors and bearers of socialist culture, the characters in *Mosaik* often paralleled the understood racism of the West and West Germany, becoming guilty of the aspects of capitalism criticized in these very publications.[41] Although these claims cannot be made of all the stories found in *Mosaik*, specifically because travel allowed the characters access to locales not necessarily populated by these "child-like" natives, that same ability to travel afforded the Digedags and the Abrafaxe opportunity to represent socialism in a setting to which it was entirely foreign. Socialism was demonstrated as a productive and important voice for change not only in the Third World, but also in parts of the world as developed as the GDR itself. This depiction was demonstrative of the perceived superiority of the socialist system. Through these cultural representatives, *Mosaik* poised the GDR to demonstrate itself as a world power, regardless of the reality of such a claim.[42]

Unlike the other comics such as the political stories appearing in *Atze*, *Mosaik* was never intended to draw attention to Germany's Cold War division. From the beginning, *Mosaik*'s purpose was the passive dissemination of socialist ideology and education and the comic accomplished this objective on two fronts. First, the characters involved, whether the Digedags or the Abrafaxe, quite literally spread this message beyond the borders of those states friendly to Soviet-style communism through their physical travels and throughout history within the context of the comic book world they occupied. Second, and at the same time, these stories imparted socialist wisdoms to the child-readership while travel was but one device obfuscating that educational content in the minds of those readers, transforming state power into the passive notion of Fulbrook's benign power through appeals to reader desire. In the mind of the readership, then, the inclusion of such good-natured story devices and tropes allowed the perception of *Mosaik* as an ideologically-free space.[43] Of course, the publication demonstrated difference in the conceptualization and representation of socialism and capitalism, touting socialism as the superior of the two as it acted in service to society, improving conditions through the sharing of technologies, the removal of exploitation, or the demonstration of the evils of profit-motivations. *Mosaik*, however, often fell into the same patterns as the *Schund und Schmutz* of Western comics against which it was positioned. The comic used many of those same tropes and drew direct and obvious influence from those banned publications, attempting to foster the socialist personality among children. This also meant that *Mosaik* represented Third World peoples as either a threat or as inferior to the comic's protagonist characters.[44] Travel as a device to export socialist ideology and "aid" in *Mosaik* often effaced actual differences between the socialism of which it was demonstrative and the capitalism it criticized. Political differences remained, but the moral ground upon which the comic stood was much less stable, often characterizing the Developing World in the same terms used by the antagonistic capital-imperialists.

In the immediate postwar and during the decline in popularity of the superhero genre of the 1930s and the war years, one of the more popular comic genres to emerge was that of the "Jungle comic." As with comics such as *Tarzan*, this genre was typified by infantilized Indigenous populations ruled and protected by a white-skinned and blond-haired lord or queen. Needless to say, that to draw in young boys, however, more often than not the protagonist of the "Jungle comic" was a scantily clad queen such as Camilla or Sheena. Although the cast of *Mosaik* never took up the mantle of Jungle King or Lord per se, instead choosing friendship over domination, the Digedags were often frustrated by the failure of Indigenous groups, defined racially in the comics, to modernize.[45]

By comparison, *Pats Reiseabenteuer* was a fairly recent creation and not influenced to the same degree by those Western publications. *Pats Reiseabenteuer* was a product of the post-*Bitterfelder Weg* and post-Berlin Wall period and the subsequent processes of normalization and stabilization that followed.[46] As part of Editor-in-Chief Wolfgang Altenburger's proposal to reinvigorate *Atze* in 1966, the adventures of Pat through nineteenth-century Germany emerged under conditions vastly different than those influencing the creation of *Mosaik*. FDJ officials and educators demarcated a uniquely East German comic language in the post-Wall space, drawing on historically German tropes, discussed elsewhere by John D. Benjamin in the context of *Mosaik von Hannes Hegen*, that addressed the needs of the regime and of the child-readers in the construction of the socialist personality. *Atze* was renewed under Altenburger's guidance specifically to fill gaps in the ideological education of children left by *Mosaik*. For the state, this meant that Pat's comic adventures were indicative of greater historical accuracy and employed travel in a way that hewed closer to the motivations and goals of the FDJ's publishing regime.

The Berlin Wall gave East German politics the freedom to expand at the same time that they addressed the concerns of a now captive population. This implied an expansion of internal openness through the offer of engagement with the state. With the implementation of reform under the auspices of Walter Ulbricht's Youth Communiqué, participation within the state fostered the perception of freedom for youth tempered by discretion under the condition that this supposed freedom did not hinder East German modernization or modernity. The control and planning of youth leisure time had "both real and symbolic meaning" for securing ideological borders as Westernized attitudes among youth persisted after 1961.[47] The Eleventh Plenum of the Central Committee of the SED brought a renewed period of controls surrounding East German society and culture, particularly relating to those films produced by DEFA, and repealed most of the reforms passed in the wake of Ulbricht's Communiqué. As this liberalization placated the "border-crossing attitudes" of youth by catering to the "Western" interests and influences of those youth, the larger controls introduced at the Plenum drove youth further into the privacy of the niche society and made the social spaces of youth, including comics, accessible to FDJ officials and educators.[48] This retreat into the private or the domestic space and the perceived impermeability of the Berlin Wall also fostered a desire for adventure and travel among those youth.[49] As much as this applied to youth who were age-appropriate for the FDJ, and thus considered by the regime to be too old for these children's publications and comics, the same can be said of the children who actually read those *Kinderzeitschriften*.[50]

The state's expansion of the Stasi in the shadow of the Berlin Wall's construction placed a premium on the domestic space as the perceived last bastion of freedom despite the state's efforts to penetrate and infiltrate that private sphere. But the resulting retreat among youth as a means of escaping state control over leisure time also meant that the FDJ never truly won the hearts and minds of East German youth despite the organization's massive membership numbers (about 86 percent in 1987).[51] And although the private sphere was never ideologically recognized by the state, its existence was important as a space in which the individual, here meaning the child-reader of these *Kinderzeitschriften*, could expand their own sense of self and their imaginary without the formal influence of the state, the organized activities of the FDJ, or the malign institutional structures of the SED state. This retreat is often characterized in terms of resistance and, certainly, in some instances this was indeed the case.⁵² However, more often the withdrawal into niche society was apolitical, driven by individual *Eigensinn* to effectively live an ordinary life away from the intrusions of the state.⁵³ This apolitical disengagement is no different in terms of the effects of comics and *Kinderzeitschriften* on child-readers within the domestic space and how those publications fostered this retreat.⁵⁴ In other words, the sheltered nature of East German niche society afforded children opportunity to read their comics in peace.

Most often in the wake of the Berlin Wall, West German television provided East Germans the ability to emigrate to the West on a nightly basis. Indeed, the SED regime and the FDJ were not oblivious to the function of the private or domestic space as the FDJ employed its members to turn those western-facing television antennae as part of a campaign against imperialist bourgeois programming.⁵⁵ This campaign extended to comics publications as polemics were published in the pages of some issues of *Atze* during the 1970s, standing against Western television and the perceived development of false consciousness resulting from such activity and specifically targeting those child-readers.⁵⁶ In restructuring *Atze* in the mid-1960s, the FDJ sought to channel the desires of the readership. Fully aware of what the private sphere politically represented to the SED state, regardless of children's apolitical understanding of the domestic space, the FDJ's purpose behind the publication of comics was to generate the readers' genuine enthusiasm toward the protagonists on the page. This approach, ideally, harnessed children's desires for travel and adventure which then directed those child-readers toward educationally valuable avenues.⁵⁷ As children sought out comics as escapist fiction as an imaginary accompaniment of the characters on their adventures, the FDJ conceptualized this desire in terms of its ability to educate and effectively socialize readers in the supposedly untouchable sphere of the private.⁵⁸

Pats Reiseabenteuer thus appeared within this environment of increasing controls over youth leisure time and state security, torn between its obligations to the FDJ to be educational and historically relevant children's literature and to appear to children as apolitical entertainment. As part of the new profile adopted by *Atze* in 1966, Altenburger argued that comics were more effective than either film or television in transmitting the motivations and feelings of the stories' protagonists. A continuing series, in addition to the popular but politically lacking *Fix und Fax*, was recommended to serve the interpretation of socialist philosophy in a way understandable to the child-readers.⁵⁹ Although this proposal did not make explicit the need for travel, travel

Figure 4.3. *Fix und Fax* 32: "Ballonfahrt" (Balloon trip), *Atze* 8 (1960). Traveling by balloon, Fix and Fax become unintentional visitors to the javelin medal podium at the 1960 Summer Olympic Games in Italy. Illustrations by Jürgen Kieser © Familie Kunow.

allowed *Pats Reiseabenteuer* to fulfill the required interpretation of the political situation. Altenburger's proposal for *Atze* stressed the importance of clarity of both word and image on the comics' pages to express the ideological positions of the characters and of the publishing regime.[60] Comics, as a medium, effectively conveys complex political ideas to children as their visual nature affects the child's imagination in more long-lasting ways than the written word. The medium's visuality creates retention, making it easier for children to recall the material regardless of their awareness of its political content.[61] This aspect was significant to the FDJ as the regime felt children would typically accept the political indoctrination apparent in comics, *Kinderzeitschriften*, and children's literature without question. The supposed or perceived lack of ideology in those publications marked the effectiveness of comics to transmit the regime's educational requirements.[62]

Travel allowed *Pats Reiseabenteuer* to retain a central purpose, reflecting the required clarity in the interplay of image and text. Although not created in an environment necessitating the mimicry of Western comic tropes such as dialogue balloons, *Pats Reiseabenteuer* used the concept of travel to transplant socialism. As one of the few constants in *Atze*, Pat was indicative of the values and morality of the GDR and of state-socialist society. As discussed in the previous chapter, by the early 1970s, readers praised the character for his persistent desire to help the poor, the underprivileged, and the exploited peoples encountered in his travels and as an example of the (socialist) revolutionaries of the nineteenth century.[63] As the embodiment and representative of East German socialism, Pat wandered the nineteenth-century Central German countryside where he was continually embroiled in political turmoil arising from conflicts between himself and those landlords and bourgeois shop-owners who caused problems for the poor.[64] Travelling streamlined the story as only Pat himself and his (socialist) outlook on the world remained focal points for the reader.

Not guilty of following the representation of the colonized other in the same way as Uncle Scrooge, Franco-Belgian comics such as *Tintin*, or even the above-mentioned example of *Mosaik von Hannes Hegen* for that matter, *Pats Reiseabenteuer* limited itself to the German countryside.[65] This did not mean that the stories written by Altenburger did not use tropes of European imperialism and representation. *Pats Reiseabenteuer* borrows from this European, particularly Franco-Belgian, tradition of storytelling through the lens of empire. In this instance, it should be noted that the empire under the microscope is that forged by the 1848 revolutions and German unification in 1871.[66] While this avoided the exoticism and disfigurement of the colonized body exemplified elsewhere, *Pats Reiseabenteuer* addressed socialist representation of German colonialism in that it employed the voyage to re-appropriate perceived "colonies." Pat's journey spoke directly to the FDJ's desires to stir children's historical consciousness through an education in proletarian history.[67] But in situating these stories in the German past, specifically in the previous century, *Pats Reiseabenteuer* addressed East German concerns over a unified and socialist German state at the same time that it engaged with desires for travel and adventure that partially defined youth motivations in the shadow of the Berlin Wall.[68] This journey positioned (East) Berlin as the center of an implied historic German socialist empire, one that not only effaced Cold War division and the Berlin Wall from the reality of the child-readers but removed a history of imperialist and fascist war from the German landscape. As Pat constantly found himself in such "political turmoil" that fueled the ideological and educational thrust of the stories, Pat was ambassador of the proletariat, socialism, and, perhaps more importantly, FDJ youth policy and the SED's doctrine over a potential future (re)unified German state.

To facilitate this, *Pats Reiseabenteuer* notoriously incorporated elements of the modern world into Pat's adventures. As discussed in the previous chapter, these were used for contest purposes and as a means of gauging the child-readers' engagement with the stories and, specifically, its educational and ideological content. The anachronistic items were seemingly random and innocuous, ranging from a hair-dryer (*Haarfön*, Atze 10/86), to latex paint (*Latexfarbe*, Atze 7/84), to a shirt with MMM (Masters of Tomorrow Exposition) printed on it (*Atze* 1/84).[69] They spoke to the importance of technology in the GDR not only in the establishment of industry, but as a construction of East German identity and its role within the Soviet Bloc. Plastic as an industry and an industrial product was understood along the lines of soft or benign power, operating through the trappings of everyday life and, as a result, proved difficult to resist. Much the same was made of comics, bringing ideology into the perceived confines of the domestic space. More importantly, plastics fostered an "ersatz consumer culture" wherein science and technology compensated for the shortcomings and shortages of a state poor in natural resources.[70] Likewise, (East) Germans associated themselves with modernity, locating science and technology at the very center of German identity constructions. Notions of modernity and modernization suited constructions of a decidedly East German identity as socialism, like technology, was capable of making the world better. Technology brought about a utopian future hand-in-hand with socialism.[71] With relation to *Pats Reiseabenteuer* and its role within *Atze*, these objects of the East German everyday established associational connections between the idyllic *Heimat* (homeland) of the nineteenth-century countryside and the GDR's socialist present.[72] Through the ideological ramifications of the development of socialism toward a utopian future, and Pat's own task of spreading socialist humanism across this rendered landscape, his comic-adventures arguably established the perceived past of a unified, socialist Germany as a potential future projected into the imaginations of child-readers.

Already children and adults alike employed different sets of skills to decode the meaning and narrative of comics. But the addition of modern and presumably common objects into *Pats Reiseabenteuer* forced children to perform close readings of the comics.[73] These inclusions taught children to identify objects seemingly misplaced in the comics and, at the same time, expected that those children possessed at least a partial, historical knowledge of the nineteenth century and of the modern (East) German state. Beyond the pure ideological educational work derived from the imposition of Pat's socialist worldview on Germany's past landscape, children's ability to decode the text/image narrative constructed meaning and interpretation.[74] The contest portion of *Pats Reiseabenteuer* visibly rendered the impact of the GDR's scientific technology and how that improved the lives of those living under socialism. The appearance of these items in (East) Germany's past century affected a form of time travel in *Pats Reiseabenteuer*, bringing the present into the past for the child-reader for the supposed benefit of those living without the technological improvements made possible through socialism.

Travel in these publications, while demonstrating and celebrating the achievements of socialism, effaced the perceived omnipresence and repressiveness of the SED regime and the Stasi. Of course, rarely do comic book villains ruminate on their own evilness, just as supposed real world "villains" typically do not consider their actions evil, but these comics specifically removed the characters and thus the child-readers from the lived reality of East German "real existing socialism" and Cold War division to produce fantasy on the page.[75] These publications were indicative of the regime's benign power, relatively innocuousness in their representation of socialism, socialist ideology, and the socialist worldview and the difficulty with which these representations may be resisted by the child-readers. *Pats Reiseabenteuer* penetrated the perspectives of its child-readership with relative ease and was instrumental to the SED exercising power over that readership. The ability of these publications to transgress the supposed safety and apolitical nature of the domestic space, treated by the East German population as a space free of state intervention through either naiveté or willful ignorance, speaks to this notion of soft power at the same time that it undermines the supposed separation of public and private necessitated by Günter Gaus's conceptualization of the GDR as a "niche society." But in removing the characters from the GDR, both temporally and geographically, the publishing regime demonstrated to children the perceived ideal socialism, arguably closer to its nineteenth-century roots, without sacrificing the publications' cultural capital.

As these characters traveled to and fro across the invisible borders of Europe, the comics and stories they contained treated Cold War division as a nonissue. The publications themselves ignored division and the difficulties of East–West travel in the German twentieth century despite the realities of the Berlin Wall, the inner-German border, and the SED's travel restrictions on the population. Moreover, as the protagonists of these publications were, effectively, ambassadors of East German socialism, they demonstrated a kind of cultural imperialism beyond the more apparent demonstrations of imperial influence, cloaked in socialist rhetoric. Symbolically, this ambassadorial status made manifest the porousness of the Berlin Wall itself and the artificiality of Germany's Cold War division as the characters—characters the regime demanded be made relatable to children—spread familiar cultural and ideological tenets to those points of the globe inaccessible to East German children. Still, this cultural influence was decidedly one-way in its representation. That is to say, socialist influence was spread throughout the nonsocialist world and, supposedly, not in the other direction. The characters as they were written, especially those appearing in *Mosaik von Hannes Hegen* given the derided interchangeability of those characters, sought to educate those they encountered, exploited and exploiter alike, though they remained immutable fixtures within the series. Their characters were never influenced by those they encountered. The exception here would be the Neosian Republic, already possessing a socialist worldview when they encountered the Digedags at the beginning of the *Weltraum-Serie*. Nor could the imperialists mount sufficient course to have the Digedags, the Abrafaxe, or even Pat question the core beliefs written into their personalities, such as they were. Nonetheless, exporting ideology demonstrated that ideas could not be contained despite the promises and threats made over the construction of the Berlin Wall as an antifascist protection rampart.

Perhaps more importantly, this approach to the characters and the comic stories in which they starred provided children a perceived escape from the demands and restrictions of the SED, the Stasi, and the FDJ's publishing regime. It is true that comics, like Western television, provided escape for many children. In this way, an argument can be made that even East German cultural productions provided escape for the child (and adult) audience. Heather Gumbert suggests that *Unser Sandmännchen* provided escapist fantasy as the program and the character fostered dreams of travel while whisking children into the arms of sleep. Likewise, television programming produced by DFF fostered border-crossing mentalities with shows such as *Tele-BZ* (a variety show in the tradition of a political *Kabarett*) and *Blaulicht* (The Blue Light) which explored pan-German themes in a police procedural setting. Particularly in the example of *Blaulicht*, the show occupied the "liminal space between East and West Berlin" prior to the construction of the Berlin Wall. After that, the show foregrounded themes of the border, division, and "criminality arising from the German-German Cold War."[76]

Not only in the East German context, but as part of the global anti-comics campaign more generally, comics were criticized as escapist and inconsequential in terms of a literary art form.[77] Certainly the FDJ, Verlag Junge Welt, and Verlag Neues Leben were concerned that the escapism provided by Western comics served no purpose and was, as a result, dangerous, contributing to the belief that Western publications for children, comics specifically, were "trashy" literature. These publications were thought to turn children toward crime and hooliganism more than it turned them toward socialism.[78] That said, the escapism provided by comics is exactly what children required to develop through imaginative play.[79] But this escapism was arguably more than the "inner emigration" in that both *Mosaik von Hannes Hegen* and *Atze* demonstrated the possibility and reality of movement beyond the artificially constructed boundaries of the GDR. The characters transcended borders in what could be construed as adventures of cultural colonialism. Travel was not counterintuitive to Soviet-style communism. Rather, travel operated hand-in-hand with the spread of ideology and was represented in a form that was easily and readily digestible by children as the ideal means of inciting global revolution, regardless of official rhetoric surrounding border closures and the construction of the Berlin Wall.

Notes

1. Barks was considered the "Good Duck Artist" even after his identity was discovered by fans. His comics were popular throughout Europe not only in divided Germany. Barks was also responsible for the creation of the characters of Scrooge McDuck, the Beagle Boys, and Magica De Spell, the city of Duckburg, and the Junior Woodchucks scout troop to which Donald's

nephews, Huey, Dewey, and Louie belonged. These are, of course, only a handful of the more well-known additions to the comic's lore for which Barks was responsible. Many of these stories, characters, and background elements found a new audience and popularity in the animated series *Ducktales* (1987–1990), following the adventures of Scrooge McDuck and his grandnephews, based on those comics by Barks; see Thomas Andrae, *Carl Barks and the Disney Comic Book: Unmasking the Myth of Modernity* (Jackson: University Press of Mississippi, 2006).
2. Pfeiffer, *Von Hannes Hegen*, 128.
3. See also Dr. Fredric Wertham's association between comics and European dictatorships following World War II, in Wright, *Comic Book Nation*, 154–64.
4. Poiger, *Jazz, Rock, and Rebels*, 1–2.
5. Frederick Kempe, *Berlin 1961: Kennedy, Khrushchev, and the Most Dangerous Place on Earth* (New York: Berkley, 2011), 46–48.
6. Harrison, *Driving the Soviets*, 145–50.
7. Fabian Rueger, "Kennedy, Adenauer and the Making of the Berlin Wall," (PhD diss., Stanford University, 2011), 93–95.
8. Major, *Behind the Berlin Wall*, 188–90.
9. Here, Corey Ross suggests the border closure was only of limited use in the regulation of youth as youth were most likely to protest the decision. Although this action allowed for the physical regulation of bodies, particularly those of youth, and their movement, as a political move this turned against the FDJ as 300,000 members left the youth group in the immediate aftermath of the Wall's construction, see Ross, *Constructing Socialism*, 174–77. Elsewhere, Edith Sheffer describes this process of creating division between East and West and how the citizens themselves ultimately bought into the state's political ideology (on both sides of the border), intensifying those divisions in a space that was previously unified through economic, industrial, and even familial bonds, see Edith Sheffer, *Burned Bridge: How East and West Germans Made the Iron Curtain* (Oxford: Oxford University Press, 2011).
10. Gumbert, *Envisioning Socialism*, 85–86 and 88. For further, see also Major, *Behind the Berlin Wall*, 93–96.
11. Kate Connolly, "The Sandmannchen, Germany's cutest communist, turns 50," *The Guardian*, retrieved 15 June 2016 from https://www.theguardian.com/world/2009/nov/23/sandmannchen-germany-communist. This was especially true of popular culture for children. Gaby Thompson-Wohlgemuth considers that popular culture a site of the state's initiatives toward social progress, see Thompson-Wohlgemuth, *Translation under State Control*, 2–4.
12. BArch DY 26/173, "5.6.5. Die Bildgeschichte in den Kinderzeitungen und–zeitschriften," pag. 195–96. The much more ideologically driven *Weltraum-Serie* began at this point.
13. BArch DY 26/173, 195–97.

14. Weißhahn, "Die Digedags im Mosaik," and "Die Digedags und Ritter Runkel," *DDR Comics* retrieved 16 June 2016 from http://www.ddr-comics.de/dig buch4.htm.
15. Catrin Gersdorf, "Digedags Go West," 42.
16. Pfeiffer, *Von Hannes Hegen*, 128.
17. Gerd Lettkemann, "Comics in der DDR," 321–26.
18. Shari Sabeti suggests that the comics medium operates on multiple levels, providing multiple entry points for readers from a pedagogical standpoint. Moreover, due to the spatial organization of comics, readers are encouraged to find their own point of entry and construct their own meanings in regard to the educational message. Characters are but one of these entry points, providing a blank slate in the comic's surroundings upon which secondary characters and actions may inscribe knowledge and meaning. See Shari Sabeti, "The 'Strange Alteration' of *Hamlet*: Comic Books, Adaptation and Constructions of Adolescent Literacy," *Changing English: Studies in Culture and Education* 21, no. 2 (2014): 182–85.
19. Pfeiffer, *Von Hannes Hegen*, 127.
20. Gersdorf, "Digedags Go West," 36.
21. *Seemühle* literally translates to Sea-(wind)mill. The image on the cover of the *Mosaik* issue 8 (1957), also the cover used for the collected volume, uses a drawing of the Digedags in what appears to be a flat-bottom boat with a windmill mounted at the back and turning the boat's paddles. As such, Fan-boat seemed a better translation than the literal, see Hannes Hegen and Mosaik-Kollektiv, "'Mosaik' Heft 8: Strichzeichnung—Seite 1 (Titelseite)," *Stiftung Haus der Geschichte der Bundesrepublik Deutschland*, retrieved 11 March 2016 from http://sint.hdg.de:8080/SINT5/SINT/?wicket:interface=:1:14:::.
22. Stroemberg, *Comic Art Propaganda*, 69.
23. Barker, *Comics*, 286.
24. Ariel Dorfman and Armand Mattelart, *How to Read Donald Duck: Imperialist Ideology in the Disney Comic*, trans. David Kunzle (New York: International General, 1975), 48–60 and Andrae, *Carl Barks*, 9–12.
25. BArch DY 26/173, "5.6.5 Die Bildgeschichte in den Kinderzeitungen und – zeitschriften," pag. 190.
26. BArch DY 26/114, "Dokumentation zur Bildzeitschrift 'Mosaik', 1976," pag. 2.
27. BArch DY 26/173, "5.6.5 Die Bildgeschichte in den Kinderzeitungen und – zeitschriften," pag. 197 and Augustine, *Red Prometheus*, 236 and 243–44.
28. Gersdorf, "Digedags Go West," 40 and 42.
29. Much the same can be said of the comics medium more generally and its perceived connections with American culture and society. For more on (US) cultural imperialism, comics, and how those narratives take specific cues from their Western forebears, see Mila Bongco, *Reading Comics: Language, Culture, and the Concept of the Superhero in Comic Books* (London: Routledge, 2000), 1–18; Nandini Maity, "From Comic Culture to Cyber Cul-

ture: Cultural Imperialism and its Impact on Youth since 1960s," *IOSR Journal of Humanities and Social Science* 8, no. 4 (Mar.–Apr. 2013): 10–14; and Suchitra Mathur, "From Capes to Snakes: The Indianization of the American Superhero," in *Comics as a Nexus of Cultures: Essays on the Interplay of Media, Disciplines and International Perspectives*, ed. Mark Berninger, Jochen Ecke, and Gideon Haberkorn (Jefferson: McFarland & Company, Inc., 2010), 175–86.
30. Chris York and Rafiel York, "Introduction: Fredric Wertham, Containment, and Comic Books," in *Comic Books and the Cold War, 1946–1962: Essays on Graphic Treatment of Communism, the Code, and Social Concerns*, ed. Chris York and Rafiel York (Jefferson: McFarland & Company, Inc., 2012), 14.
31. Danny Fingeroth, *Superman on the Couch: What Superheroes Really Tell Us about Ourselves and Our Society* (New York: Continuum, 2005), 36 and John Lees, "On Comics Custodianism and the Illusion of Change," John Lees Comics, retrieved 13 March 2016 from https://johnleescomics.wordpress.com/2014/07/17/on-comics-custodianism-and-the-illusion-of-change/.
32. BArch DY 26/173, "5.6.5 Die Bildgeschichte in den Kinderzeitungen und – zeitschriften," pag. 197.
33. BArch DY 24/8674, Letter from the Central Committee FDJ on the 20th anniversary of *Mosaik*.
34. Like the Digedags, the Abrafaxe trio was composed of goblin-like individuals. Similarly, one was a blonde, the second a brunette, and the third a redhead to provide a sense of continuity from one character grouping to the next.
35. BArch DY 24/8674, Letter from the Central Committee FDJ on the 20th anniversary of *Mosaik*.
36. BArch DY 24/8674, proposal to award the editors of the magazine *Mosaik* with the "Medal for outstanding achievements in socialist education in the Pioneer Organization Ernst Thälmann" in gold, 31 October 1975.
37. BArch DY 26/173, "2.2. Funktion und Aufgaben der Kinderzeitungen und – zeitschriften in der DDR," pag. 11 and BArch DY 26/42, "Die Kinderzeitschrift 'Mosaik'," pag. 1. Jim Willis also suggests that fostering child groups and friendships at home and internationally was one of the primary tasks of socialist education and of the Young Pioneers specifically, see Jim Willis, *Daily Life Behind the Iron Curtain* (Santa Barbara: Greenwood, 2013), 68.
38. BArch DY 24/8674, Proposal to award the editors of the magazine *Mosaik* with the "Medal for outstanding achievements in socialist education in the Pioneer Organization Ernst Thälmann" in gold, 31 October 1975.
39. Jan Fleischhauer, "Germany's Best-Loved Cowboy: The Fantastical World of Cult Novelist Karl May," Spiegel Online International, retrieved 16 June 2016 from http://www.spiegel.de/international/germany/marking-the-100th-anniversary-of-german-cult-author-karl-may-s-death-a-824566.html.
40. Tim Bergfelder, *International Adventures: German Popular Cinema and European Co-Productions in the 1960s* (New York: Berghahn Books, 2005), 177.

41. Augustine, *Red Prometheus*, 236–43.
42. Augustine, 244.
43. Augustine, 230 and Christoph Richter and Kate Bowen, "East German Comic Celebrates 400 Editions of Slapstick Adventure," *DW Deutsche Welle*, retrieved 18 March 2016 from http://www.dw.com/en/east-german-comic-celebrates-400-editions-of-slapstick-adventure/a-4156898.
44. Barker, *Comics*, 282 and Augustine, *Red Prometheus*, 243.
45. Augustine, *Red Prometheus*, 243. For the racism apparent in American comics and for the "Jungle comic" genre more broadly, see Wright, *Comic Book Nation*, 72–75 and 90–95.
46. Fulbrook, "Concept of 'Normalisation,'" 12–13.
47. Wierling, "Youth as Internal Enemy," 166.
48. Wierling, 164.
49. Wierling, 160–67.
50. This does not suggest that youth or even adults did not read Western or GDR comics. The FDJ noted that there was an audience for these publications beyond the suggested age range, though the vast majority of readers recognized by the regime were under sixteen years of age and considered children within East German society.
51. McDougall, *Youth Politics*, 234 and 240.
52. Wolfgang Kaschuba, "Popular Culture and Workers' Culture as Symbolic Order: Comments on the Debate about the History of Culture and Everyday Life," in *The History of Everyday Life: Reconstructing Historical Experiences and Ways of Life*, ed. Alf Lüdtke, trans. William Templer (Princeton: Princeton University Press, 1995), 169–97. Kaschuba discusses the operation and overlap of popular and proletarian cultures and how each informs the other through their mutual intersection point of everyday life. At the same time, Kaschuba warns that, in recognizing this and the *Eigensinn*, there is no single or simple definition or representation of the *Eigensinn* as it is an individual experience negotiated by "'culture,' conceived as a constant process of communication and interaction."
53. Betts, *Within Walls*, 9–14. See also, Lindenberger, "SED-Herrschaft als soziale Praxis," 23–47.
54. Corey Ross argues that in the wake of youth criminality in the border areas of Berlin, prior to the Wall's construction, the FDJ attempted to further organize itself and make itself more attractive to youth. However, the youth group found the dual task of proselytizing socialism and convincing youth of Western evils impossible. Ross contends that this, paired with youths' perspective that the FDJ was only interested in them when it had something to gain, caused the rise of subcultures outside the control of, and dangerous to, the FDJ's organization of leisure time and activities. Efforts to increase this organization only added to the attraction of Western popular culture as that culture was further politicized. See Ross, *Constructing Socialism*, 140–42. Uta Poiger then suggests that, as the SED authorities had

the power to organize and control culture and economics and which aspects of those were consumed by youth, the state's politicization of leisure time and the *Eigensinn* constructed identities of resistance within youth culture. See Poiger, *Jazz, Rock, and Rebels*, 222–26.
55. Fulbrook, *People's State*, 129.
56. BArch DY 24/23769, "Leserpostanalyse für das 2. Halbjahr 1972," pag. 5.
57. BArch DY 24/1581, "Vorlage an das Sekretariat des Zentralrates der FDJ, 22.7.66," pag. 6. H. Glenn Penny argues that an essential component to the German desire for education and acculturation (*Bildung*) was "the corresponding desire to gain and demonstrate a sense of worldliness." Germans were encouraged to consider the interconnectivity between people and places encountered through travel and how they related to the place of Germans and their origins. This "promoted open-minded voyages of self-discovery as well as explorations of foreign territory" that was demonstrated in GDR comics. See Penny, *Kindred by Choice*, 33.
58. Richter and Bowen, "East German Comic Celebrates."
59. While some of the stories that appeared in *Atze* were told over the course of a number of issues, aside from *Fix und Fax*, none ran long enough to be considered "ongoing." *Pats Reiseabenteuer* filled this void as both an ongoing and political comic story, running from 1967 until 1991 when the magazine folded in the wake of (re)unification.
60. BArch DY 24/1581, "Vorlage an das Sekretariat des Zentralrat der FDJ, 22.7.66," pag. 4.
61. Sabeti, "Irony of 'Cool Club,'" 138.
62. Brock, "Producing the 'Socialist Personality'?" 250.
63. BArch DY 24/23769, "Leserpostanalyse für die Monate Januar bis Juni 1972 Redaktion ATZE/Mosaik," pag. 7.
64. Weißhahn, "Pats Reiseabenteuer."
65. Tintin's adventures, by the Belgian illustrator Georges Remi (Hergé), often took the reporter to exotic locales, many of which were designed as educational propaganda by the publisher. Following *Tintin in the Land of the Soviets*, Hergé published *Tintin in the Congo* (1930–31) as part of this process of education and generating interest in the Belgian Congo. In the study of *bande dessinée*, it is often cited as one of the more influential examples of colonial ideology in comics, see McKinney, *Colonial Heritage*, 3 and Pierre Assouline, *Hergé, the Man Who Created Tintin*, trans. Charles Ruas (Oxford: Oxford University Press, 2009), 24–29.
66. It should also be noted that this is around the same time in which the *Communist Manifesto* by Karl Marx and Friedrich Engels first saw publication.
67. Jeanette Madarasz argues that the FDJ fostered connections between this historical, humanist-based education with a broad array of youth culture wherein responses to the desires of youth were shaped by specific political and educational goals, see Madarasz, *Conflict and Compromise*, 62–65. For similar arguments in relation to more specific areas of culture, see McDou-

gall, "Liberal Interlude," 123–55 and Poiger, *Jazz, Rock, and Rebels*, on the influence of Western music in divided Germany; H. Glenn Penny, "Red Power: Liselotte Welskopf-Henrich and the Indian Activist Networks in East and West Germany," *Central European History* 41, no. 3 (September 2008): 447–76 for the American "Wild West" in GDR films; and Thompson-Wohlgemuth, "Official and Unofficial," 32–52 for Children's Literature in the GDR.
68. Wierling, "Youth as Internal Enemy," 167.
69. MMM stood for *Messe der Meister von Morgen* (Masters of Tomorrow Exposition) and was a trade fair, of sorts, and youth competition designed to generate youth interest and, if you will, enthusiasm towards technology and the sciences. Comparable to the *Junge forscht* (Youth Research) in the Federal Republic after 1965, the MMM was created by the FDJ and held annually in the GDR from 1958 until 1990.
70. Rubin, *Synthetic Socialism*, 5 and 10.
71. Augustine, *Red Prometheus*, 242–43.
72. *Heimat* is a much more complicated concept than a direct translation allows. It is bound in both the local and national identifications of the self. Simultaneously, it involves a nostalgic eye toward the national past and draws on modern constructions of the present; the past as a space of perpetual stability despite the instabilities of modernity. Alon Confino, *The Nation as a Local Metaphor: Württemberg, Imperial Germany, and National Memory, 1871–1918* (Chapel Hill: University of North Carolina Press, 1997), 120–23.
73. Augustine, *Red Prometheus*, 232–34.
74. McCloud, *Understanding Comics*, 27–36, 58–59, and 68–69; Eisner, *Comics and Sequential Art*, 7, 8, and 24; and Hatfield, "Comic Art," 343–44.
75. This does not suggest that the SED and the FDJ publishing regime were evil, per se. They were undeniably repressive and an increasing amount of literature on the subject points to this. However, evil and villain are relative terms based on the perspective of the protagonist observer. During the Cold War, Western assumptions undoubtedly cast these terms across the entire Soviet Bloc. There is no evidence to suggest that the child-readers of East German comics and *Kinderzeitschriften* considered the regime using this same terminology. The terms are used here to draw a comparative between the regime and comic book villains, suggesting a sense of evildoing for altruistic intentions or, more simply, an obliviousness surrounding the perceived wrongdoing of one's actions.
76. Gumbert, *Envisioning Socialism*, 85–86 and 90–93.
77. Barker, *Comics*, 246.
78. Nothnagle, *East German Myth*, 57–60.
79. Jobs, "Tarzan Under Attack," 716.

CHAPTER 5

Western Influence, Popular Taste, and the Limitations of the FDJ's Publishing Regime

When Hannes Hegen approached Verlag Neues Leben in 1955 with his idea for *Mosaik* and the Digedags, he had a relatively clear idea of the characters he wanted to create and their journey. I have already made much of the inspiration Hegen drew from the Disney comics popularized in both halves of divided Germany in the decade following the end of World War II.[1] Some of this inspiration came from the Free German Youth itself, issuing orders to the publishing director of Verlag Neues Leben to create a socialist counterpart to Mickey Mouse.[2] Presumably, this directive included other characters such as Donald Duck and Uncle Scrooge in the wake of the Europe-wide popularity of Carl Barks's work with those characters.[3] However, the similarities in these perceived starting points for the Digedags and their globe-trotting adventures, not to mention their forays through both time and space, does not suggest that Hegen and the FDJ were ever of the same mind regarding the direction and contents of *Mosaik von Hannes Hegen*.

This chapter follows developments within *Mosaik* from the early 1960s through Hegen's departure from the publisher in 1975. Earlier chapters have already made much of the socialist content found in the publication despite observers' suggestions that East German comics were sites free from ideology and propaganda. Of course, many of these observations were made after (re)unification as former East Germans reclaimed an identity thought lost during the process of Westernization in the former-German Democratic Republic (GDR), adopting domestic and private spaces and the *Alltag* as sites supposedly free of the SED regime's influence.[4] Here, state influence is often understood in terms of the overt intrusion of SED and Stasi authority over the lives of East German citizens. At the same time, this rose-colored retrospective typically ignores the more benign cultural incursions affected through forms of popularly consumed media in an effort to claim perceived normalcy over the experience of everyday life.[5] This being the case and not to suggest that *Mosaik* and East German comics broadly were devoid of state-sponsored propaganda, this chapter explores the often tumultuous relationship between Hegen and the editorial regime of Verlag Junge Welt and the FDJ.[6] This point of departure was not selected randomly but was a turning point in Hegen's relationships with his creation and with the publishers and organizations responsible for the approval, mediation, and distribution of those comics to their child-readership. As with the transformation undertaken by *Atze* in 1966, this chapter begins with a similar transformation in *Mosaik* as the publication and its creative team came under fire from the FDJ and educators in the GDR.

Despite the FDJ's ties to the comic, the state's educational program, and the overall growth of the publication, the comic and the adventures of the Digedags were rarely considered as ideological as the regime requested or required. Early stories found the Digedags often associating with royalty and drawing the ire of the publishing regime. By the mid-1960s, the Digedags were mandated to demonstrate in a clear fashion their motives and to clarify their role as "funny folk heroes" (*lustige Volkshelden*), helping the exploited and poor against the bourgeoisie and their lackeys. They needed to show the production of materials and their appropriation by the ruling classes, representing the ideological and historical principles of the SED regime in their actions and behavior.[7] In other words, the FDJ required that *Mosaik von Hannes Hegen* embody the socialist educational content necessary for their comics and other publications for children. The inclusion of ideology was not new, but one that was long marginalized, if not outright ignored, by Hegen. As the ideological demands of the regime grew alongside the demands of a rigorous publishing schedule, Hegen chafed in his role as creative voice and director of the Mosaik-Kollektiv.

Despite the socialist, cultural policies promoted during Mitteldeutscher Verlag's conference in Bitterfeld in 1959, *Mosaik* remained a holdout of the Western comics tradition and influence and of the relative ideological freedom among the bevy of East German children's publications. Even after the construction of the Berlin Wall and the subsequent control of Western publications in the East German marketplace, as much as the GDR can be said to have a marketplace, *Mosaik* was less apparently motived by ideology than its contemporary publications *Frösi, Junge Welt*, and even *Atze*. Of course, *Mosaik* was never completely free of this ideological impetus.[8] Yet *Mosaik* continued to draw the FDJ's criticisms and, perhaps more importantly as far as Hegen was concerned, its interference. Though, it should not be concluded that the SED regime, the FDJ, or Verlag Junge Welt were wholly responsible for the chasm growing between publisher and creator. The FDJ and Verlag Junge Welt were not interested in seeing through their particular form of ideology when it came to *Mosaik von Hannes Hegen*, partially due to internal conflicts among the editorial collective, but also because the genre itself did not support it. In this instance, the perceived tastes of the child-readership won out over propaganda. This matter of taste is arguably responsible for the perception of a supposed ideology-free zone that developed around GDR comics and the *Alltag* in the post-unification period.[9]

Perhaps nowhere are the limits of dictatorship more noticeable or important than among East German children and youth given the significance the regime put upon their collective role in society and the model of the socialist personality.[10] As a comic creator and, for the first five years of *Mosaik*'s publication, one of the few creative voices behind the Digedags, Hegen was on the frontlines of constructing the socialist personality even as he sought to entertain. Given the restrictions on Western children's publications, *Mosaik* was indicative of a supposed socialist alternative not only among comics publications but within the sphere of children's and youth culture and of socialism and Soviet-style communism as a superior tool in child-rearing. Regardless, *Mosaik*'s popularity stemmed from its emulation of the Western comics tradition, influenced by the United States. Perhaps in spite of the FDJ's intentions, then, this apparent influence and its associated popularity made changing the comics' formula not nearly as simple a process as it was with *Atze*.

The directives established in Bitterfeld encouraged professional writers "to write about the work of building socialism," following the established principles of Socialist Realism imported from the Soviet Union.[11] Novels emerging in the wake of this conference prescribed the ideal way a committed socialist citizen and Party member would act and think through the construction of the socialist personality.[12] This program was evident throughout the East German arts and nowhere more so than in the children's literature of the day, raising the bar for the production of children's literature that grew too sophisticated for the young audience for whom it was intended.[13]

The effects of the *Bitterfelder Weg* on GDR comics are more difficult to ascertain as connections to the conference and these literary circles are not explicit. Prior to the drastic changes made to East German comics in the shadow of the Berlin Wall, comics were largely ignored, considered irrelevant and derivative at best or as a continuation of Western *Schund- und Schmutzliteratur* at worst. The timing of the East German variation of the anti-comics campaign circulating through the capitalist world and calling for changes to *Mosaik* appears suspect. In the mid-1960s, around the same time that similar recriminations were made against *Atze*, criticisms were levelled against *Mosaik von Hannes Hegen* with particular attention to the motivations of the Digedags, their characterizations and respective personalities, and, most important, the accuracy of historical representation in the comics' stories. Likewise, comics were intended to develop a space central to the construction and formation of the socialist personality among children. While these specific criticisms came down on the publication and those involved in its production in the mid-1960s, similar accusations were directed toward the publication at the beginning of the decade when Hegen himself came under attack from the FDJ and East German educators.[14] Although *Mosaik* and *Atze* were not included in the *Bitterfelder Weg* by name, nor were comics considered part of a literary scene that required close cooperation between the creators and the working class due to their association with childhood, decisions taken in Bitterfeld extended beyond the realm of literary "arts" to the harmful influence (*schädlicher Einfluß*) of bourgeois comic books.[15]

Despite *Mosaik*'s early objective of providing a socialist bulwark against the influence of American comics that were illegally crossing the border and the perceived public outcry in both halves of postwar Germany, *Mosaik* followed its American inspiration more closely than the dictates of the FDJ.[16] Because of this perceived lack of ideology, children purchased approximately a quarter million issues of the comic every month by the late 1950s.[17] After the initial stories of the Digedags, Hegen began the *Weltraum-Serie* in 1958. This did not stem directly from the dictates of the *Bitterfelder Weg* as the *Weltraum-Serie* launched a year before the conference. But the *Weltraum-Serie* shared goals similar to those of the *Bitterfelder Weg* through its demonstration of alien technologies suspiciously reminiscent to those already found in the GDR. *Mosaik* privileged industrial technologies at the expense of consumer desires.[18] This served the FDJ's educational objectives at the forefront among the comics' editorial mandate during the 1960s. At the same time, it addressed the scientific-technological revolution at the heart of an East German and decidedly socialist education and identity while still being both nationalistic and imperialistic in character and representation.[19]

However, following the *Bitterfelder Weg*, *Mosaik* came under attack for the contents of the publication and Hegen himself was attacked on a personal level, alienating him from the FDJ and the state-owned publisher Verlag Junge Welt. This was a transitional moment for the publication having recently moved from its original publisher, Verlag Neues Leben, in June 1959. Thälmann Pioneer Chairman Robert Lehmann thought the comics should be tended by editors familiar with and responsible for the production of similar works suitable for children. It was hoped this change in editorial would influence *Mosaik*'s content and intensify its sense of socialist education.[20] The change in the publication's home preceded suggestions to include educational leaflets in issues of *Mosaik*, providing readers with obvious demonstrations of the GDR's success in areas relevant to the comics' stories and arguably stretching the limits of what may be considered the state's benign exercise of power. These leaflets, *Steinchen auf Steinchen* (stone on stone) as they were known in official parlance because of the cornerstones they laid in the construction of socialism for children, emphasized the stories' educational aspects in ways the comics themselves lacked, providing technical and historical information not included in those comics. And despite the additions of Lothar Dräger, Gisela Zimmermann, and Horst Boche to the Mosaik-Kollektiv in 1958, preparing the groundwork for a monthly publication schedule and bringing the publication in line with criticisms emerging from the Pioneer organization, the FDJ and Wolfgang Altenburger (in a retrospective of Hegen's association with *Mosaik* drafted in 1975 following his departure) thought Hegen placed a premium on the stories' fable aspects at the expense of their socialist educational content. Moreover, the FDJ contended that Hegen's contract with Verlag Junge Welt was in non-compliance with statutes pertaining to the publisher and editor's responsibilities in that Hegen often overturned demands on his artistic influence within the publication.[21]

Hegen drew on the tropes of Western "schlock" because of the perceived popularity of genres such as science fiction and the detective thriller among young readers.[22] Regardless, in 1960 the *Deutsche Lehrerzeitung* (German Teachers' News) questioned the role of *Mosaik*'s editorial board in the proper construction of the comic's ideological function. Hegen himself came under suspicion of having a bourgeois background and potentially being part of a remote campaign to undermine the GDR through its children. The editor of the children's magazine

Frösi argued that Hegen was irresponsible, setting his stories in the past without the proper representation of reality. As a result of these attacks against Hegen and *Mosaik*'s role for East German children and society more broadly, Hegen's contract was amended. While fundamentally similar, Hegen's consolidated influence within the children's publication was reduced as his creative role was immediately subjected to the editorial authority of Hans Erhardt, and later of Wolfgang Altenburger, as Hegen himself became director of the Mosaik-Kollektiv. Hegen's name remained on the publication's masthead, providing the illusion of his role as sole creator.[23]

The effects of Hegen's marginalization within his own comic was arguably the "exercise of power caus[ing] a perceptible . . . extreme change for the worse in the position of the victim and . . . his relationship to the world."[24] Though Hegen broke no recognized law or convention during his stewardship and production of *Mosaik*, his failure to toe the Party line in terms of these publications was previously chastised through the hiring of Dräger, Zimmermann, and Boche. Arguably, the dilution of Hegen's influence was noticeable in the ideological shift of the *Weltraum-Serie* compared to the Digedags' adventures that came before. Hegen's loss of status during *Mosaik*'s transfer to Verlag Junge Welt, a publisher experienced in the production of children's magazines, came from an established set of norms acceptable and expected from East German children's literature, but particularly comics magazines in this case. The *Bitterfelder Weg* was the codification of norms previously understood though perhaps not explicitly stated, even in the publication of comics.[25] Specifically, the work of the publishers, comics publishers included, through the enforcement of these ideals toward representation in *Mosaik* became a struggle to maintain a high level of culture in the construction of socialism. This combated the negative and consumerist influences of Western comics before the Berlin Wall significantly reduced the availability of those children's publications.[26]

For Hegen, the radical shift in the publisher's approach to *Mosaik* meant the supposed end to his monopoly over the comic's creative direction. As Verlag Junge Welt brought Erhardt aboard as editor of the publication, Hegen, Dräger, Zimmermann, and Boche were incorporated into the Mosaik-Kollektiv in June 1960. *Mosaik* and the associated *Kollektiv* were initially under direction of the Thälmann Pioneers' leadership, but quickly fell under the purview of the FDJ's Central Committee as the managing editorial board.[27] These changes were intended to chastise Hegen's supposed bourgeois tendencies, eliminate *Mosaik*'s Western influence, and return the comic to the directives of the publisher and the FDJ, regardless of the outside influence from the *Bitterfelder Weg* earlier in the year. Perhaps Hegen perceived these changes to the publishing environment around him as the threat they were, given his loss of status within the publication and potentially also in the estimation of the publisher, the FDJ, and the Party. But the FDJ's use of power should have been expected given the history of criticism laid at *Mosaik*'s door and the youth group's continuing concerns over the comic's content. This censure suggested the FDJ's desire to bring *Mosaik* into the ideological and educational fold of East German educators following the *Deutsche Lehrerzeitung*'s problems with the publication and the desires of FDJ functionaries to have greater influence over the space afforded by comics to penetrate the niche society and children's otherwise unregulated leisure time.

But this change came a year into a planned story, the *Weltraum-Serie*. Whether or not plans for the story originally envisioned it to continue four years, and given subsequent developments adopted by the publication and the gradual return of the Digedag character at the advent of the *Erfinder-Serie* while Dig and Dag remained in space this appears unlikely, little immediately changed regardless of the alterations to Hegen's contract or situation. The *Weltraum-Serie* was itself a product of Hegen's reduced influence within these editorial changes. Earlier stories utilized the Digedags effectively, though not explicitly, practicing cultural imperialism and racism through the perceived superiority of East German politics, society, and culture.[28] This is particularly the case in the *Orient-Südsee-Serie* and aspects of the *Amerika-Serie* (well after the formation of the Mosaik-Kollektiv); it involved the American Indigenous population and continued through the era of unification with the representation of island populations as primitive, child-like, and racial stereotypes. The *Weltraum-Serie* was a significant step away from the fantasy and historical inaccuracies criticized in earlier stories. Though not specifically of the Socialist Realist model described by the *Bitterfelder Weg*, Dig and Dag's abduction into space demonstrated a socialist worldview and dedicated antifascism necessary to East German fiction, including science fiction and comics.[29] The ongoing *Weltraum-Serie* ensured the temporary continuation of these narrative and editorial modes. But as that series concluded in 1962, Erhardt passed his authority as Editor-in-Chief to Wolfgang Altenburger. Altenburger already enjoyed success as an editor with Verlag Junge Welt. He was a dedicated and reliable Party member, having joined the SED in 1948 while a member of the FDJ since the end of World War II.[30] Though tasked with broadening the appeal and expanding the readership of *Mosaik*, Altenburger proved something of a collaborator to Hegen when and where he could, even if he was not exactly an ally.

The *Erfinder-Serie* concluded in 1964, allowing the FDJ and the comic's editorial regime to demonstrate the GDR's penchant toward scientific and technological progress around which they could rally constructions of an East German identity. Meanwhile, Hegen returned the Digedags to settings more familiar, the medieval courts and journeys through the Middle East during the Crusades of the *Ritter Runkel-Serie*.[31] In this same moment, the FDJ declared that the ideological role of *Kinderzeitschriften*, including *Mosaik*, was to "fight against western comics with distinct, humanistic means," particularly those comics from the United States.[32] The FDJ understood and represented East German comics as a tool to combat the influence of Westernization, Americanization, and the consumerism sifting through the supposedly impervious Berlin Wall.[33] This struggle was met through a cultural confrontation with the likes of Scrooge McDuck and *Fix und Foxi* on one side against the perceived superiority of socialist morality demonstrated in the pages of comic books published by Verlag Junge Welt. Comics, particularly *Mosaik* as the best-selling publication of its kind among East German children, were the regime's most potent weapons in this regard, apparent through the publication's increased paper quota and circulation.[34] Despite accusations that *Mosaik* followed Western patterns and tendencies far too closely even before the *Erfinder-Serie* concluded, it was the perceived adherence to those Western tropes that endeared the publication to children and replaced American and West German comics in the minds of that readership after the Wall's construction.[35]

As editor of both of the significant comic magazines published by Verlag Junge Welt, Altenburger used his position as writer and *Chefredakteur* of *Atze* to deflect the regime's attention from *Mosaik*. East German authors often used flagrant political statements to attract the censors' attention, keeping eyes away from the more subtle criticisms that peppered their works. At the same time, editors and publishing houses were often as much authors of the work as were the authors themselves.[36] This does not suggest that Altenburger assisted Hegen with the scripting of *Mosaik*. Since the late 1950s, Lothar Dräger was the comic's credited co-writer.[37] Rather, Altenburger used *Atze*'s glaring deficiencies to obfuscate some of those same problems in *Mosaik*, maintaining *Mosaik* in a form recognizable to its readership. As discussed in the first chapter, before the mid-1960s *Atze* was an uneven publication with questionable quality in terms of its writing, art, and the entwined operation of the two. Some conventions of the comics' form, deriving from the Americanization of the medium, were considered by the FDJ to intrude on the meaning of the images and interfered with children's ability to understand the required political message. In this regard, *Atze* suffered more than *Mosaik*, particularly due to its irregular publishing schedule, murky artwork, the creators' insistence upon experimentation, and the lack of a politically driven, serialized story to carry readers not only through the comic but from one issue to the next. As such, in their first decade of publication, East German comics failed to meet the FDJ's expectations despite the FDJ's own reports on the comics medium's supposed superiority, given the medium's relative permanency and re-readability as means of delivering informational content, over televised children's programming.[38] Moreover, Heather Gumbert suggests that television was particularly popular among children and youth and although authorities hoped it would prevent a latchkey-kid phenomenon and keep youth out of Western cinemas, the variety of entertainment available in Berlin would not hold youth attention for long. At the same time, Gumbert contends that programming was relatively irregular and as such, few shows had the chance to become cornerstones of a programming schedule. *Unser Sandmännchen* was one of the exceptions, generating popularity on both sides of the inner-German border even though children's entertainment accounted for only 8.9 percent of DFF's total programming in 1960.[39]

Altenburger assumed *Mosaik*'s policy matters to have the publication conform to the declared objectives of the FDJ and of SED youth policy more broadly. Not only did Altenburger's involvement give *Mosaik* the veneer of acceptability with the FDJ leadership, but also kept Hegen, and Dräger to a lesser degree, out of the publication's politics, keeping discussions of politics and ideology within the comic itself to a minimum. And despite the Digedags' role as the cultural ambassadors of East German socialism, this great burden now fell to *Fix und Fax*.[40] The perception of *Mosaik*'s acceptance was accomplished through the early conceptualization of stories by Altenburger and Verlag Junge Welt publishing director, Rudolf Barbarino, often years in advance and beginning with "Auf den Spuren der Marco Polo" (On the Trail of Marco Polo, appearing as part of the *Ritter Runkel-Serie*) in 1964. Regarding the GDR's broader publishing culture, Robert Darnton suggests that editors and publishers left intentional gaps in the publishing plan to allow the last-minute inclusion of books deemed too "hot" for publication, as approval from the Ministry of Culture was more forthcoming on an ad hoc basis. However, if the Central Committee was unhappy with what went on in a publishing office, restricting resources to the publishing office was a frequent punishment that hobbled the publisher's ability to function on a daily basis. Advance planning, not only with regard to *Mosaik* but with East German publications at large, dealt with these potential political problems well ahead of time.[41] Editorial influence significantly interfered with Hegen's creative process, but *Mosaik* largely avoided these last-minute and often impossible changes to the comics' fundamental design and execution. Due to the connectivity between text and image in comics and with the Mosaik-Kollektiv often working right up to its deadlines, changes to the comics on political grounds or over historical accuracy were often difficult, if not impossible, to carry forward. This policy of planning and approving *Mosaik*'s stories before the involvement of the Mosaik-Kollektiv allowed the publisher, and by extension the FDJ, more input into the creation of those stories for the political and educational content mandated by the regime. The policy also expanded Altenburger's role in *Mosaik*. Developing *Mosaik*'s stories in advance and beyond the reach of Hegen and the Mosaik-Kollektiv's writers meant that only minor corrections were later required between the publisher and printer as Altenburger took responsibility for the publication's overall direction and content.[42]

Hegen and his collaborators on *Mosaik* drew the criticisms of the regime and East German educators since 1958 despite the *Weltraum-Serie* story's inclusion of ideological and educational content through the portrayal of the analogous Cold War conflict and the creation of a utopian future. Criticism stemmed from *Mosaik*'s perceived adherence to the tropes and traditions of Western comics. Critics believed those in the Mosaik-Kollektiv came from petite-bourgeois (*kleinbürgerlich*) backgrounds and moved in bourgeois circles. The FDJ considered this perceived problem of Western influence serious enough to potentially dissolve the publication completely. Of course, this did not happen. As the most popular children's publication of its kind in the GDR, *Mosaik* was Verlag Junge Welt's financial backbone and the publisher's continued existence depended upon the comic as a stable source of revenue. And yet, the comic drew the regime's ire for suggesting Western tendencies in a publication that was supposed to be a child-rearing tool and aid in children's humanist and moral educational development.[43] Introducing Altenburger to the Mosaik-Kollektiv introduced a control lever previously absent from the publication and provided *Mosaik* with a new degree of perceived respectability from the regime.

The FDJ agreed that because of its content and peculiarities, *Mosaik* could not be substantially changed and still maintain its existing readership.[44] This impotence, however, did not mean change could not occur in the offices of Verlag Junge Welt or within the Mosaik-Kollektiv itself. In this regard, despite his position as creator of *Mosaik* and of the Digedags, Hegen was more an employee of the state, a work-for-hire comic creator, rather than an autonomous author or artist.[45] In such a case, which applies in the East German context despite Hegen's criticisms and accusations following his departure from *Mosaik* in 1975, copyright of a work remained with the employer, or publisher, rather than the artist or author of that work. The editorial regime argued that Hegen was contracted to provide his work to *Mosaik*.[46] Indeed, no real effort was made to normalize the idea of *Autorencomics* (creator-owned comics) with West German publishers until the 1980s, and with East German publishers not at all.[47] With changes enacted over the first half of the 1960s, particularly Altenburger and Barbarino drafting story ideas for *Mosaik* and an attempted break with *Mosaik*'s series publication model, Verlag Junge Welt demonstrated a firmer grasp over what would and would not be allowed in the comic. Moreover, Hegen's contracts were initially renewed on an issue-by-issue basis as the publisher had no previous experience with comic book contracts. Treating Hegen as a contracted employee of Verlag Junge Welt serves to explain how the publisher followed the dictates of the *Bitterfelder Weg* without Hegen's apparent consent.[48]

Among the changes wrought on the publication in the mid-1960s, the FDJ required Verlag Junge Welt to organize a reader group for *Mosaik*. This reader group was appointed by Kurt Feitsch, the Publishing Director who took over for Barbarino in 1965, but who remained under Altenburger's direct authority.[49] The group examined the text and graphics of each issue, and consulting with Hegen, drew attention to ideological and historical inaccuracies. At the same time, the group ensured that the guiding principles and ethical behavior of the Digedags were clear to the reader as the obscurity of these principles was a problem often pointed out in the past. For all intents and purposes, though the FDJ recognized Hegen as the creative force behind *Mosaik*, Hegen's name on the title masthead represented the last of his influence within the publication.[50] The formation of this group brought *Mosaik* closer to East German publishing practices carried out in the areas of fiction and *Belles-Lettres* as the first line of censorship, even before manuscripts were vetted by the Hauptverwaltung Verlage und Buchhandel (Office of Publishers and Booksellers) or HV in the Ministry of Culture. To the publication's benefit, this shift meant that *Mosaik* was treated by the editorial regime as part of the internationally respected children's literature and not with the Western *Unkultur* with which it was first associated. The reading group's introduction to oversee *Mosaik*'s production subverted Hegen's influence alongside the supposed bourgeois elements of the Mosaik-Kollektiv, tendencies of which included the Western comic tropes and "schlock" used in the adventures of the Digedags. The first step of censorship in the GDR, a state in which censorship did not officially occur given the inclusion of free speech in the East German constitution, came from planning.[51] And during the meeting of the Secretariat of the Central Committee FDJ that took place on 4 October 1966, at which time *Mosaik*'s reading group was mandated, the FDJ required annual plans be drafted for the editorial board and the reading group to smooth the progress and process of the publication.[52]

Opposed to what was considered standard procedure, publishing in the GDR involved deals made between authors, publishers, and proxies for those in the HV behind closed doors. This was the case for authors like Volker Braun, Christa Wolf, and Christoph Hein, to name a few, and was necessary to pass their works through the various levels of East German (unofficial) censorship and receive a publishing license while still producing a text that, for the most part, reflected the author's original intent.[53] This system of "negotiation, accommodation, resistance, and compromise" remained largely untouched throughout the entire lifespan of the GDR, despite the effects of *glasnost* (openness) trickling in from the Soviet Union from the mid-1980s until the final collapse of the SED regime in 1989.[54] However, this approach was arguably not the case in Verlag Junge Welt's dealings with Hegen. Gerd Lettkemann and Michael F. Scholz suggest that, due to the existing political order and the construction of the GDR as an independent state with its own history separate from that of the Federal Republic and the need to support and develop this history, Hegen was forced to yield to those criticisms levelled against him in the mid-1960s.[55] *Mosaik*'s editorial policies removed Hegen from the creation of his own comics, placing restrictions on his creative abilities and voice. At the same time, Hegen and his wife, Edith, were monitored by the Stasi until the end of the 1980s. This does not appear to have impacted the couple's work on *Mosaik*. Rather, Stasi interest was piqued exactly because of Hegen's work and the perceived level of influence he and his wife wielded over East German children through the comic book page.[56] Hegen grew generally resistant, not only to these changes but to any further alterations of the publication and to his creations. As a result, the publisher was forced to make concessions that made dealing with Hegen easier and smoothed over those changes required of the publication itself. Attention turned to Altenburger as Verlag Junge Welt constructed *Atze* as the ideological backbone of comics publishing in the GDR.[57]

Altenburger's creation of *Pats Reiseabenteuer* shifted the FDJ's focus to *Atze*. Meanwhile, *Mosaik* continued largely unchanged in form from what came before despite the changes to its presentation of historical accuracy and ideological content. Since even before the publication of *Mosaik*'s first issue, the SED charged the FDJ with the systematic education of youth as part of its recruitment into the military and its larger participation in socialist society.[58] This directive was renewed in the wake of the *Bitterfelder Weg* as publishers endorsed a program toward a uniform representation of East German socialism across the arts.[59] Throughout the 1960s, particularly following the construction of the Berlin Wall and the failure of Walter Ulbricht's Youth Communiqué by the middle of the decade, the FDJ found itself in a stronger position than just a few years earlier, firmly establishing its role and responsibilities in the Volkskammer and as a mass party organization.[60] Despite the FDJ's increased visibility, the Digedags travelled Europe, the Middle East, and Asia as the youth group discovered its inability to fundamentally reshape the publication without also affecting reader perceptions of security and privacy within the space afforded by comics and within the domestic niche itself. The need to revitalize *Atze*, particularly with regard to the bar of quality established by *Mosaik*, allowed Altenburger opportunity to draw the regime's attention from *Mosaik* as he corrected *Atze*'s failings.[61] This did not completely shelter *Mosaik* or Hegen from the FDJ's interests, but it made permissible the publication's continuation with Hegen's reduced influence.

By the end of the decade, *Mosaik* was arguably at its most successful point, publishing hundreds of thousands of copies domestically and expanding publication to include exports to Western Europe, specifically the Netherlands. The numbers in this latter endeavor were modest, licensing only twenty thousand copies for the initial shipment in July 1969 with the debut of the *Amerika-Serie*, but with the hope of gaining a successful foothold in the Western European comic book market.[62] The publisher approved the requested allocation of precious paper, constantly in short supply throughout the existence of the GDR, finding the timing favorable with the launch of the *Amerika-Serie* and the demonstration of capitalist development and the social contrasts and antagonisms (*Gegensätzen*) at work in North America contained therein.[63] By the late 1960s, the FDJ found *Mosaik* ideologically reliable enough to represent East German socialism through the Digedags and their interactions on the American frontier. While this was arguably not the case, it begs questioning why the least ideological comic was ideal to provide "a positive, political balance to the flood of Western comics."[64]

Of the comics available in the GDR, and admittedly this list is extremely short compared to those available in the Western world during the postwar, *Mosaik* was arguably the one most influenced by the West and the Western comic book tropes.[65] Moreover, the *Amerika-Serie* addressed the Americanisms of the *Mosaik* comics through their interactions with the Digedags and their socialist worldview.[66] *Mosaik* here addressed American racism, particularly through the nation's history of slavery and exploitation. The writers, however, did not look toward their own brand of racism apparent in the cultural imperialism and perceived superiority of socialism evident in earlier issues.[67] The introduction of the *Amerika-Serie* put *Mosaik* in a unique position for the purposes of export. The publication closely resembled the "funny animal" comics that were already popular among children in Western Europe, drawing inspiration from those same books, giving *Mosaik* the best chance of success in the international market while still serving the agenda of the FDJ, the SED, and German communism broadly.

That said, the editorial regime's actions and Hegen's own reduced influence proved sticking points as the *Amerika-Serie* and the FDJ's plans for *Mosaik*'s export moved forward. When *Mosaik* was transferred to Verlag Junge Welt at the beginning of 1960, Hegen's contract remained relatively unchanged despite the changes affected around him and the changing tasks of socialist ideology and cultural policy in *Mosaik*. Unlike Hegen's contracts with Verlag Neues Leben that were renewed quarterly with each new issue, contracts between Hegen and the Verlag Junge Welt were for fixed periods and renewed every few years. This allowed the publisher opportunity to revise the terms and the fundamentals of the relationship with Hegen as the publisher licensed use of the Digedags, but it guaranteed Hegen very little control after the creation of the *Chefredakteur* position and the reading-group. Throughout the 1960s, Hegen had opportunity to periodically renegotiate the contractual terms with Verlag Junge Welt. Why then his contract remained relatively unchanged despite his obvious dissatisfaction is unclear, unless the terms of those contracts were imposed upon him by the FDJ and the publisher. However, there is insufficient evidence to indicate that this was the case.[68] As suggested elsewhere by Darnton, publication, and especially the publication of *Mosaik* for our purposes here, was indeed subject to processes of resistance, compromise, and accommodation.[69] Regardless, as the 1960s wore on, Hegen grew increasingly resistant to the demands of the FDJ's editorial regime. By 1969, Dr. Anselm Glücksmann, Verlag Junge Welt's legal counsel since 1967, recommended that the publisher negotiate a new contract with

Hegen for an indeterminate amount of time. The FDJ hoped that Hegen's inability to revise his contract for the foreseeable future would force him to settle any misgivings as revisions to the terms within were made difficult and the contract required a full year's notice prior to termination. At the same time, this contract bound the regime to Hegen's ownership, insofar as the regime recognized intellectual property, of the Digedags and of the comic magazine itself. Indeed, the FDJ conceded Hegen's ownership of the Digedag characters, their stories, and of the title *Mosaik von Hannes Hegen*. The FDJ was admittedly unwilling to fight Hegen on the matter. That being the case, this unwillingness did not extend to the title *Mosaik* more generally for the purposes of recognition and appeal with the established readership.[70]

As the FDJ considered Hegen to be a contracted employee of Verlag Junge Welt, Hegen's expressed problems with the publisher drew upon this relationship, not turning to the issue of control over the comic's creative direction, but to its perceived deficiencies. Not unlike the children writing into the editorial of *Atze* discussed in Chapter Three, Hegen's complaints to the editorial regime employed the language of the workers and of the regime that was supposed to represent them.[71] In 1972, three years after the completion of the open-ended contract suggested by Glücksmann and the same amount of time into the publication of the *Amerika-Serie*, Hegen informed Kurt Feitsch that the continued publication of twelve issues of *Mosaik* per year was impossible under the current working conditions. Since 1958, *Mosaik* published on a monthly schedule. In the autumn of 1972, however, Hegen argued that the monthly schedule demanded a physical and psychological overload compounded by understaffing, the insufficient qualifications of the *Kollektiv's* new employees, and the retirement of some older colleagues. By the end of the year, Lona Rietschel, a member of the Mosaik-Kollektiv since 1960, and Joachim Arfert, associated with the *Kollektiv* since the late 1950s, wrote to the publisher on Hegen's behalf, requesting increased wages for the *Kollektiv*. Hegen demanded a renegotiation of his and the *Kollektiv's* contracts, as Altenburger reported to Feitsch in early 1973 following a conversation with Dräger. If a new contract was not agreed upon, Hegen threatened to withdraw from his existing contract, taking the Digedags with him, at the end of June 1974.[72]

As far as *Mosaik*, Hegen, and the Mosaik-Kollektiv were concerned, the space of negotiation provided by West German Chancellor Willy Brandt's *Ostpolitik* (Eastern policy) and the ratification of the German-German Basic Treaty in late-1972 found form in the *Amerika-Serie*. It is tempting to suggest that the exportation of *Mosaik* in 1969 was related to the introduction of *Ostpolitik* in the West as the two coincided, relatively speaking. But due to the nature of East German economic planning, the letter from Verlag Junge Welt of 8 May 1969 suggests a much longer process of preparations and approvals to develop a story adequately representative of the socialist worldview and the workers' and farmers' state that produced it. That said, *Ostpolitik* itself did not emerge from thin air in 1969 and existed in arguably similar forms during Willy Brandt's tenure as Mayor of West Berlin, as Minister of Foreign Affairs during Chancellor Kurt Georg Kiesinger's Grand Coalition, and as West German Vice Chancellor. The initial relations addressed between the states were more concerned with mutual recognition and transit regulations than they were with the import and export of comic books. Nonetheless, the development of *Ostpolitik* over the course of the 1960s did have a certain effect on comic creators, the editorial regime's outlook on the United States, and their ability to discuss and adequately represent the American continent in *Mosaik* almost as a response to the construction of the Berlin Wall at the beginning of the decade.[73]

The *Amerika-Serie* represented the United States as a place of fun, serving as a more appropriate setting for the Digedags story.[74] This portrayal deconstructed the SED's rhetoric over the evils of capitalist society and of the worker's role in it as the fault-line for class conflict in the United States. East German detective and crime novels were often set in the West, providing the most fertile literary ground for social criticisms, at least insofar as the editorial regime and the Ministry of Culture were concerned. Setting *Mosaik* in the United States gave the FDJ the opportunity to demonstrate the Western world's supposed failings and the constant class-based agitations as part and parcel of the American *Unkultur* that so completely influenced East German youth culture during the 1960s.[75] As *Mosaik* was arguably the least overtly propagandistic of the *Kinderzeitschriften* and possessed Western tropes from the supposedly petite-bourgeois of the Mosaik-Kollektiv, these aspects made the publication ideal for the distribution of socialist ideology in the capitalist marketplace.[76] Export provided the publisher and the state with much needed hard, Western currency. And though *Ostpolitik* made for a nice backdrop against which this seemingly well-timed penetration of the Western market occurred, the larger patterns of German-German relations and détente made possible Hegen's criticisms of Verlag Junge Welt's practices regarding his comics.

Despite initiatives such as the *Bitterfelder Weg* and the more direct assaults on comics in the GDR, their adherence to socialist educational principles, and their abilities (or lack thereof) to develop the socialist personalities of children, youth policy in the 1960s was relatively uneven. The state's desire for international recognition and the Federal Republic's own advance toward détente made a degree of flexibility in that policy possible. But the SED state had no clear policy to deal with authors and artists in terms of carrots and sticks, instead dealing with each case by case.[77] As a result, by 1972 the FDJ was not in a position to either force Hegen to continue or to wrest control of the comic from him entirely. Locking Hegen into a contract without an expiration date attempted to restrain Hegen's and the Mosaik-Kollektiv's Western influences and have the comics address the concerns of the FDJ and Party educators; concerns that were only marginally addressed since these issues were first raised nearly a decade before. The *Amerika-Serie* contractually obligated the FDJ to exports if they hoped to demonstrate *Mosaik*'s competitiveness in a global market, comparable to the regime's celebrated children's literature. Hegen was neither willing to budge, insisting that the *Kollektiv* could not produce more than six issues per year as most involved in their production were freelance or part-time, nor would he transfer outright ownership of *Mosaik* and the Digedags to Verlag Junge Welt. Given Altenburger's position as *Chefredakteur* and perhaps resulting from his dealings with Hegen, as soon as Hegen's position was made clear in late 1973 and early 1974, Altenburger suggested the creation of a new monthly children's comic to replace the existing *Mosaik von Hannes Hegen*.[78] By June–July 1974, as the *Amerika-Serie* saw its final issue, Hegen reminded Glücksmann of GDR copyright laws, threatening to charge the publisher with plagiarism should it choose to continue *Mosaik* without his express permission. This ultimatum forced the FDJ to finally, though begrudgingly, accept the creator's resignation and resolve the matter of existing contracts with Edith Hegenbarth and Lothar Dräger, as co-copyright holder and scripter of *Mosaik* respectively. In August–September of the same year, the publisher's Central Party Leadership (*Zentrale Parteileitung* or ZPL) approved the termination of existing contracts with Hegen, his wife, and Dräger. In the same moment, however, the ZPL approved Altenburger's newly developed direction for the comic, immediately renewing contract negotiations with Dräger.[79]

This suggests a relatively measured reaction from the FDJ and the editorial regime. Though Honecker insisted on the supposed lack of taboos within the arts, this does not indicate that censorship mechanisms ceased to function or exist entirely.[80] But if censorship was at fault for Hegen's departure from *Mosaik*, it was because of censorship embedded in the foundations of the East German publishing system through the annual plan.[81] Arguably, the situation did not warrant repressive measures from the FDJ or suggest that comics in the East German state did not "matter." *Mosaik* was not only a financial pillar for the publisher but a fundamental, though unofficial, platform for the regime's educational agenda and the construction of the socialist personality more broadly. But releasing Hegen from his contract was the easiest and most beneficial solution for all involved. West German media sought any aberration in the arts as evidence of the SED's repressiveness and the general lack of freedom pervasive in the East German literary scene, including children's literature, particularly after Honecker's ascendency.[82] Abiding by the terms of GDR copyright law and respecting Hegen's ownership of the Digedags, the FDJ demonstrated to observers the perceived legality of the regime's actions and evidenced the GDR as a *Rechtstaat* (state governed by the rule of law).[83] The state, the FDJ, and the publisher all attempted to placate Hegen. When that apparently failed, however, given the importance of societal concerns surrounding the Basic Treaty and the normalization of relations with the Federal Republic, not to mention the perceived normalization of life within the GDR itself, and as the publisher already had the mechanisms available to produce a successor to *Mosaik von Hannes Hegen*, the only viable recourse was a mutual and "amicable" dissolution of Hegen's contract with Verlag Junge Welt.[84]

An article published in *Der Tagesspiegel* on 24 April 2014 suggests that the sudden disappearance of the Digedags in *Mosaik* had no political basis or motivation (*Das plotzliche Verschwinden der Digedags . . . hatte keine politischen Gründe*). I would counter that this observation is motivated by the presumption that East German comics were spaces free from the state's ideology, as cited earlier by Augustine. While this position argues in favor of the perceived normalcy associated with the *Alltag* in East Germany, thus making childhood an experience comparable across the Cold War division, it misrepresents the SED regime and *durchherrschte Gesellschaft* conceptualized by Jürgen Kocka. It is not my purpose to deconstruct the perception of normalcy within the East German *Alltag*. Indeed, the necessity of constructing a common, or comparative, history is arguably necessary in overcoming the *Mauer im Kopf* (Wall in the Head) apparent with some Germans, from both East and West, since (re)unification in 1990. Likewise, nostalgia for the former GDR (*Ostalgie*) is predicated upon the insistence that the niche society, the domestic, the everyday, was an apolitical space free from the regime's influence and conducive to practices of the *Eigensinn* discussed in earlier chapters. However, ignoring the SED's power structures, both malign or benign, and their penetration of the most routine practices does a disservice to those who lived under the communist regime.[85]

In January 1976 and after a year of reprinted issues featuring the Digedags, Verlag Junge Welt launched the first issue of *Mosaik*'s new era, this time starring three characters known collectively as the Abrafaxe. The comics did away with the notion of "series" that saddled the publication with storylines continuing for years on end. The numbering scheme ended with the Abrafaxe's introduction and, after this, *Mosaik* was numbered by the year and month of publication stylistically similar to *Atze* following Altenburger's rejuvenation of that series a decade earlier. Beyond the cosmetic changes, though, the comics were extremely familiar to children. Similarly referred to as "goblins" like their predecessors, the Abrafaxe was a trio of friends, arguably as interchangeable as the Digedags themselves. They travelled the world, sometimes visiting locales previously explored by the Digedags, though the time-jumps that arguably defined the Digedags' era were no longer as apparent.

The Abrafaxe was indicative of a continuity within the publication that was as important for the readers as it was for the regime. Drawing on available resources, Verlag Junge Welt ensured relative consistency in *Mosaik*'s presentation as it transitioned from the Digedags to the Abrafaxe. Uniformity was apparent in the stories, the art, the presentation, and the quality of all three, drawing obvious inspiration from what came before. Like the Digedags, the Abrafaxe featured a blonde, a brunette, and a red-haired imp with short, tall, and middling builds, travelling the landscape of a bygone world. Additionally, the Abrafaxe had a naming convention similar to and no less confusing than that of the Digedags. Just as the Digedags were named Dig, Dag, and Digedag, the Abrafaxe were Abrax, Brabax, and Califax. While not entirely the same, this was yet another perceived similarity that Hegen would later consider in his accusations of plagiarism against Verlag Junge Welt. As the Abrafaxe were seemingly interchangeable with the Digedags, just as the Digedags were supposedly interchangeable with one another, readers were welcomed into the new world of the Abrafaxe as though it was exactly the same as before.[86] This ensured that the child-readership, both at home and abroad, found familiarity and was not alienated by the publication's changing status quo. Paper quotas for the comic's exports were increased yet again as the comics were translated, most notably into English and Dutch, for wider distribution throughout the Soviet Bloc and the Western world during the late-1970s and continuing well into the 1980s.[87] The attention doted on the Abrafaxe suggested that this new incarnation of *Mosaik* faced few of the same political hurdles encountered by *Mosaik von Hannes Hegen* as Hegen himself no longer proved a creative bulwark against the stories' ideological contents. More importantly, perhaps, Verlag Junge Welt was the sole copyright holder to the Abrafaxe characters and this latest iteration of the comic and, as a result, the characters were beholden to socialist values and representations of socialist history and the state in ways the Digedags never were.

Problematically, the Abrafaxe were directly inspired and influenced by the Digedags. This meant they were equally subject to the Western comic book tropes and traditions of their predecessors. As a result, the Abrafaxe were equally guilty of cultural imperialism. The representation of populations in the Developing World tumbled into the same patterns of cultural racism that afflicted the Digedags under Hegen's guidance, as the Abrafaxe and socialism were the only forces demonstrably strong enough to free those populations from exploitation and enslavement.[88] The need for continuity during this transitional period to maintain *Mosaik*'s readership shackled the Abrafaxe to the same conventions that hamstrung the Digedags. Moreover, the German-German Basic Treaty and the exportation of *Mosaik* to Western Europe placed the comics squarely in the battleground of the Western capitalist marketplace where *Mosaik* had to compete with established and popular "imperialist" comics. The FDJ's imperative to prove the humanistic and moral strength of *Mosaik* against the capitalist comics caused the warranted socialist transformation of *Mosaik* to remain incomplete. This only perpetuated the misconstrued notion that *Mosaik* provided a space free from ideology compared to publications such as *Atze* and *Frösi* in the minds of the readership, arguably serving the comic's transgression into the private and domestic space associated with East Germany's niche society.

As with the unsubstantiated accusations levelled against the American comic book industry in the 1940s and 1950s prior to the publication of Fredric Wertham's *Seduction of the Innocent* in 1954, *Mosaik* was long thought to be misrepresentative of socialism, the socialist worldview, and of the FDJ's educational mandate that produced it. Socialists in the emerging postwar Soviet Bloc claimed comics were evil, indicative of capital-imperialism wielding influence over children in North America, Western Europe, and in the socialist states of Eastern Europe. Among other characters and issues, these socialists cited DC Comics' Superman as an extension of the National Socialist conceptualization of the superman (*der Übermensch*).[89] Though East German comics were created to combat this supposed influence over children and youth, *Mosaik* too closely resembled the comics it was meant to critique. Throughout the 1960s, decisions taken for the *Bitterfelder Weg* held sway over the representation of comics in the GDR throughout the decade. These directives maneuvered *Mosaik*, Hannes Hegen, and the Mosaik-Kollektiv toward the conservative course of youth policy determined by SED educators and the FDJ following the untimely failure of Ulbricht's liberal Youth Communiqué. But Hegen, himself influenced by Disney comics as were many East German comic creators and the children for whom they wrote, fought the inclusion of ideology despite the very obvious American morality encoded in those same Disney comics. The 1960s and 1970s marked *Mosaik* by the push and pull of creative forces as the regime eroded Hegen's influence, reconstituting the comic along lines acceptable to the regime and endorsed by the *Bitterfelder Weg*.

While books in the GDR were spaces of negotiation between author and editor toward consensus acceptable to the Ministry of Culture's censors, Hegen largely lacked similar oversight until Hans Erhardt was hired as editor-in-chief. Without this perceived oversight and given Hegen's contractual ownership of the characters and the perceived freedom such ownership entailed, Hegen was relatively free to continue the comics following those Western models that initially inspired their creation. As a result, the Digedags represented socialism and the interests of the SED state only insofar as their expressed morality ran counter to FDJ assumptions and perceptions of capital-imperialism. However, the brand of socialism practiced by the Digedags mirrored the same capital-imperialism of Disney comics as *Mosaik*'s socialist morality was supposedly superior to the developing social cultures of the people the Digedags were meant to help. This depiction contradicted the fundamental precepts of utopian socialism. As the Digedags demonstrated cultural racism toward those in developing nations, they distorted the perceived idealism of the socialist worldview regardless of how near or far that representation was from the practices of "real existing socialism" in the GDR.

And yet, the SED regime never deployed the full weight of its power against Hegen to bring *Mosaik* in line with the other children's publications from Verlag Junge Welt. Given Hegen's and the Mosaik-Kollektiv's position and the presumed importance of their work in the socialist education of East German youth, ostensibly the future of the SED state, observations by the regime and the Stasi are not only understandable but expected. However, the publisher and the editorial regime pursued legal means to dilute Hegen's influence and remake *Mosaik* in a medium typified by Western *Schund– und Schmutzliteratur*. The FDJ pursued this course to keep Hegen loyal or, at the very least, to maintain

Hegen's outward demonstration of that loyalty and not turn him toward open dissent. The regime tried to accommodate Hegen and *Mosaik*, tolerating historical inaccuracies and the relatively absent sense of developing socialist consciousness to maintain the publication and its connections between the regime, the schools, and the East German domestic niche.[90]

An arts scene free of taboos as articulated by Honecker in 1971 obviously did not extend to comics as they were perceived part of the regime's youth education. When Hegen complained of overwork and the *Kollektiv's* inability to fulfill the FDJ's plan for the publication, threatening his departure if the regime did not agree to his requests, Altenburger, one of Hegen's defenders to that point and perhaps the one who understood Hegen's relationship with the publication best, suggested change. The Abrafaxe characters emerging from that suggestion were intentionally similar to Hegen's Digedags for the sake of the publication's continuity with the child-readership. This provided the regime the illusion of control over the publication and the characters as it was no longer restricted by the terms of Hegen's contract and his ownership of the Digedags. However, as the FDJ moved forward with its dual objectives of exporting *Mosaik* to the West and preserving a loyal domestic readership, releasing Hegen did not have the desired effect. In this atmosphere, the Abrafaxe found themselves as locked into Western tropes as were the Digedags before them. The publisher attempted to exert its own control over *Mosaik* while quelling Hegen's minor rebellions for the perceived benefit of the comics' educational content. Still, Hegen's absence from the publication did nothing to prevent him from creating further problems for the regime, the publisher, and the Abrafaxe, engaging the editorial regime in copyright disputes extending well beyond German (re)unification in 1990.[91]

Notes

1. Lent, "Comics Debate Internationally," 21.
2. Pfeiffer, *Von Hannes Hegen*, 128.
3. Brian Cronin, *Was Superman a Spy?: And Other Comic Book Legends Revealed* (New York: Plume, 2009), 198.
4. Cooke, *Representing East Germany*, 93–94.
5. Anselma Gallinat, *Narratives in the Making: Writing the East German Past in the Democratic Present* (New York: Berghahn Books, 2017), 3–8.
6. BArch DY 26/114, "Dokumentation zur Bilderzeitshrift 'Mosaik' Berlin den 23.9.76," pag. 3

7. BArch DY 24/1585, "Information über die Weiterführung der Bilderzeitschrift 'Mosaik,'" pag. 2–4.
8. See Lettkemann, "Comics in der DDR," 317–61 and Sebastian Unterrainer, "Comics in der DDR," in *Comic-Kunst vom Weberzuklus zum Bewegten Mann Deutschsprachige Bildergeschichten des 20. Jahrhunderts*, ed. Dietrich Grünewald (Koblenz: Görres, 2004), 26–27.
9. Augustine, *Red Prometheus*, 230. See also the discussions of nostalgia and its association with intentional misrememberings of an apolitical private space and attachments to popular culture in Daphne Berdahl, "*Good Bye, Lenin!* Aufwiedersehen GDR: On the Social Life of Socialism," in *Post-Communist Nostalgia*, eds. Maria Todorova and Zsuzsa Gille (New York: Berghahn Books, 2010), 177–89; Borneman, *After the Wall*; Svetlana Boym, *The Future of Nostalgia* (New York: Basic Books, 2001); Cooke, *Representing East Germany*; Eli Rubin, "Understanding a Car in the Context of a System: Trabants, Marzahn, and East German Socialism," in *The Socialist Car: Automobility in the Eastern Bloc*, ed. Lewis H. Siegelbaum (Ithaca: Cornell University Press, 2011), 124–40; and Elizabeth A. Ten Dyke, "Memory and Existence: Implications of the Wende," in *The Work of Memory: New Directions in the Study of German Society and Culture*, ed. Alon Confino and Peter Fritzsche (Urbana: University of Illinois Press, 2002), 154–69.
10. For further, see Brock, "Producing the 'Socialist Personality'?" 220–52 and Saunders, *Honecker's Children*.
11. Leask, "Humiliation as a Weapon," 243.
12. Leask, 243.
13. Thompson-Wohlgemuth, "Official and Unofficial," 37–40.
14. Lettkemann and Scholz, *"Schuldig ist schließlich jeder,"* 37–38.
15. BArch DY 26/173, "5.6.5. Die Bildgeschichte in den Kinderzeitungen und -zeitschriften," pag. 190–91.
16. BArch DY 26/173, 191; BStU Zentralarchiv MfS Zentralarchiv Allg. P. Band 10321/64, *Hauptabteilung II –Abteilung 3—Bericht Betr. Werksbungskandidaten Reitzel, Egon—österrichischer Staatsbürger, Berlin, den 17.1.1964*; and Lettkemann, "Comics in der DDR," 320–22.
17. Augustine, *Red Prometheus*, 230.
18. Augustine, 232.
19. Augustine, 230–39.
20. BArch DY 24/5790, "Abschrift an der Zentralrat der Freien Deutschen Jugend—Sekretariat—Berlin, 29. Juni 1959."
21. BArch DY 26/114, "Dokumentation zur Bilderzeitschrift 'Mosaik,'" pag. 3–5.
22. Darnton, *Censors*, 151 and 167–68. In the early 1980s, even Erich Honecker expressed his love of the American western novels of the author Karl May. Honecker went so far as to inquire with the East German Ministry of Culture as to the possibility of adapting them into DEFA-produced films.
23. Lettkemann and Scholz, *"Schuldig ist schließlich jeder,"* 37–38.

24. Leask, "Humiliation as a Weapon," 238–39.
25. For further see, Lothar Köhn, "Von der Formalismus-Debatte zum <<Bitterfelder Weg>>," in *Geschichte der deutschen Literatur von 1945 bis zur Gegenwart: Zweite, aktualisierte und erweiterte Auflage*, ed. Wilfried Barner (Munich: Verlag C.H. Beck: 2006), 287–306.
26. Darnton, *Censors*, 163.
27. Lettkemann and Scholz, *"Schuldig ist schließlich jeder,"* 38–40.
28. Dorfman and Mattelart mark numerous examples of this in the pages of *Donald Duck* and *Scrooge McDuck* written by Carl Barks, arguing that Barks's Duck characters negatively impacted the peoples they encountered due to their material exploitation and capitalist cultural imperialism. As this was the Western example the FDJ wished to follow with *Mosaik*'s creation, it comes as little surprise that Hegen employed those same tropes demonstrated by Disney characters and comic books. Although perceived as a "socialist alternative," *Mosaik*, for all intents and purposes, was a reflection and derivative of the same Western comics against which it supposedly protested. See Dorfman and Mattelart, *Donald Duck*, 96–98.
29. Darnton, *Censors*, 153–54 and Sonja Fritzsche, *Science Fiction Literature in East Germany* (Bern: Peter Lang, 2006), 80–85. Fritzsche argues here that due to the nature of science fiction in a socialist state, the representation of the future as dystopic was impossible. Moreover, she suggests that much of the science fiction was influenced by and incorporated elements from earlier authors including Jules Verne, Hans Dominik (a science journalist, engineer, and novelist, publishing during the interwar period), and Karl May. Fritzsche specifically notes the example of the East German children's science fiction novel *Das Weltraumschiff* (The Spaceship, 1952) by Arthur Bagemühl.
30. BStU MfS AIM 9409/69, "Ermittlungsbericht—Altenburger, Wolfgang, Berlin, den 4.12.1959," pag. 1 and BStU MfS AIM 9409/69 Zentral Archiv, "Hauptabteilung II/1C, Bericht über Kontaktaufnahme, Berlin, den 23.2.1960," 1–2;"*Lebenslauf—Wolfgang Altenburger;*" and "Hauptabteilung II/1c, Vorschlag zur Werbung als DA, Berlin, den 17.5.1960," pag. 1–6.
31. Augustine, *Red Prometheus*, 230.
32. Lettkemann and Scholz, *"Schuldig ist schließlich jeder,"* 44.
33. For more on the porous nature of the Berlin Wall and its effects on East German society, see April A. Eisman, "East German Art and the Permeability of the Berlin Wall," *German Studies Review* 38, no. 3 (October 2015): 597–616; Poiger, *Jazz, Rock, and Rebels*; and McDougall, "Liberal Interlude."
34. Lettkemann and Scholz, *"Schuldig ist schließlich jeder,"* 43.
35. BStU Zentralarchiv MfS Zentral-Archiv Allg. P Band 10321/64, "Hauptabteilung II—Abteilung 3—Bericht, Betr: Werkungskandidaten Reitzl, Egon—österreichischer Staatsbürger-, Berlin, den 17.1.1964," pag. 1–2.
36. Darnton, *Censors*, 183–84.

37. BArch DY 26/114, "Dokumentation zur Bilderzeitschrift 'Mosaik,'" pag. 3.
38. BArch DY 24/1581, "Vorlage an das Sekretariat des Zentralrates der FDJ, Betr. Konzeption für das neue Profil der Bilderzeitschrift 'Atze', Berlin, den 22.7.66," pag. 1–4.
39. Gumbert, *Envisioning Socialism*, 56–57, 78, and 85.
40. Lettkemann and Scholz, *"Schuldig ist schließlich jeder,"* 40–43.
41. Darnton, *Censors*, 151, 159 and 162.
42. BArch DY 26/114, "Dokumentation zur Bilderzeitschrift 'Mosaik,'" pag. 5–6.
43. BStU Zentralarchiv MfS Zentral-Archiv Allg. P Band 10321/64, "Hauptabteilung II—Abteilung 3—Bericht, Betr: Werkungskandidaten Reitzl, Egon—österreichischer Staatsbürger-, Berlin, den 17.1.1964," pag. 1–2.
44. BArch DY 24/1585, "Information über die Weiterführung der Bilderzeitschrift 'Mosaik,'" pag. 2–4.
45. "Circular 9—Works Made for Hire," United States Copyright Office—Library of Congress, retrieved 28 April 2016 from http://www.copyright.gov/circs/circ09.pdf. Work for hire means a work that is created by an author or artist as part of the job for which they were hired by an employer. More often than not, this is the current practice among American comic book publishers such as Marvel and DC so that copyright over the characters and stories remains with the publisher. For more on German comics publishing and the problems and perceptions associated with the American industry as *Massenzeichenware* (mass bulk commodity), see Malone, "Periphery," 17, 19, and 24.
46. BArch DY 24/5790, "Abschrift—Pionierorganisation 'Ernst Thälmann,' Berlin 29. Juni 1959"; and BArch DY 26/114, "Dokumentation zur Bilderzeitschrift 'Mosaik', Berlin den 23.9.1976," pag. 1–2.
47. Malone, "Periphery," 21.
48. BArch DY 26/253, "Standpunkt zum Schriftsatz von Johannes Hegenbarth," pag. 1. As Verlag Neues Leben had no prior experience publishing comic books, initial contracts with Hegen were drawn up along the lines of published books and on an issue by issue basis. While ownership of the characters remained with Hegen as it would with any novelist, Hegen's presence on the publication and subsequent issues were published at the pleasure and discretion of the publisher and the FDJ.
49. "Stiftung Archiv der Parteien und Massenorganisationen der DDR im Bundesarchiv—Verlag Junge Welt, DY 26," Jugendwerkhof-Treffen.de, retrieved 28 April 2016 from http://www.jugendwerkhof-treffen.de/CMS_FILES_2.1/images/content/doku/organisation_ddr/junge_welt.pdf.
50. BArch DY 24/1585, "Information für die Weiterführung der Bilderzeitschrift 'Mosaik,' 1966," pag. 2–4.
51. Darnton, *Censors*, 149–51.
52. BArch DY 24/1585, "Protokol Nr. 169 der Sitzung des Sekretariats des Zentralrats der Freien Deutschen Jugend an 4. Oktober 1966," pag. 1–4; and "Information für die Weiterführung der Bilderzeitschrift 'Mosaik,' 1966," pag. 4.

53. Darnton, *Censors*, 212–13.
54. Darnton, 227.
55. Lettkemann and Scholz, "*Schuldig ist schließlich jeder*," 44–46.
56. BStU MfS HA VIII Nr. 2608.
57. Lettkemann and Scholz, "*Schuldig ist schließlich jeder*," 49.
58. Ross, *Constructing Socialism*, 73.
59. Heather L. Gumbert, "East German Television and the Unmaking of the Socialist Project, 1952–1965" (PhD diss., University of Texas at Austin, 2006), 135–36.
60. McDougall, *Youth Politics*, 234–35.
61. Lettkemann and Scholz, "*Schuldig ist schließlich jeder*," 49.
62. BArch DC 9/1628, "Verlag Junge Welt Zeitungen und Zeitschriften, Presseamt beim Vorsitzenden des Ministerrates, Betr. Export, 8 Mai 1969."
63. BArch DC 9/1628.
64. BArch DC 9/1628.
65. Pragar, Review of *Micky, Marx und Manitu*, 364 and Fritzsche, "Dreams of 'Cosmic Culture,'" 85.
66. Gersdorf, "Digedags Go West," 42.
67. Augustine, *Red Prometheus*, 243.
68. BArch DY 26/253.
69. Darnton, *Censors*, 157–59.
70. BArch DY 26/114, "Dokumentation zur Bilderzeitschrift 'Mosaik,' Berlin, den 23.9.1976," pag. 6–8 and BArch DY 26/253.
71. Alf Lüdtke, "Sprache und Herrschaft in der DDR. Einleitende Überlegungen," in *Akten, Eingaben, Schaufenster. Die DDR und ihre Texte: Erkunden zu Herrschaft und Alltag*, ed. Alf Lüdtke and Peter Becker (Berlin: Akademie Verlag, 1997), 11–26. See also, Esther von Richthofen, *Bringing Culture to the Masses: Control, Compromise and Participation in the GDR* (New York: Berghahn Books, 2009), 97 and Patrick Major, "Introduction," in *The Workers' and Peasants' State: Communism and Society in East Germany under Ulbricht 1945–71*, ed. Patrick Major and Jonathan Osmond (Manchester: Manchester University Press, 2002), 7. Both suggest the authors of letters of complaint in the GDR drew weight to their grievances through the appropriation of the language of socialism. That is, they used the Party's own rhetoric in framing their complaints and in the constructions of positive images of both themselves and the state. Richthofen suggests that while this was perhaps not reflective of reality or of how the authors acted in society, it demonstrated a "willingness to adapt and submit to SED supremacy." This is exactly what Hegen did in his complaints rendered to the publisher and the FDJ.
72. BArch DY 26/114, "Dokumentation zur Bilderzeitschrift 'Mosaik,' Berlin, den 23.9.1976," pag. 7–9 and "Entwicklung des neuen 'Mosaik,' Presserecht: Dr. Glücksmann über die Zeitschrift 'Mosaik' am 5.2.1974, Anlage 3."
73. BArch DC 9/1628, "Verlag Junge Welt Zeitungen und Zeitschriften, Presseamt beim Vorsitzenden des Ministerrates, Betr. Export, 8. Mai 1969."

74. Gersdorf, "Digedags Go West," 42.
75. By way of example, see attitudes surrounding Deutschlandtreffen 1964 and the subsequent founding of East German rock radio station DT64 as a means of the regime demonstrating liberal attitudes when it came to issues of youth entertainment and consumer culture. McDougall, "Liberal Interlude," 131–39.
76. Augustine, *Red Prometheus*, 230 and BStU Zentralarchiv MfS Zentralarchiv Allg. P Band 10321/64, "Hauptabteilung II—Abteilung 3—Bericht, Betr. Werksbungskandidaten Reitzl, Egon—österreichischer Staatsbürger, Berlin, den 17.1.1964," pag. 1–2.
77. Darnton, *Censors*, 171.
78. BArch DY 26/114, "Dokumentation zur Bilderzeitschrift 'Mosaik,' Berlin, den 23.9.1976," pag. 7–10 and Guido Weißhahn, "Das MOSAIK," *DDR Comics*, retrieved 6 May 2016 from http://ddr-comics.de/mosaik.htm. Following the completion of the *Amerika-Serie* (issue 211), the series ran for another year (issue 223) to conclude the planned stories as well as Hegen's contract with the publisher. Reprint issues were released between July 1974 and December 1975 and the Abrafaxe made their debut in *Mosaik*, no longer *Mosaik von Hannes Hegen*, in January 1976.
79. BArch DY 26/114, "Dokumentation zur Bilderzeitschrift 'Mosaik,' Berlin, den 23.9.1976," pag. 14.
80. Shortly after coming to power in 1971, Honecker declared that there should be no taboos in the arts. Although this stood in stark contrast to statements made during his tenure as head of the FDJ, and he would renege on this statement in the 1980s, this represented the SED's attempt to come to terms with the prevailing westernized youth culture including jeans, long hair, and beat music. Honecker wanted to present the GDR as youthful and dynamic, particularly in the run up to the German-German Basic Treaty and the perceived normalization of relations between the two German states as a means of garnering international recognition from the West. See McLellan, *Love in the Time of Communism*, 28.
81. Darnton, *Censors*, 149.
82. Darnton, 181.
83. Cooke, *Representing East Germany*, 29–30. The GDR was rife with western accusations, some well-founded, of the state's supposed status as an *Unrechtsstaat* (state without the rule of law) due to the SED regime's repressive hold on power and the Stasi's coercive measures in maintaining order in the state. This point was problematic in terms of formal recognition of the GDR during negotiations of the Basic Treaty and reared again when questions of the normality of the East German everyday and memory were broached in the (re)unification era.
84. Fulbrook, "Concept of 'Normalisation,'" 1–30.
85. Bodo Mrozek, "Ausstellung über DDR-Comichelden: Reisefreiheit für die Fantasie," *Der Tagesspiegel*, retrieved 21 June 2016 from http://www.tagesspiegel.de/kultur/ausstellung-ueber-ddr-comichelden-greuliche-zeich

nungen-in-rekordauflage/9755588-2.html. See also, Cooke, *Representing East Germany*, 7–8 and Kocka, "Eine durchherrschte Gesellschaft," 547–53.
86. As discussed, the Digedags were often criticized for their lack of individual personalities and the unnecessary continuation of the group as a trio. In 1958, following the addition of Dräger and the first artists hired to what became the Mosaik-Kollektiv, this resulted in the sudden transition from the *Römer-Serie* to the *Weltraum-Serie*. During this story, the character Digedag was left behind as Dig and Dag were abducted aboard a Neosian spaceship. The publication seemed to suffer no apparent ill effects from the multiyear absence of one of *Mosaik*'s core characters.
87. BArch DC 9/1628, "Auflagenstatistik 1984 Januar-September, Mosaik"; "Presseamt beim Vorsitzenden des Ministerrates der DDR, Betrifft: Lizenzhöhung für die Zeitschrift Mosaik ab 1985"; "Antrag zur Lizenzhöhung für die Zeitschrift 'Mosaik' zur Gewährleistung der Export-Aufträge, Berlin 6. April 1979"; "VOB Zentrag Bereich Verlagsentwicklung, z.H. Gen. Jeschke, Betr. Lizenznachtrag 1979 für Mosaik-Sammelbände."
88. Augustine, *Red Prometheus*, 243 and McKinney, *Colonial Heritage*, 4–5.
89. Wright, *Comic Book Nation*, 101–2.
90. Darnton, *Censors*, 212–27.
91. BArch DY 26/253.

CONCLUSION

Contesting SED Power in the Comic Book Space

In the preceding pages, I sought to describe East German society and the SED regime's perceptions of childhood through the lens offered by the comic books and the *Kinderzeitschriften* published by that regime. It was never my intention to provide a comprehensive and definitive history of comics in the GDR. Instead, I attempted to characterize the comic books published by Verlag Junge Welt and the Free German Youth as an intersection, a meeting point, between benign state power and the children that read those publications, where the will of the state confronted the desires of children. Sometimes these children recognized their supposed role in socialist society. At other times, they seemed to willfully ignore the state's preconceptions of childhood, of children, and of the socialist personality. Moreover, these comics, specifically *Mosaik von Hannes Hegen* and *Atze*, but also including the *Kinderzeitschriften* that contained comic strips such as *Frösi, Bummi, ABC-Zeitung,* or *Trommel,* are sites of negotiated power between the state, its educational and social institutions and infrastructure, (child) citizens, and the differing perceptions of childhood and youth responsibility in the socialist state that circulated between these groups.

For the Socialist Unity Party, comics were proxies for its own authority. The FDJ deployed comics as demonstrations of the socialist personality, indicative of the state's educational and ideological agendas directed toward the child-readership. The use of state power evident in these comics attempted to steer youth activity in ways largely invisible, and thus more pervasive, to the audience. As children and youth were increasingly viewed as both the future of the state and as potential threats to the stability of the state with juvenile delinquency arguably on the rise in the early postwar years, it was the FDJ's responsibility to organize the newly discovered leisure time of East German youth.[1] Of course, this supposed problem was not limited to the GDR, but occurred throughout Western Europe and the United States accompanying the generational shift in the aftermath of World War II. Whereas the United States blamed the content and popularity of comic books for this turn toward delinquency, European states, the GDR included, saw this problem as one of Americanization of which comic books were a small, but important part.[2] As a medium, comics had the potential to influence children toward the goals of the SED state exactly because of the popularity that also made them a threat to the FDJ's efforts to organize and control the leisure time of youth. Filling the ever-increasing leisure time of the postwar *Freizeitgesellschaft*, though this concept applied less to the GDR than it did to the Federal Republic, created "needs" for which there were also ample solutions offered.[3] The concept of leisure time was important to the FDJ and the SED regime, appearing in numerous official reports on comics that questioned the most effective uses of leisure and what individuals did during that time.[4] Publishing these comics, Verlag Junge Welt, and the FDJ by extension, directed children's leisure time that went unaccounted with activities from school and organized youth groups, both the FDJ and Ernst Thälmann Pioneers. Comics were read by children largely without the supervision of adults. This absence of authority figures empowered children to interpret the stories they read in their own ways, but it also provided the FDJ a space to control and subvert the private reading of those children within the developing niche society.[5]

State power can be separated between the capacity to enforce one's will upon others and the likelihood that issued directives will be obeyed by a population; that is, the difference between "power" and "authority."[6] Comics in the German Democratic Republic tended to follow the latter as comics themselves and their content demonstrated a mode of state power typically unnoticed by its readership, which easily transgressed the perceived boundaries between the public and the private sphere, between the political and the apolitical. Effectively, within the comics and *Kinderzeitschriften* published by the FDJ, the state exercised a benign mode of power. This is to say that while these publications were possessed of the same ideological imperatives and the educational and moral values associated with the East German socialist state, the regime wielded these with a soft touch not often associated with the boogiemen of Soviet-style communism and the Stasi as demonstrated elsewhere in the existing historiography. Often, the propagandistic ideology was obfuscated by the adventurous nature of the comic stories being told and the tropes and trappings of the medium more broadly. In keeping with the attestations of GDR comics after the fall of the Berlin

Wall and the collapse of Soviet power in Eastern Europe, comics were thus perceived by readers to be sites free from that ideology despite the obvious inclusions of socialist educational stories and content. Engaging and interacting with the comics published by the FDJ, children gave comics and other similar reading material the opportunity to cross the threshold separating state power from the assumed privacy of the niche society, allowing comics' state-sanctioned influence into the domestic space and into the privacy of imagination. Comic publications thus infiltrated and organized the leisure time of its readership in ways that were arguably beneficial to the state through the perceived development of the socialist personality through that ideological material. These comics were, as suggested by the FDJ itself, a means of conveying the importance of a socialist education more effectively and permanently than was available through television due to the comics medium itself and the reader-participation that was required by that medium. Reading comics requires the act of "closure" to create meaning between seemingly disparate images. This "closure" is entirely voluntary on the part of the reader and completely invisible, according to Scott McCloud, as the act of reading and interpreting comics is one that does not draw attention to itself, occurring in the readers' imaginations.[7] In effect, closure demonstrates its own notion of benign power over the reader through the invisible means by which it leads the reader through the story and the movement suggested in the gutters between illustrated panels. By comparison, television is a static and passive medium requiring nothing from its audience. Comics and the required reader participation are reflective of the participation required of youth and of the citizenship broadly by the FDJ and the SED state itself, as a result. Internalizing the content of these comics, children, consciously or not, were required to engage with the SED state's imperatives and with their own collective role as citizens under socialism.

However, precisely because of comics' ability and need to transgress the bounds of privacy and infiltrate the everyday life of the East German state, these *Kinderzeitschriften* opened themselves to the ersatz public sphere as the meanings and constructions of state power included in their pages were accessed through the interpretive lens of the child-readers' *Eigensinn*. The domestic spaces of the East German niche society was significant as sites in which citizens were able to express themselves and exercise the *Eigensinn* that itself shaped the private sphere.[8] It is the result of the understanding and association of comics with the domestic that opens them to the interpretation of the reader. Although the regime imbued these publications with varying degrees of ideological influence, the expectation that these comics would be consumed during the reader's leisure time in the home made them subject to the ersatz public sphere that arguably existed within the walls of the domestic space. This was particularly the case after the turn of the 1960s with calls for the close monitoring of the educational imperatives of these publications following the construction of the Berlin Wall and the subsequent controls over Western media in East German shops. As such, themes of travel, education, race relations, and even the ideological divide between capitalism and state socialism had the capacity to take on new and different meanings for the children reading these comics beyond their socialist educational intentions exactly because of that act of "closure" and of the child's interactions and interactivity with those comics and, thus, with the state.

The ways children interacted with these comics, emerging from the ersatz public sphere of the home, is comparable to the criticisms of state socialism and the production of *Eingaben* by adults, predominantly women, in the GDR. The FDJ and Verlag Junge Welt's editorial regime insisted on connections between comics, *Kinderzeitschriften*, and the broader educational regime of the SED state. Part of this requirement stemmed from criticisms aimed at the publications by the educators themselves and their demand to be included in determining these comics' content. At the same time, this educational ideological requirement came equally from the FDJ's need to control children's leisure time and to organize those spaces that arguably existed without the influence of state power—in short, the home. East German comics were supposed to remake children's leisure time and space into one where the child would not or could not avoid the state. Entertainment was structured around the improvement of the individual and of the individual's private space for the benefit of socialist society, as opposed to the mindless entertainment found in the capitalist West. East German comics, and this was certainly the case after the early 1960s, were created around the development of the children's socialist personality so that the next generation could be successfully deployed in service of the state. Incorporating those comics into a perceived aspect of the private space, and their consumption within a period of time assumed to be private, made them subject to the perceived rules of that space. The private was by no means an apolitical space. Indeed, the private was politicized entirely through the consumption of music, of Western television, of books, and, in this instance, of comics. *Eigensinn* was a means of dealing with the larger nature of politicization in the GDR that allowed for the perception, if not the reality, of an apolitical niche society.[9]

And while the private operated as a site for the construction of state power, precisely due to this consideration of the private as the ersatz public sphere, the distinction between public and private and the criticisms permissible within the private were made possible by the individual's need to negotiate the perceived panopticon. Comics provided children with sites through which to engage the regime directly, whether or not they did so in a critical way. Through the consumption of comics and the interaction provided by editorials and by the children's own letters to the publishers, children carved out their own understanding of the comics' contents, how they should respond to it, and developed their own criticisms of those comics. These were, in turn, criticisms of the socialist imperatives behind those comics more broadly. Children, as readers, both understood those ideological imperatives and subverted them to draw entertainment from the comics in ways that did not negate the state's educational objectives but marginalized them. This was not always the case, though, and just as often children complained of their inabilities to connect comics and the classroom as the FDJ intended. Typically, these complaints came as a result of problems associated with the comics' production plan or of the editorial regime's own failure when implementing and concretizing that plan. This is not the same as direct criticism of the SED regime itself, though. *Eigensinn* was more than simply being a means of "doing things one's own way," as the term is often translated. It took on the much more significant role of acting independent of the East German state to construct a "plethora of interpretations and patterns of behavior by an individual confronted with the political, social, and cultural structures" of the SED state and the FDJ for the purposes of exploring the "space of citizens' personal negotiations between public and private demands and opportunities."[10] As a result, East German comics provided a site common to both children and the state. Independent of the other, each group could determine its own ideas of childhood and what that meant to citizenship and obligation in East German state-socialism. In the same moment, comics provided both groups space to subvert and redefine the meanings and understandings associated with the *Kinderzeitschriften* and its consumption within an ersatz public sphere.

Notes

1. Jarausch and Geyer, *Shattered Past*, 288–90.
2. Jobs, "Tarzan Under Attack," 687–725; Jovanovic and Koch, "Comics Debate in Germany," 93–128; and Wright, *Comic Book Nation*, 91–96.

3. Führer and Ross, "Mass Media," 2.
4. BArch DY 26/118; BArch DY 26/173; and BStU MfS HA VIII Nr. 2608.
5. Sabin, *Comics, Comix & Graphic Novels*, 28.
6. Fulbrook, *People's State*, 236.
7. McCloud, *Understanding Comics*, 63–69 and 91.
8. See Betts, "Building Socialism," 96–132; Betts, *Within Walls*; Fulbrook, *People's State*; Jan Palmowski, "Between Conformity and Eigen-Sinn," 494–502; and Eli Rubin, "The Trabant: Consumption, Eigen-Sinn, and Movement," *History Workshop Journal* 68, no. 1 (2009): 27–44.
9. Jarausch and Geyer, *Shattered Past*, 272–81; Poiger, *Jazz, Rock, and Rebels*; and Betts, "Building Socialism."
10. Palmowski, "Between Conformity and Eigen-Sinn," 495.

Bibliography

Archives and Libraries

Bundesarchiv Berlin-Lichterfelde (BArch)
DC 9 Presseamts beim Ministerrat der DDR
   9/1628
DC 207 Palast der Republik (Bestand)
   207/686
DY 24 Zentralrat der FDJ
   24/1581 1 von 2
   24/1581 2 von 2
   24/1585
   24/2398
   24/5790
   24/8662
   24/8674
   24/8675
   24/23769
DY 25 "Ernst Thälmann" Pionier Organisation
   25/315
DY 26 Verlag "Junge Welt"
   26/42
   26/52
   26/63
   26/69
   26/114
   26/118
   26/173
   26/253

Bundesbeauftragte für die Unterlagen des Staatssicherheitsdienstes der ehemaligen Deutschen Demokratischen Republik (BStU)
   MfS AIM 9409/69
   MfS AP 803/70

MfS AP 10321/64
MfS HA VIII 1406/2
MfS HA VIII 2608
MfS HA XX 10915
MfS HA XX 11285
MfS HA XX 11510
MfS HA XX 12353
MfS HA XX 18546
MfS HA XX/AKG 6680

Comic Bibliothek Renate, Berlin, DE

Haus der Geschichte der Bundesrepublik Deutschland, Leipzig, DE

Wende Museum, Culver City, CA, USA

Films and Television Programs

Becker, Wolfgang, dir. *Good Bye, Lenin!* DVD. Berlin: X-Filme Creative Pool, 2003.
Beyer, Frank, dir. *Spur der Steine*. DVD. Berlin: DEFA, 1966.
Blaulicht. Berlin: DFF, 1959–1968.
Carow, Heiner, dir. *Sheriff Teddy*. DVD. Berlin: DEFA, 1957.
Haußmann, Leander, dir. *Sonnenallee*. DVD. Berlin: Delphi Filmverleih GmbH, 1999.
Mach, Josef, dir. *Die Söhne der großen Bärin*. DVD. Berlin: DEFA, 1966.
Prisma. Berlin: DFF, 1963–1991.
Tele-BZ. Berlin: DFF, 1960–1990.
Unser Sandmännchen. Berlin: DFF, 1958–1990.

Published Primary Sources

ABC-Zeitung (Berlin, DE, 1946–1996)
Atze (Berlin, DE, 1955–1991)
Bummi (Berlin, DE, 1957–1991)
Frösi (Berlin, DE, 1953–2005)
Junge Welt (Berlin, DE, 1947–present)
Mosaik (Berlin, DE, 1976–present)
Mosaik von Hannes Hegen (Berlin, DE, 1955–1975)
Trommel (Berlin, DE, 1958–1991)

Secondary and Online Sources

Anderson, Benedict. *Imagined Communities: Reflections on the Origin and Spread of Nationalism*. London: Verso, 1983.

Andrae, Thomas. *Carl Barks and the Disney Comic Book: Unmasking the Myth of Modernity*. Jackson: University Press of Mississippi, 2006.

Assouline, Pierre. *Hergé, the Man Who Created Tintin*. Translated by Charles Ruas. Oxford: Oxford University Press, 2009.

Augustine, Dolores L. *Red Prometheus: Engineering and Dictatorship in East Germany, 1945–1990*. Cambridge, MA: MIT Press, 2007.

Barker, Martin. *Comics: Ideology, Power and the Critics*. Manchester: Manchester University Press, 1989.

Barthes, Roland. *Mythologies*. Translated by Richard Howard and Annette Lavers. New York: Hill and Wang, 1957.

Beaty, Bart. *Unpopular Culture: Transforming the European Comic Book in the 1990s*.Toronto: University of Toronto Press, 2007.

Benjamin, John D. "Relocating the Text: *Mosaik* and the Invention of a German East German Comics Tradition." *The German Quarterly* 92, no. 2 (Spring 2019): 148–65.

Bensing, Manfred. "Thomas Müntzer." *Encyclopedia Britannica*. Retrieved 9 February 2016 from https://www.britannica.com/biography/Thomas-Muntzer.

Berdahl, Daphne. "*Good Bye, Lenin!* Aufwiedersehen GDR: On the Social Life of Socialism." In *Post-Communist Nostalgia*, edited by Maria Todorova and Zsuzsa Gille, 177–89. New York: Berghahn Books, 2010.

Bergfelder, Tim. *International Adventures: German Popular Cinema and European Co-Productions in the 1960s*. New York: Berghahn Books, 2005.

Berghahn, Daniela. *Hollywood Behind the Wall: The Cinema of East Germany*. Manchester: Manchester University Press, 2005.

Bergmann, Werner. *Antisemitismus in öffentlichen Konflikten: Kollektives Lernen in der politischen Kultur der Bundesrepublik 1949–1989*. Frankfurt: Campus Verlag, 1997.

Berninger, Mark, Jochen Ecke, and Gideon Haberkorn. "Introduction." In *Comics as a Nexus of Cultures: Essays on the Interplay of Media, Disciplines, and International Perspectives*, edited by Mark Berninger, Jochen Ecke, and Gideon Haberkorn, 1–6. Jefferson: McFarland & Company, Inc., 2010.

Betts, Paul. "Building Socialism at Home: The Case of East German Interiors." In *Socialist Modern: East German Everyday Culture and Politics*, edited by Katherine Pence and Paul Betts, 96–132. Ann Arbor: University of Michigan Press, 2008.

———. *Within Walls: Private Life in the German Democratic Republic*. Oxford: Oxford University Press, 2010.

Blessing, Benita. "DEFA Children's Films: Not Just for Children." In *DEFA at the Crossroads of East German and International Film Culture*, edited by Marc Silberman and Hennig Wrage, 243–62. Berlin: Walter de Gruyter GmbH, 2014.

———. "Defining Socialist Children's Films, Defining Socialist Childhoods." In *Re-Imagining DEFA*, edited by Seán Allan and Sebastian Heiduschke, 248–67. New York: Berghahn Books, 2016.

Bongco, Mila. *Reading Comics: Language, Culture, and the Concept of the Superhero in Comic Books*. London: Routledge, 2000.

Borneman, John. *After the Wall: East Meets West in the New Berlin*. New York: Basic Books, 1991.

Boym, Svetlana. *The Future of Nostalgia*. New York: Basic Books, 2001.

Brock, Angela. "Producing the 'Socialist Personality'? Socialisation, Education, and the Emergence of New Patterns of Behavior." In *Power and Society in the GDR, 1961–1979: The 'Normalisation of Rule'?*, edited by Mary Fulbrook, 220–52. New York: Berghahn Books, 2009.

Brockman, Stephen. "The Eleventh Plenum and Film Criticism in East Germany." *German Life & Letters* 66, no. 4 (October 2013): 432–48.

Bruce, Gary. *The Firm: The Inside Story of the Stasi*. Oxford: Oxford University Press, 2010.

Calloway, Colin G., Gerd Gemunden, and Susanne Zantop, eds. *Germans and Indians: Fantasies, Encounters, Projections*. Lincoln: University of Nebraska Press, 2002.

Carleton, Sean. "Drawn to Change: Comics and Critical Consciousness." *Labour/Le Travail*, no. 73 (Spring 2014): 151–77.

Chapman, James. *British Comics: A Cultural History*. London: Reaktion Books, 2011.

Childs, David. *The GDR: Moscow's German Ally*. New York: Routledge, 2015.

Chute, Hilary L. *Graphic Women: Life Narrative & Contemporary Comics*. New York: Columbia University Press, 2010.

"Circular 9—Works Made for Hire." United States Copyright Office—Library of Congress. Retrieved 28 April 2016 from http://www.copyright.gov/circs/circ09.pdf.

"Complete Carl Barks Library #14. Walt Disney's Uncle Scrooge: The Seven Cities of Gold." Grand Comics Database. Retrieved 29 December 2015 from http://www.comics.org/issue/1264699/.

Confino, Alon. *The Nation as a Local Metaphor: Württemberg, Imperial Germany, and National Memory, 1871–1918*. Chapel Hill: University of North Carolina Press, 1997.

Connolly, Kate. "The Sandmannchen, Germany's cutest communist, turns 50." *The Guardian*. Retrieved 15 June 2016 from https://www.theguardian.com/world/2009/nov/23/sandmannchen-germany-communist.

Cooke, Paul. *Representing East Germany since Unification: From Colonization to Nostalgia*. Oxford: Berg, 2005.

Cronin, Brian. *Was Superman a Spy?: And Other Comic Book Legends Revealed*. New York: Plume, 2009.

Danziger-Russell, Jacqueline. *Girls and Their Comics: Finding a Female Voice in Comic Book Narrative*. Lanham: The Scarecrow Press, Inc., 2013.

Darnton, Robert. *Censors at Work: How States Shaped Literature*. New York: Norton, 2014.
Dennis, Mike, and Jonathon Grix. *Sport under Communism: Behind the East German 'Miracle.'* Houndmills: Palgrave, 2012.
"Dig, Dag, Digedag. DDR-Comic Mosaik." Stiftung Haus der Geschichte der Bundesrepublik Deutschland. Retrieved 11 March 2016 from http://www.hdg.de/leipzig/ausstellungen/wechselausstellungen/ausstellungen/dig-dag-digedag-ddr-comic-mosaik/.
Di Napoli, Thomas. "Thirty Years of Children's Literature in the German Democratic Republic." *German Studies Review* 7, no. 2 (May 1984): 281–300.
Donovan, John. "Parody and Propaganda: Fighting American and the Battle Against Crime and Communism in the 1950s." In *Comic Books and American Cultural History*, edited by Matthew Pustz, 110–19. New York: Continuum, 2012.
Dorfman, Ariel, and Armand Mattelart. *How to Read Donald Duck: Imperialist Ideology in the Disney Comic*. Translated by David Kunzle. New York: International General, 1975.
Eedy, Sean. "Animating the Socialist Personality: DEFA Fairy Tale *Trickfilme* in the Shadow of 1968." In *Celluloid Revolt: German Screen Cultures and the Long 1968*, edited by Christina Gerhardt and Marco Abel, 183–200. Rochester: Camden House, 2019.
———. "Back to the (Socialist) Future: History, Time Travel, and East German Education in *Mosaik von Hannes Hegen*, 1958–1974." In *Drawing the Past: Comics and the Historical Imagination*, edited by Michael Goodrum, David Hall, and Philip Smith. Jackson: University Press of Mississippi, forthcoming.
———. "Four Colour Anti-Fascism: Postwar Narratives and the Obfuscation of the Holocaust in East German Comics." *Journal of Modern Jewish Studies* 17, no. 1 (2018): 24–35.
———. "Reimagining GDR Comics: *Kultur*, Children's Literature and the Socialist Personality." *Journal of Graphic Novels and Comics* 5, no. 3 (September 2014): 245–56.
Eghigian, Greg. "The Psychologization of the Socialist Self: East German Forensic Psychology and its Deviants, 1945–1975." *German History* 22, no. 2 (2004): 181–205.
Eisman, April A. "East German Art and the Permeability of the Berlin Wall." *German Studies Review* 38, no. 3 (October 2015): 597–616.
Eisner, Will. *Comics and Sequential Art: Principles & Practice of the World's Most Popular Art Form*. Paramus: Poorhouse Press, 1985.
Ewers, Hans-Heino. "Children's Literature Research in Germany." *Children's Literature Association Quarterly* 27, no. 3 (Fall 2002): 158–65.
Feinstein, Joshua. *The Triumph of the Ordinary: Depictions of Daily Life in the East German Cinema 1949–1989*. Chapel Hill: University of North Carolina Press, 2002.

Fingeroth, Danny. *Superman on the Couch: What Superheroes Really Tell Us about Ourselves and Our Society*. New York: Continuum, 2005.

Fitzpatrick, Sheila. *Everyday Stalinism: Ordinary Life in Extraordinary Times: Soviet Russia in the 1930s*. Oxford: Oxford University Press, 1999.

Fleischhauer, Jan. "Germany's Best-Loved Cowboy: The Fantastical World of Cult Novelist Karl May." Spiegel Online International. Retrieved 5 January 2016 from http://www.spiegel.de/international/germany/marking-the-100th-anniversary-of-german-cult-author-karl-may-s-death-a-824566.html.

Foucault, Michel. "Discipline and Punish, Panopticism." In *Discipline and Punish: The Birth of the Prison*, edited by Alan Sheridan, 195–228. New York: Vintage, 1977.

"Four Color #62." Grand Comics Database. Retrieved 29 December 2015 from http://www.comics.org/issue/4095/.

Fritzsche, Sonja. "Dreams of 'Cosmic Culture' in *Der schweigende Stern* [The Silent Star, 1960]." In *Re-Imagining DEFA: East German Cinema in its National and International Contexts*, edited by Seán Allan and Sebastian Heiduschke, 210–26. New York: Berghahn Books, 2016.

———. *Science Fiction Literature in East Germany*. Bern: Peter Lang, 2006.

Führer, Karl Christian, and Corey Ross. "Mass Media, Culture, and Society in Twentieth-Century Germany: An Introduction." In *Mass Media, Culture and Society in Twentieth-Century Germany*, edited by Karl Christian Führer and Corey Ross, 1–22. Houndmills: Palgrave, 2006.

Fulbrook, Mary. "The Concept of 'Normalisation' and the GDR in Comparative Perspective." In *Power and Society in the GDR 1961–1979: The 'Normalisation of Rule'?*, edited by Mary Fulbrook, 1–30. New York: Berghahn Books, 2009.

———. *Interpretations of the Two Germanies, 1945–1990*. Houndmills: Macmillan, 2000.

———. "'Normalisation' in the GDR in Retrospect: East German Perspectives of Their Own Lives." In *Power and Society in the GDR 1961–1979: The 'Normalisation of Rule'?*, edited by Mary Fulbrook, 278–319. New York: Berghahn Books, 2009.

———. *The People's State: East German Society from Hitler to Honecker*. New Haven: Yale University Press, 2005.

———. "Putting the People Back In: The Contentious State of GDR History." *German History* 24, no. 4 (November 2006): 608–20.

———. "Structures and Subjectivities in GDR History." In *Becoming East German: Socialist Structures and Sensibilities after Hitler*, edited by Mary Fulbrook and Andrew I. Port, 277–90. New York: Berghahn Books, 2013.

Gallinat, Anselma. *Narratives in the Making: Writing the East German Past in the Democratic Present*. New York: Berghahn Books, 2017.

Gaus, Günter. *Wo Deutschland liegt*. Munich: Deutscher Taschenbuch Verlag, 1986.

Gersdorf, Catrin. "The Digedags Go West: Images of America in an East German Comic Strip." *Journal of American Culture* 19, no. 2 (Summer 1996): 35–45.

Geyer, Michael. "America in Germany: Power and the Pursuit of Americanization." In *The German-American Encounter: Conflict and Cooperation between Two Cultures, 1800–2000*, edited by Frank Trommler and Elliot Shore, 121–44. New York: Berghahn Books, 2001.

Grieder, Peter. *The German Democratic Republic*. Houndmills: Palgrave, 2012.

Grix, Jonathon. "Non-Conformist Behaviour and the Collapse of the GDR." In *East Germany: Continuity and Change*, edited by Paul Cooke and Jonathon Grix, 69–80. Amsterdam: Rodopi, 2000.

Gumbert, Heather L. "East German Television and the Unmaking of the Socialist Project, 1952–1965." PhD diss., University of Texas at Austin, 2006.

———. *Envisioning Socialism: Television and the Cold War in the German Democratic Republic*. Ann Arbor: University of Michigan Press, 2014.

Habel, F. B. "Biografie-Gojko Mitić—Schauspieler, Stuntman, Autor, Regisseur." Cinegraph-Lexikon zum deutschsprachigen Film. Retrieved 14 January 2016 from http://www.cinegraph.de/lexikon/Mitic_Gojko/biografie.html.

Habermas, Jürgen. "The Public Sphere: An Encyclopedia Article (1964)." *New German Critique* no. 3 (Autumn 1974): 49–55.

———. *The Structural Transformation of the Public Sphere: An Inquiry into a Category of Bourgeois Society*. Cambridge, MA: MIT Press, 1991.

Harris, Cheryl. "Introduction Theorizing Fandom: Fans, Subculture and Identity." In *Theorizing Fandom: Fans, Subculture and Identity*, edited by Cheryl Harris and Alison Alexander, 3–8. Cresskill: Hampton Press, Inc., 1998.

Harrison, Hope M. *Driving the Soviets up the Wall: Soviet-East German Relations, 1953–1961*. Princeton, NJ: Princeton University Press, 2003.

Harsch, Donna. *Revenge of the Domestic: Women, the Family, and Communism in the German Democratic Republic*. Princeton, NJ: Princeton University Press, 2008.

Hatfield, Charles. "Comic Art, Children's Literature, and the New Comic Studies." *The Lion and the Unicorn* 30, no. 3 (September 2006): 360–82.

Hatfield, Charles, and Craig Svonkin. "Why Comics Are and Are Not Picture Books: Introduction." *Children's Literature Association Quarterly* 37, no. 4 (Winter 2012): 429–35.

Heermann, Christian. *Old Shatterhand Ritt Nicht im Auftrag der Arbeiterklasse: Warum war Karl May in SBZ und DDR 'Verboten'?* Dessau: Anhaltische Verlagsgesellschaft, 1995.

Hegen, Hannes, and Mosaik-Kollektiv. "'Mosaik' Heft 8: Strichzeichnung—Seite 1 (Titelseite)." *Stiftung Haus der Geschichte der Bundesrepublik Deutschland*. Retrieved 11 March 2016 from http://sint.hdg.de:8080/SINT5/SINT/?wicket:interface=:1:14:::.

Heiduschke, Sebastian. *East German Cinema: DEFA and Film History*. New York: Palgrave, 2013.

Heretz, Leonid. "Petitions from Peasants." In *From Supplication to Revolution: A Documentary History of Imperial Russia*, edited by Gregory Freeze, 170–79. Oxford: Oxford University Press, 1988.

Ho'omanawanui, Ku'ualoha Meyer. "Hero or Outlaw? Two Views of Kaluaiko'olau." In *Navigating Islands and Continents: Conversations and Contestations in and around the Pacific*, edited by Cynthia Franklin, Ruth Hsu, and Suzanne Kosanke, 232–63. Honolulu: University of Hawai'i, 2000.

Howard, Marc Morjé. *The Weakness of Civil Society in Post-Communist Europe*. Cambridge: Cambridge University Press, 2003.

Jarausch, Konrad H. "Care and Coersion: The GDR as Welfare Dictatorship." In *Dictatorship as Experience: Toward a Socio-Cultural History of the GDR*, edited by Konrad H. Jarausch, translated by Eve Duffy, 47–69. New York: Berghahn Books, 1999.

Jarausch, Konrad H., and Michael Geyer. *Shattered Past: Reconstructing German Histories*. Princeton, NJ: Princeton University Press, 2003.

Jenkins, Henry. "Introduction: Should We Discipline the Reading of Comics?" In *Critical Approaches to Comics: Theories and Methods*, edited by Matthew J. Smith and Randy Duncan, 1–14. New York: Routledge, 2012.

Jobs, Richard Ivan. "Tarzan under Attack: Youth, Comics, and Cultural Reconstruction in Postwar France." *French Historical Studies* 26, no. 4 (Fall 2003): 687–725.

Jones, Matthew, and Joan Ormrod. "Introduction: Contexts and Concepts of Time in the Mass Media." In *Time Travel in Popular Media: Essays on Film, Television, Literature, and Video Games*, edited by Matthew Jones and Joan Ormrod, 5–18. Jefferson, NC: McFarland & Co, 2015.

Jovanovic, Goran, and Ulrich Koch. "The Comics Debate in Germany: Against Dirt and Rubbish, Pictoral Idiotism, and Cultural Analphabetism." In *Pulp Demons: International Dimensions of the Postwar Anti-Comics Campaign*, edited by John A. Lent, 93–128. Cranbury: Associated University Presses, Inc., 1999.

Jüngst, Heike Elisabeth. *Information Comics: Knowledge Transfer in a Popular Format*. Frankfurt: Peter Lang, 2010.

Kaiser, Monika. "Reforming Socialism? The Changing of the Guard from Ulbricht to Honecker during the 1960s." In *Dictatorship as Experience: Towards a Socio-Cultural History of the GDR*, edited by Konrad H. Jarausch, translated by Eve Duffy, 325–40. New York: Berghahn Books, 1999.

Kaschuba, Wolfgang. "Popular Culture and Workers' Culture as Symbolic Order: Comments on the Debate about the History of Culture and Everyday Life." In The *History of Everyday Life: Reconstructing Historical Experiences and Ways of Life*, edited by Alf Lüdtke, translated by William Templer, 169–97. Princeton, NJ: Princeton University Press, 1995.

Kempe, Frederick. *Berlin 1961: Kennedy, Khrushchev, and the Most Dangerous Place on Earth*. New York: Berkley, 2011.

Klocke, Sonja E. "Teddy Boys in Ost und West: Eine generationenspezifische Metamorphose in Heiner Carows Sheriff Teddy (1957)." In *Von Pionierin und Piraten: Der DEFA-Kinderfilm in seinen kulturhistorischen, filmästhetischen und ideologischen Dimensionen*, edited by Bettina Kümmerling-Meibauer and Steffi Ebert. Heidelberg: Universitätsverlag, forthcoming.

Kocka, Jürgen. "Eine durchherrschte Gesellschaft." In *Sozialgeschichte der DDR*, edited by Hartmut Kaelbe, Jürgen Kocka, and Hartmut Zwahr, 547–53. Stuttgart: Klett-Cotta, 1994.

Köhn, Lothar. "Von der Formalismus-Debatte zum <<Bitterfelder Weg>>." In *Geschichte der deutschen Literatur von 1945 bis zur Gegenwart: Zweite, aktualisierte und erweiterte Auflage*, edited by Wilfried Barner, 287–306. Munich: Verlag CH Beck, 2006.

Kotkin, Stephen. *Uncivil Society: 1989 and the Implosion of the Communist Establishment*. New York: Modern Library, 2009.

Kramer, Thomas. "Die DDR der fünfziger Jahre im Comic Mosaik: Einschienenbahn, Agenten, Chemieprogramm." In *Akten, Eingaben, Schaufenster: Die DDR und ihre Texte. Erkundungen zu Herrschaft und Alltag*, edited by Alf Lüdtke, 167–88. Berlin: Akademie Verlag, 1997.

———. "Donald, Asterix and Abrafaxe: Die Verarbeitung amerikanischer und französischer Comic-Serien in den Mosaik-Bildgeschichten der DDR (1955–1990)." In *Kinder- und Jugendliteraturforschung 1999/2000*, edited by Hans-Heino Ewers, Ulrich Nassen, Karin Richter, and Rüdiger Steinlein, 40–66. Stuttgart: Verlag J.B. Metzler, 2000.

———. *Micky, Marx und Manitu: Zeit- und Kulturgeschichte im Spiegel eines DDR-Comics 1955–1990: "Mosaik" als Fokus von Medienerlebnissen im NS und in der DDR*. Berlin: Weidler Buchverlag, 2002.

Kussmann, Jens. "'Nothing but Exclamation Points?' Comics in the Bavarian Academic High School." In *Novel Perspectives on German-Language Comic Studies*, edited by Lynn Marie Kutch, 67–92. Lanham: Lexington Books, 2016.

Leask, Phil. "Humiliation as a Weapon within the Party: Fictional and Personal Accounts." In *Becoming East German: Socialist Structures and Sensibilities after Hitler*, edited by Mary Fulbrook and Andrew I. Port, 237–56. New York: Berghahn Books, 2013.

Lee, Peter. "Decrypting Espionage Comic Books in 1950s America." In *Comic Books and the Cold War, 1946–1962: Essays on Graphic Treatment of Communism, the Code and Social Concerns*, edited by Chris York and Rafiel York, 30–44. Jefferson: McFarland & Company, Inc., 2012.

Lees, John. "On Comics Custodianism and the Illusion of Change." John Lees Comics. Retrieved 13 March 2016 from https://johnleescomics.wordpress.com/2014/07/17/on-comics-custodianism-and-the-illusion-of-change/.

Lefèvre, Pascal. "The Battle over the Balloon: The Conflictual Institutionalization of the Speech Bubble in Various European Countries." *Image & Narrative: Online Magazine of the Visual Narrative*, issue 14. Retrieved 5 June 2016 from http://www.imageandnarrative.be/inarchive/painting/pascal_levevre.htm.

Lent, John A. "Introduction: The Comics Debate Internationally: Their Genesis, Issues, and Commonalities." In *Pulp Demons: International Dimensions of the Postwar Anti-Comics Campaign*, edited by John A. Lent, 9–41. Cranbury: Associated University Presses, Inc., 1999.

Lettkemann, Gerd. "Comics in der DDR." In *Fortsetzung folgt: Comic Kultur in Deutschland*, edited by Andreas C. Knigge, 317–61. Frankfurt: Verlag Ullstein GmbH, 1985.

Lettkemann, Gerd, and Michael F. Scholz. *"Schuldig ist schließlich jeder...der Comics besitzt verbreitet oder nicht einziehen läßt" Comics in der DDR— Die Geschichte eines ungeliebten Mediums (1945/49–1990)*. Berlin: MOSAIK Steinchen für Steinchen Verlag GmbH, 1994.

"A Liberal Western Journalist Praises the Progress of the GDR (1986)." German History in Documents and Images. Retrieved 1 February 2016 from http://germanhistorydocs.ghi-dc.org/sub_document.cfm?document_id=74.

Lindenberger, Thomas. "Alltagsgeschichte und ihr möglicher Beitrag zu einer Gesellschaftsgeschichte der DDR." In *Die Grenzen der Diktatur: Staat und Gesellschaft in der DDR*, edited by Richard Bessel and Ralph Jessen, 298–325. Gottingen: Vanderhoeck & Ruprecht, 1996.

———. "'Asociality' and Modernity: The GDR as a Welfare Dictatorship." In *Socialist Modern: East German Everyday Culture and Politics*, edited by Katherine Pence and Paul Betts, 211–33. Ann Arbor: University of Michigan Press, 2008.

———. "SED-Herrschaft als soziale Praxis—Herrschaft und 'Eigen-Sinn': Problemstellung und Begriffe." In *Staatsicherheit und Gesellschaft. Studien zum Herrschaftsalltag in der DDR*, edited by Jens Gieseke, 23–47. Göttingen: Vandenhoeck & Ruprecht, 2007.

Lorenz, Christa. ">>Bummi<< und der Weg ins Leben: Erziehung zur Gesellschaft in einer Kinderzeitschrift." In *Fortschritt, Norm und Eigensinn: Erkundungen im Alltag der DDR*, edited by Andreas Ludwig, 211–32. Berlin: Christoph Links Verlag, 1999.

Lüdtke, Alf. "Cash, Coffee-Breaks, Horseplay: Eigensinn and Politics among Factory Workers in Germany circa 1900." In *Confrontation, Class Consciousness and the Labor Process: Studies in Proletarian Class Formation*, edited by Michael Hanagan and Charles Stephenson, 65–96. New York: Greenwood Press, 1982.

———. "'Helden der Arbeit'—Mühen beim Arbeiten. Zur mißmutigen Loyalität von Industriearbeitern in der DDR." In *Sozialgeschichte der DDR*, edited by Harmut Kaelbe, Jürgen Kocka, and Hartmut Zwahr, 188–213. Stuttgart: Klett-Cotta, 1994.

———. "Practices of Survival—Ways of Appropriating 'the Rules': Reconsidering Approaches to the History of the GDR." In *Power and Society in the GDR*

1961–1979: The 'Normalisation of Rule'?, edited by Mary Fulbrook, 181–93. New York: Berghahn Books, 2009.
———. "Sprache und Herrschaft in der DDR. Einleitende Überlegungen." In *Akten, Eingaben, Schaufenster. Die DDR und ihre Texte: Erkunden zu Herrschaft und Alltag*, edited by Alf Lüdtke and Peter Becker, 11–26. Berlin: Akademie Verlag, 1997.
———. "Wo blieb die 'rote Glut?' Arbeitererfahrungen und deutscher Faschismus." In *Alltagsgeschichte, Zur Rekonstruktion historischer Erfahrungen und Lebenweisen*, edited by Alf Lüdtke, 224–82. Frankfurt: Campus Verlag, 1989.
Lüdtke, Alf, ed. *Akten, Eingaben, Schaufenster: Die DDR und ihre Texte. Erkundungen zu Herrschaft und Alltag*. Berlin: Akademie Verlag, 1997.
Madarasz, Jeanette Z. *Conflict and Compromise in East Germany, 1971–1989: A Precarious Stability*. Houndmills: Palgrave, 2003.
Mah, Harold. "Phantasies of the Public Sphere: Rethinking the Habermas of Historians." *Journal of Modern History* 72, no. 1 (March 2000): 153–82.
Maity, Nandini. "From Comic Culture to Cyber Culture: Cultural Imperialism and its Impact on Youth since 1960s." *IOSR Journal of Humanities and Social Science* 8, no. 4 (Mar.–Apr. 2013): 10–14.
Major, Patrick. *Behind the Berlin Wall: East Germany and the Frontiers of Power*. Oxford: Oxford University Press, 2010.
———. "Introduction." In *The Workers' and Peasants' State: Communism and Society in East Germany under Ulbricht 1945–1971*, edited by Patrick Major and Jonathan Osmond, 1–20. Manchester: Manchester University Press, 2002.
———. "'Smut and Trash': Germany's Culture Wars against Pulp Fiction." In *Mass Media, Culture and Society in Twentieth-Century Germany*, edited by Karl Christian Führer and Corey Ross, 234–50. Houndmills: Palgrave, 2006.
Malone, Paul M. "A Periphery surrounded by centres: The German-Language comics market, transnational relationships, and graphic novels." *Journal of Graphic Novels and Comics* 11, no. 1 (2020): 10–30.
Mathur, Suchitra. "From Capes to Snakes: The Indianization of the American Superhero." In *Comics as a Nexus of Cultures: Essays on the Interplay of Media, Disciplines and International Perspectives*, edited by Mark Berninger, Jochen Ecke, and Gideon Haberkorn, 175–86. Jefferson: McFarland & Company, Inc., 2010.
Maxwell, Alexander. "East Europeans in the Cold War Comic *This Godless Communism*." In *Comic Books and the Cold War, 1946–1962: Essays on Graphic Treatment of Communism, the Code and Social Concerns*, edited by Chris York and Rafiel York, 190–203. Jefferson: McFarland & Company, Inc., 2012.
McAllister, Matthew P., Edward H. Sewell Jr., and Ian Gordon. "Introducing Comics and Ideology." In *Comics & Ideology*, edited by Matthew P. McAllister, Edward H. Sewell Jr., and Ian Gordon, 1–14. New York: Peter Lang, 2001.
McCloud, Scott. *Reinventing Comics: How Imagination and Technology are Revolutionizing an Art Form*. New York: Harper, 2000.
———. *Understanding Comics: The Invisible Art*. New York: Harper, 1993.

McCulloch, Mark. "The Sword and Shield of Consumption: The Police-Society Relationship in the Former East Germany." *Past Tense: Graduate Review of History* 1 (2012): 67–83.
McDougall, Alan. "The Liberal Interlude: SED Youth Policy and the Free German Youth (FDJ), 1963–65." *Debatte* 9, no. 2 (2001): 123–55.
———. *Youth Politics in East Germany: The Free German Youth Movement 1946–1968*. Oxford: Clarendon Press, 2004.
McGuire, Patrick L. *Red Stars: Political Aspects of Soviet Science Fiction*. Ann Arbor: UMI Research Press, 1985.
McKinney, Mark. *The Colonial Heritage of French Comics*. Liverpool: Liverpool University Press, 2011.
McLellan, Josie. *Love in the Time of Communism: Intimacy and Sexuality in the GDR*. Cambridge: Cambridge University Press, 2011.
Merkel, Ina. "'. . . in Hoyerswerda leben jedenfalls keine so kleinen viereckigen Menschen.' Briefe an das Fernsehen der DDR." In *Akten, Eingaben, Schaufenster: Die DDR und ihre Texte. Erkundungen zu Herrschaft und Alltag*, edited by Alf Lüdtke, 279–310. Berlin: Akademie Verlag, 1997.
Merkel, Ina, and Felix Mühlberg. "Eingaben und Öffentlichkeit." In *Wir sind doch nicht die Meckerecke der Nation!: Briefe an das Fernsehen der DDR*, 2nd ed., edited by Ina Merkel, 11–46. Berlin: Schwarzkopf & Schwarzkopf, 2000.
Meyer, Michael. *The Year That Changed the World: The Untold Story Behind the Fall of the Berlin Wall*. New York: Scribner, 2009.
"'Micky Maus' vs 'Fix und Foxi' fürs Leben gezeichnet." *Spiegel Online*. Retrieved 13 August 2013 from http://www.spiegel.de/einestages/micky-maus-vs-fix-und-foxi-fuers-leben-gezeichnet-a-949644.html.
Mrozek, Bodo. "Ausstellung über DDR-Comichelden: Reisefreiheit für die Fantasie." *Der Tagesspiegel*. Retrieved 21 June 2016 from http://www.tagesspiegel.de/kultur/ausstellung-ueber-ddr-comichelden-greuliche-zeichnungen-in-rekordauflage/9755588-2.html.
Mühlberg, Felix. "Konformismus oder Eigensinn? Eingaben als Quelle zur Erforschung der Alltagsgeschichte der DDR." *Mitteilungen aus der kulturwissenschaftlichen Forschung* (February 1996): 331–45.
Naftzinger, Joseph. "Policy-Making in the German Democratic Republic: The Response to West German Trans-Border Broadcasting." PhD diss., University of Maryland at College Park, 1994.
Neuhaus, Jessamyn. "How Wonder Woman Helped My Students 'Join the Conversation': Comic Books as Teaching Tools in a History Methodology Course." In *Comic Books and American Cultural History*, edited by Matthew Pustz, 11–25. New York: Continuum, 2012.
Nikolajeva, Maria. "Russian Children's Literature Before and After Perestroika." *Children's Literature Association Quarterly* 20, no. 3 (Fall 1995): 105–11.
Nothnagle, Alan L. *Building the East German Myth: Historical Mythology and Youth Propaganda in the German Democratic Republic, 1945–1989*. Ann Arbor: University of Michigan Press, 1999.

Nowak, Bernd. "Erinnerung an Atze aus der 'Atze.'" Altes und Neues von Bernd Nowak, Dessau. Retrieved 17 May 2018 from http://barrynoa.blogspot.ca/2014/08/erinnerung-atze-aus-der-atze.html.

Palmowski, Jan. "Between Conformity and Eigen-Sinn: New Approaches to GDR History." *German History* 20, no. 4 (2002): 494–502.

———. "Learning the Rules: Local Activists and the Heimat." In *Power and Society in the GDR 1961–1979: The 'Normalisation of Rule'?*, edited by Mary Fulbrook, 151–77. New York: Berghahn Books, 2009.

Pence, Katherine. "Schaufenster der sozialistichen Konsums: Texte der ostdeutschen 'Consumer Culture.'" In *Akten, Eingaben, Schaufenster: Die DDR und ihre Texte. Erkundungen zu Herrschaft und Alltag*, edited by Alf Lüdtke, 91–118. Berlin: Akademie Verlag, 1997.

———. "Women on the Verge: Consumers between Private Desires and Public Crisis." In *Socialist Modern: East German Everyday Culture and Politics*, edited by Katherine Pence and Paul Betts, 287–322. Ann Arbor: University of Michigan Press, 2008.

Penny, H. Glenn. *Kindred by Choice: Germans and American Indians since 1800*. Chapel Hill: University of North Carolina Press, 2013.

———. "Red Power: Liselotte Welskopf-Henrich and the Indian Activist Networks in East and West Germany." *Central European History* 41, no. 3 (September 2008): 447–76.

Pfeiffer, Reinhard. *Von Hannes Hegen bis Erich Schmitt: Lexikon der Karikaturisten, Presse-und Comic-Zeichner der DDR*. Berlin: Schwarzkopf & Schwarzkopf Verlag, 1998.

Pilz, Michael. "Der erste Superheld der DDR heißt Ronny Knäusel." *Die Welt*. Retrieved 10 July 2016 from http://www.welt.de/kultur/literarischewelt/article122884381/Der-erste-Superheld-der-DDR-heisst-Ronny-Knaeusel.html.

Poiger, Uta G. "Amerikanischer Jazz und (ost)deutschen Respektabilität." In *Akten, Eingaben, Schaufenster: Die DDR und ihre Texte. Erkundungen zu Herrschaft und Alltag*, edited by Alf Lüdtke, 119–36. Berlin: Akademie Verlag, 1997.

———. *Jazz, Rock, and Rebels: Cold War Politics and American Culture in a Divided Germany*. Berkeley: University of California Press, 2000.

Port, Andrew I. *Conflict and Stability in the German Democratic Republic*. Cambridge: Cambridge University Press, 2007.

Prager, Brad. Review of *Micky, Marx und Manitu. Zeit- und Kulturgeschichte im Spiegel eines DDR-Comics 1955–1990. Mosaik als Fokus von Medienerlebnissen im NS und in der DDR*, by Thomas Kramer. *German Quarterly* 76, no. 3 (Summer 2003): 363–64.

Puaca, Brian M. *Learning Democracy: Education Reform in West Germany, 1945–1965*. New York: Berghahn Books, 2009.

Pustz, Matthew J. *Comic Book Culture: Fanboys and True Believers*. Jackson: University Press of Mississippi, 1999.

———. "Introduction: Comic Books as History Teachers." In *Comic Books and American Cultural History*, edited by Matthew J. Pustz, 1–8. New York: Continuum, 2012.
Reagin, Nancy. "Dances with Worlds: Karl May, 'Indian' Hobbyists, and German Fans of the American West since 1912." *Participations: Journal of Audience & Reception Studies* 13, no. 1 (May 2016): 553–83.
Richter, Christoph, and Kate Bowen. "East German Comic Celebrates 400 Editions of Slapstick Adventure." *DW Deutsche Welle*. Retrieved 18 March 2016 from http://www.dw.com/en/east-german-comic-celebrates-400-editions-of-slapstick-adventure/a-4156898.
Richthofen, Esther von. *Bringing Culture to the Masses: Control, Compromise and Participation in the GDR*. New York: Berghahn Books, 2009.
———. "Communication and Compromise: The Prerequisites for Cultural Participation." In *Power and Society in the GDR 1961–1979: The 'Normalisation of Rule'?*, edited by Mary Fulbrook, 130–50. New York: Berghahn Books, 2009.
Robinson, Ronald E. "Introduction: Railway Imperialism." In *Railway Imperialism*, edited by Clarence B. Davis, Kenneth E. Wilburn, Jr., and Ronald E. Robinson, 1–6. Westport: Greenwood, 1991.
Ross, Corey. *Constructing Socialism at the Grass-Roots: The Transformation of East Germany*, 1945–65. Houndmills: Palgrave, 2000.
———. *The East German Dictatorship: Problems and Perspectives in the Interpretation of the GDR*. London: Arnold, 2002.
Rubenstein, Anne. *Bad Language, Naked Ladies, & Other Threats to the Nation: A Political History of Comic Books in Mexico*. Durham, NC: Duke University Press, 1998.
Rubin, Eli. *Amnesiopolis: Modernity, Space, and Memory in East Germany*. Oxford: Oxford University Press, 2016.
———. *Synthetic Socialism: Plastics & Dictatorship in the German Democratic Republic*. Chapel Hill: University of North Carolina Press, 2012.
———. "The Trabant: Consumption, Eigen-Sinn, and Movement." *History Workshop Journal* 68, no. 1 (2009): 27–44.
———. "Understanding a Car in the Context of a System: Trabants, Marzahn, and East German Socialism." In *The Socialist Car: Automobility in the Eastern Bloc*, edited by Lewis H. Siegelbaum. Ithaca: Cornell University Press, 2011.
Rueger, Fabian. "Kennedy, Adenauer and the Making of the Berlin Wall." PhD diss., Stanford University, 2011.
Sabeti, Shari. "The Irony of 'Cool Club': The Place of Comic Book Reading in Schools." *Journal of Graphic Novels and Comics* 2, no. 2 (December 2011): 137–49.
———. "Reading Graphic Novels in School: Texts, Contexts and the Interpretive Work of Critical Reading." *Pedagogy, Culture & Society* 20, no. 2 (2012): 191–210.

———. "The 'Strange Alteration' of *Hamlet*: Comic Books, Adaptation and Constructions of Adolescent Literacy." *Changing English: Studies in Culture and Education* 21, no. 2 (2012): 182–97.

Sabin, Roger. *Comics, Comix & Graphic Novels: A History of Comic Art*. New York: Phaidon Press, 1996.

Sanders, Martin. "10th World Festival of Youth and Students, East Berlin, 1973." University of Warwick Library, Media Resource Centre. Retrieved 10 February 2016 from https://www2.warwick.ac.uk/services/library/mrc/explorefurther/filmvideo/worldfestival.

Sarotte, Mary Elise. *1989: The Struggle to Create Post-Cold War Europe*. Princeton, NJ: Princeton University Press, 2009.

Saunders, Anna. *Honecker's Children: Youth and Patriotism in East(ern) Germany, 1979–2002*. Manchester: Manchester University Press, 2007.

Schäder, Katharina. "Deutsche Dinge 'Das Mosaik'. Ein West-Kind und sein Ost-Comic." *Die Welt*. Retrieved 28 April 2016 from http://www.welt.de/deutsche-dinge/article3071851/Ein-West-Kind-und-sein-Ost-Comic.html.

Schneider, Matthias. "Creator of the Digedags—Hannes Hegen." Goethe-Institut: Deutschsprachige Comics. Retrieved 6 July 2016 from http://www.goethe.de/kue/lit/prj/com/pck/en363879.htm.

Scholz, Michael F. "Images of Spies and Counterspies in East German Comics." In *Comics of the New Europe: Reflections and Intersections*, edited by Martha Kuhlman and José Alaniz, 159–76. Leuven: Leuven University Press, 2020.

Schweppe, Peter. "The Politics of Removal: Kursbuch and the West German Protest Movement." *The Sixties* 7, no. 2 (2014): 138–54.

Sheffer, Edith. *Burned Bridge: How East and West Germans Made the Iron Curtain*. Oxford: Oxford University Press, 2011.

Shen, Qinna. "Barometers of GDR Cultural Politics: Contextualizing the DEFA Grimm Adaptations," *Marvels & Tales* 25, no. 1 (2011): 70–95.

Stahl, J. D. "Children's Literature and the Politics of the Nation State." *Children's Literature* 20 (1992): 193–203.

Steinkamp, Maike. "The Propagandistic Role of Modern Art in Postwar Berlin." In *Berlin: Divided City, 1945–1989*, edited by Philip Broadbent and Sabine Hake, 23–33. New York: Berghahn Books, 2010.

"Stiftung Archiv der Parteien und Massenorganisationen der DDR im Bundesarchiv—Verlag Junge Welt, DY 26." Jugendwerkhof-Treffen. Retrieved 28 April 2016 from http://www.jugendwerkhof-treffen.de/CMS_FILES_2.1/images/content/doku/organisation_ddr/junge_welt.pdf.

Stites, Richard. *Revolutionary Dreams: Utopian Vision and Experimental Life in the Russian Revolution*. Oxford: Oxford University Press, 1989.

Stitziel, Judd. "Shopping, Sewing, Networking, Complaining: Consumer Culture and the Relationship between State and Society in the GDR." In *Socialist Modern: East German Everyday Culture and Politics*, edited by Katherine Pence and Paul Betts, 253–86. Ann Arbor: University of Michigan Press, 2008.

Stroemberg, Fredrik. *Comic Art Propaganda: A Graphic History*. New York: St. Martin's Griffin, 2010.
Suny, Ronald Grigor. *The Soviet Experiment: Russia, the USSR, and the Successor States*. 2nd ed. New York: Oxford University Press, 2011.
Suvin, Darko. *Russian Science Fiction 1956–1974: A Bibliography*. Elizabethtown, NY: Dragon Press, 1976.
Tankel, Jonathan David, and Keith Murphy. "Collecting Comic Books: A Study of the Fan and Curatorial Consumption." In *Theorizing Fandom: Fans, Subculture and Identity*, edited by Cheryl Harris and Alison Alexander, 55–68. Cresskill: Hampton Press, Inc., 1998.
Ten Dyke, Elizabeth A. "Memory and Existence: Implications of the Wende." In *The Work of Memory: New Directions in the Study of German Society and Culture*, edited by Alon Confino and Peter Fritzsche, 154–69. Urbana: University of Illinois Press, 2002.
Thomson-Wohlgemuth, Gaby. "About Official and Unofficial Addressing in East German Children's Literature." *Children's Literature Association Quarterly* 30, no. 1 (Spring 2005): 32–52.
———. *Translation under State Control: Books for Young People in the German Democratic Republic*. New York: Routledge, 2009.
Timm, Annette F. *The Politics of Fertility in Twentieth-Century Berlin*. Cambridge: Cambridge University Press, 2010.
Tóth, András György. "Hungarian Avant-garde Comics in the 1990s." Stripburek. Comics from Behind the Rusty Iron Curtain. Retrieved 28 June 2016 from http://www.ljudmila.org/stripcore/burek/hungary.htm.
Unterrainer, Sebastian. "Comics in der DDR." In *Comic-Kunst vom Weberzuklus zum Bewegten Mann Deutschsprachige Bildergeschichten des 20. Jahrhunderts*, edited by Dietrich Grünewald, 26–27. Koblenz: Görres, 2004.
Weißhahn, Guido. "Atze." *DDR Comics*. Retrieved 27 August 2013 from http://www.ddr-comics.de/atze.htm.
———. "Die Digedags im Mosaik." *DDR Comics*. Retrieved 27 August 2013 from http://www.ddr-comics.de/digedags.htm.
———. "Die Digedags und Ritter Runkel." *DDR Comics*. Retrieved 16 June 2016 from http://www.ddr-comics.de/digbuch4.htm.
———. "Das MOSAIK." *DDR Comics*. Retrieved 6 May 2016 from http://ddr-comics.de/mosaik.htm.
———. "Pats Reiseabenteuer." *DDR Comics*. Retrieved 16 March 2016 from http://www.ddr-comics.de/pat.htm.
———. "Propaganda in 'Atze.'" *DDR Comics*. Retrieved 20 August 2013 from http://www.ddr-comics.de/atzepol.htm.
Wertham, Fredric. *Seduction of the Innocent*. New York: Rhinehart & Company, Inc., 1954.
Wierling, Dorothee. "The Hitler Youth Generation in the GDR: Insecurities, Ambitions, and Dilemmas." In *Dictatorship as Experience: Toward a Socio-Cul-*

tural History of the GDR, edited by Konrad H. Jarausch, translated by Eve Duffy, 307–24. New York: Berghahn Books, 1999.

———. "Der Staat, die Jugend und der Westen. Texte und Konflikten der 1960er Jahre." In *Akten, Eingaben, Schaufenster: Die DDR und ihre Texte. Erkundungen zu Herrschaft und Alltag*, edited by Alf Lüdtke, 223–40. Berlin: Akademie Verlag, 1997.

———. "Youth as Internal Enemy: Conflicts in the Education Dictatorship of the 1960s." In *Socialist Modern: East German Everyday Culture and Politics*, edited by Katherine Pence and Paul Betts, 157–82. Ann Arbor: University of Michigan Press, 2008.

Willis, Jim. *Daily Life Behind the Iron Curtain*. Santa Barbara: Greenwood, 2013.

Witek, Joseph. *Comic Books as History: The Narrative Art of Jack Jackson, Art Spiegelman, and Harvey Pekar*. Jackson: University Press of Mississippi, 1989.

Wittenberg, David. *Time Travel: The Popular Philosophy of Narrative*. New York: Fordham University Press, 2013.

Woll, Allen L. "The Comic Book in a Socialist Society: Allende's Chile, 1970–1973." *Journal of Popular Culture* 9, no. 4 (Spring 1976): 1039–45.

Wright, Bradford W. *Comic Book Nation: The Transformation of Youth Culture in America*. Baltimore: John Hopkins University Press, 2001.

York, Chris, and Rafiel York. "Introduction: Fredric Wertham, Containment, and Comic Books." In *Comic Books and the Cold War, 1946–1962: Essays on Graphic Treatment of Communism, the Code and Social Concerns*, edited by Chris York and Rafiel York, 5–15. Jefferson: McFarland & Company, Inc., 2012.

Zander, Alex. "Die Digedags sind die Beatles aller deutschen Comics." *Freestland Vorpommern: Wo die Ostsee am süßsten ist*. Retrieved 8 June 2016 from https://freestland.wordpress.com/2012/04/01/die-digedags-sind-die-beatles-des-deutschen-comics/.

Index

10th World Festival of Youth and Students, 107

ABC-Zeitung, 110, 119, 188
Abrafaxe, 16n4, 20n53, 49, 66, 103, 134, 142–44, 152, 156n34, 178–79, 181, 186n78
Act on the Integrated Socialist Education System, 120
Action Comics, 36
Adi, 83–84, 93n55
Adolph, Gerhard. *See* Adi
Adria-Serie, 143
Alisch, Horst, 83
Alltag, 2, 5–6, 17n23, 97, 124, 160, 162, 177. *See also* everyday life
Altenburger, Christina, 131n87
Altenburger, Wolfgang, 12, 39, 42, 48–49, 51–53, 55, 60n63, 65, 101–2, 109, 120, 122, 131n87, 145, 148–49, 164–72, 174, 176, 178
Americanization, 1, 36, 38, 41, 141, 167–8, 189
Amerika-Serie, 12, 28, 57, 79–81, 84, 93n43, 93n53, 120, 138, 166, 172–76, 186n78
anti-comics campaign, 12, 36, 52, 56, 67–68, 87, 134, 163
antifascism, 34, 109, 134, 166
Arfert, Joachim, 174
Asterix, 23
Atze, 12–13, 15, 22–23, 26–28, 32, 34–35, 37, 42, 45, 49–57, 65, 67–69, 77–79, 83, 85, 88–89, 92n38, 96, 98, 101–3, 105–9, 113–16, 119–20, 122, 127n40, 133, 144–45, 147–50, 153, 158n59, 161–63, 167–68, 171–72, 174, 178–79, 188
Austria, 34, 144

bande dessinée, 158n65
Barbarino, Rudolph, 168, 170
Barks, Carl, 23, 26, 56, 71, 78, 132, 136, 139–42, 153n1, 160, 183n28
Basic Treaty (1972), 89, 126n30, 174, 177, 179, 186n80, 186n83
Becker, Wolfgang, 85, 130n72
Belgium, 23, 127n43
benign power, 4–6, 12, 15, 56, 65–66, 85, 96, 99, 109, 120–21, 144, 150–51, 161, 164, 178, 188, 190
Berlin, 22, 26, 43, 133–34, 139, 157n54, 168
  Blockade, 61n70
  East, 42, 43, 107, 150, 153
  as an "escape hatch," 43, 133
  West, 36, 153, 175
Berlin Wall, 3, 7–8, 15, 43–45, 56–57, 90, 96, 133–35, 145–47, 150, 152–53, 161, 163, 165, 172, 175, 189–91
  permeability, 89–90, 133–35, 146, 152, 167, 183n33
Berliner Schülerparlament, 88
Bhur Yham, 73, 75, 77
Bitterfeld, 14, 33, 161–63
Bitterfelder Weg, 12, 14–15, 18n28, 33–35, 37, 44, 46, 127n43, 145, 163–6, 170, 172, 175, 180
Black Channel, 111
black market, 43
Boche, Horst, 164–65
Bogdanov, Alexander, 30
bourgeoisie, 9, 12, 28, 33, 79, 81, 84, 161
Brandt, Willy, 174–75
Braun, Volker, 171
Brezhnev, Leonid, 3, 47
Brothers Grimm, 41–42, 44, 66. *See also* fairy tales

Buchenwald, 92n38
Bummi, 22, 37, 67, 188
Busch, Wilhelm, 21, 40–41

capitalism, 3, 7, 14, 31, 33, 47, 73, 78–80, 132, 139, 144–45, 191
  capitalist-imperialism, 28, 31, 76, 78–79 (*see also* imperialism)
Carow, Heiner, 36
censors, 167, 180
censorship, 170–71, 176
  self-censorship, 6, 19n41
Central Committee
  FDJ, 12, 23, 36, 49–50, 79, 119, 165, 171
  SED, 146, 168
  Thälmann Pioneers, 28, 52
childhood, 2, 8, 13, 15, 18n33, 27, 87, 94n66, 123, 139, 163, 177, 187, 192
Children's and Young People's Harmful Publications Act, 21, 33
children's periodicals, 22–23, 28, 43. See also *Kinderzeitschriften*
citizenship, 4, 51, 192
  as a population, 11, 46, 190
closure, 190–91
Cold War, 29, 34, 64, 71, 73, 77, 80, 128n47, 153, 159n75, 169
  division, 135, 144, 150–53, 177
Colonel Springfield, 80, 138–39
comic(s)
  American, 12, 20n52, 23, 36, 38, 54, 56–57, 67–69, 86, 163, 184n45
  creator, 13–14, 26, 29, 31, 39, 55, 69, 85, 91, 96, 100, 105–6, 122, 140, 162–63, 165, 168, 170, 175–76, 180
  culture, 8, 13, 36, 56, 60n48, 87–89, 91, 96–97, 112
  as a medium, 3, 6, 12, 23, 27–28, 38–41, 50, 55, 69, 75, 118, 121, 136, 149, 155n18, 155n29, 167–68, 189–90
  publications, 2, 7–8, 16n4, 21, 27, 37, 46, 54, 66, 68–69, 91, 110, 123, 147, 162
  publishing, 3, 12, 36, 42, 44, 49, 96, 100, 122, 165, 171, 184n45, 184n48, 189–90
  strip, 22, 36, 41, 53, 57, 67, 83, 102–5, 109–10, 119, 127n43, 188
  tropes, 14, 27, 73, 132, 136, 140–43, 145, 149, 164, 169, 171, 173, 179, 183n28, 189

Western, 8, 12, 14, 20n53, 26, 28, 35–36, 43, 56, 60n48, 68, 70, 96, 136, 139–40, 143, 145, 153, 161–62, 165, 167, 169, 172–73, 180, 183n28
Comics Code Authority (CCA), 36
Commission for the Oversight and Control of Publications intended for Children and Adolescents, 21, 33
communism, 4, 14, 30, 32, 173
  Soviet-style, 4, 19, 30–31, 35, 46, 134, 144, 153, 162, 189
Communist Party of Germany (KPD), 7, 42
consumer, 3, 13
  choice, 42, 133
  culture, 150, 186n75
  desire, 119, 163
consumerized politics, 112
consumption, 2, 7, 15, 22, 43, 65, 75, 96, 122–23, 126n37, 133, 191–92
copyright, 16n4, 142, 170, 176–77, 179, 181, 184n45
cosmic culture, 73
counterculture, 120
cult of technology, 104
culture of complaint, 2, 5, 98, 111–12, 114, 118, 121, 130n64. See also *Eingaben*

Davis, Angela, 107
DC Comics, 179, 184n45
DEFA, 35, 41, 46, 69, 81, 84, 86, 94n66, 127n43, 146, 182n22
Dell Comics, 14, 36
détente, 175–76
Deutsche Fernsehfunk (DFF), 111, 127n43, 153, 168
Deutscher Lehrerzeitung, 164, 166
Deutschlandtreffen der Jugend, 47, 90, 186n75
Developing World, 133, 145, 179. See also Third World
dictatorship, 1–3, 113–14, 162
Digedags
  Dig and Dag, 24, 29, 37, 40, 71, 73, 137–39, 142, 166, 178, 187n86
  Digedag, 24, 29, 38, 71, 138–39, 142, 166, 178, 187n86
  as a trio, 14, 16n4, 24–32, 37–39, 46–49, 53, 57, 66, 69–71, 73, 75–80, 84, 121,

Index • 213

132, 134–37, 139–45, 152, 155n21, 156n34, 160–63, 165–68, 170–81, 187n86
Dirks, Rudolph, 41
Disney, 14, 23–24, 26–28, 36, 52, 56, 68–71, 78, 132, 136, 140–41, 160, 180, 183n28
domestic, 2, 5, 7, 10–11, 13, 19n48, 48, 64–66, 91, 96, 99, 113–5, 117–20, 122–24, 128n49, 146–47, 150–51, 160, 172, 179, 181, 190–91
Dominik, Hans, 183n29
Donald Duck
 character, 24, 26–28, 68–71, 136, 140, 153n1, 160
 comic, 23, 36, 78, 132, 136, 183n28
Dräger, Lothar, 16n4, 37, 142, 164–65, 167–68, 174, 176, 187n86
DT64, 47, 90, 186n75
durchherrschte Gesellschaft. See thoroughly ruled society

East Germany, 4, 11–12, 21–22, 27, 35, 36–37, 40, 43–44, 54, 56, 73, 85, 88, 94n61, 98, 132–34, 143, 151, 177, 179. See also German Democratic Republic (GDR)
editorial regime, 8, 15, 54, 56, 111, 116–17, 122, 161, 167, 170, 173–76, 180–81, 191–92
educational regime, 2, 7, 13, 15, 29, 35, 44–45, 81, 91, 191
Ehapa Verlag, 14
Eigensinn, 5, 9–13, 97–101, 106, 108–9, 121, 124, 147, 157n52, 158n54, 177, 190–92
Eighth Party Congress, 32, 119–20. See also "unity of economic and social policy"
Eingaben, 5, 10–11, 19n45, 106, 108–9, 111–14, 117, 122–23, 191. See also culture of complaint
Eleventh Plenum, 49, 93n53, 127n40, 127n43, 146. See also "Rabbit film"
England, 33, 36. See also Great Britain
Erfinder-Serie, 37, 44, 46, 48, 166–67
Erhardt, Hans, 39, 48–49, 165–66
everyday life, 2, 5, 10–11, 19n41, 150, 157n52, 161, 190. See also *Alltag*

export, 56, 93n43, 145, 152, 172–76, 178–79, 181

fairy tales, 41, 66, 69, 86, 94n65. See also Brothers Grimm
fantasy, 48, 94n66, 151–52, 166
fascism, 6, 133
Federal Republic of Germany (FRG), 27, 34–35, 61n70, 64, 131n87, 159n69, 171, 176–77, 189. See also West Germany
Feitsch, Kurt, 170, 174
fiction, 69, 143, 147, 166, 170
 "close aim," 30, 44
 detective, 175
 science, 6, 30–31, 90, 164, 166, 183n29
 utopian, 30–31, 44, 73, 75–76, 78
film, 6, 33, 43, 46, 49, 51, 81, 84–85, 88–90, 94n66, 127n43, 130n72, 135, 146–47, 182n22
 children's, 35–36, 41, 66, 94n66
Fix and Fax
 characters, 50, 82, 132, 148
 comic, 49–50, 53, 56–57, 66, 82, 101–2, 147–48, 158n59, 168
Fix and Foxi
 characters, 69
 comic, 52, 167
Flagg, James Montgomery, 80
four-color process, 102, 125n25
France, 36, 39, 85, 127n43
Free German Youth (FDJ), 2–4, 7–8, 11–15, 18n28, 22–24, 26–31, 33–39, 42–45, 47–57, 65–66, 68–71, 75, 77–79, 81, 83, 85–91, 92n38, 94n61, 94nn65–66, 96–102, 105–16, 118–24, 128n49, 132–37, 139–43, 145–47, 149–50, 152–53, 154n9, 157n50, 157n54, 158n67, 159n69, 159n75, 160–77, 179–81, 183n28, 184n48, 185n71, 186n80, 188–92
free time, 7, 9, 44, 76, 91, 96, 115. See also leisure
Freizeitgesellschaft, 7, 189
frontier thesis, 81
Frösi, 13, 15, 22, 37, 67, 77, 83, 85, 87, 98, 105, 108–16, 118–19, 122, 124, 162, 165, 179, 188
 Frösi-treff, 83–89, 91, 96

"funny animal" genre, 14, 27, 49, 70, 139, 173

Gaus, Günter, 9–11, 64–66, 97, 99, 107, 152
gender, 77, 109, 116–18, 121, 123
   feminized space, 11, 118, 123
   norms, 117
   roles, 117, 123
   women, 70, 77, 114, 117–19, 123, 191
German Democratic Republic (GDR), 2–12, 14–15, 21–22, 26, 31, 33–34, 38, 41–44, 46–50, 52, 56, 59n40, 64–69, 73, 78–79, 83–84, 87–88, 90–91, 97, 99–100, 104, 107, 110, 113–15, 122, 127n43, 132–35, 142–44, 149–53, 159n69, 160–64, 167–69, 171–73, 175–77, 180, 185n71, 186n80, 186n83, 188–89, 191.
   See also East Germany
glasnost, 171
Glücksmann, Anselm, 173–74, 176
Good Bye, Lenin!, 85, 130n72
governmentality, 17n23
Graupner, Ulf S., 24
Great Britain, 130n66. See also England
"grumble society," 5
Günther, Bernd, 78
Günther, Jürgen, 83
gutters, 55, 100–101, 190

Hain, Günther, 54
Hauptverwaltung Verlage und Buchhandel (HV), 170–71
Haußmann, Leander, 90
Hegen, Hannes, 14–15, 16n4, 20n53, 23–24, 27–29, 31, 37, 39, 48–49, 51, 56, 69, 78–79, 85, 89, 132, 139–40, 142–3, 160–81, 183n28, 184n48, 185n71, 186n78
Hegenbarth, Edith, 37, 176
Hegenbarth, Johannes. See Hegen, Hannes
Heimat, 150, 159n72
Hein, Christoph, 171
Hergé, 41, 158n65
High Art, 21, 38
High Culture, 33–35, 56, 67
historical
   accuracy, 14–15, 38, 52, 89, 145–46, 169–70, 181

consciousness, 30, 70–71, 89–90, 139–40, 150
representation, 28, 37–38, 52, 142, 163, 179
Hoffmann, Heinrich, 41
Holocaust, 78, 92n38
Honecker, Erich, 10, 32, 45–47, 49, 87, 106, 113, 119–20, 176–77, 181, 186n80
Honecker, Margot, 119–20
honeycomb state, 4
horror comics, 36, 68
Huey, Dewey, and Louie. See nephews
Hungary, 144
Hungarian uprising, 127n43

ideology, 3, 7, 9, 28, 31, 37, 48–49, 51, 56–57, 76, 78–80, 85, 88, 91, 94n66, 96–97, 121, 128n49, 134, 140, 144–45, 149, 151–53, 154n9, 158n65, 160–63, 168, 173, 175, 177, 180
"ideological free zone," 48, 162, 177, 179, 190
imagined communities, 105
imperialism, 26, 35, 70, 84, 87, 107, 134, 141, 149
   cultural, 21, 36, 68, 141, 152, 155n29, 166, 173, 179, 183n28
   See also capitalist-imperialism
Indigenous peoples, 27, 70, 141, 145
"inner emigration," 14, 135, 153
inner-German border, 26, 42–43, 133–34, 152, 168
inoffizielle Mitarbeiter (IM), 131n87
International Children's Day, 108
International Union of Students, 107
Italy, 127n43, 138, 148

Jähn, Sigmund, 84–87, 93n55
Japan, 127n43
June 1953 Uprising, 42, 127n43
Junge Welt, 67, 162
juvenile delinquency, 21, 36, 188

Käpt'n Lütt, 83
Katzenjammer Kids, 41, 69
Kauka, Rolf, 52
Khrushchev, Nikita, 47
Kieser, Jürgen, 22, 49, 53, 67, 85, 101

Kiesinger, Kurt Georg, 89, 175
Kinderzeitschriften, 2–3, 12–13, 15, 85, 97, 101, 105, 109–10, 112–18, 120–23, 127n43, 134, 143, 146–47, 149, 159n75, 167, 175, 188–92. *See also* children's periodicals
Kollektiv. *See* Mosaik-Kollektiv
Kultur, 1, 35, 44, 54–56, 94n65
  Kinderkultur, 34–35, 37–38, 40–41, 44–45, 56–57, 94n65, 143
  Kulturstaat, 21, 34–35, 41–42, 56–57, 69

Law on the Distribution of Writings Harmful to Young People, 21, 33
Lebensraum, 81
Lehmann, Robert, 36–37, 164
Leipzig, 23, 48, 62n91
Leipziger Schule, 62n91
leisure, 7–9, 67, 123, 146–47, 157n54, 166, 188–91. *See also* free time
Lenin, Vladimir Ilyich, 32, 53, 117
Lenin Pioneers, 105, 108, 110
letters. *See Eingaben*
literature, 12, 14, 18n28, 22–23, 28, 33–35, 38, 52, 66–67, 99–100, 127n43, 135, 153
  children's, 8, 12, 18n28, 32–35, 42, 44, 48, 55, 57, 65, 69, 73, 78, 147, 149, 162, 165, 176–77
  travel, 137, 143
Little Orphan Annie, 36
Low Art, 21, 38
Low Culture, 33–34
lowbrow, 21, 33, 118
Lunacharsky, Anatoly, 32

malign power, 4–6, 15, 65, 109, 120–22, 146, 178
Marcinelle School, 23
Marvel Comics, 184n45
Marxism, 21, 24, 38, 75, 78
  Marxist-Leninism, 3, 51
mass culture, 1, 7
mass party organization, 172
Mauer im Kopf, 177
Max and Moritz, 21, 40–2, 44, 52, 68
Max und Maxi, 53, 104
Mäxchen und Tüte, 109–10, 116

May, Karl, 81, 143, 182n22, 183n29
Mickey Mouse, 23, 27–28, 68, 132, 160
Mini-Max, 115
Ministerrat, 98
Ministry of Culture, 168, 170, 175, 180, 182n22
Mitić, Gojko, 84, 86–87
Mitteldeutscher Verlag, 33, 161
modernity, 31, 66, 75–76, 79, 146, 150, 159n72
Modrow, Hans, 98
Mosaik (1976–present), 16n4, 24, 134, 142–4, 178–9, 186n78
Mosaik von Hannes Hegen (1955–1975), 3, 12–15, 16n4, 23, 26–33, 35–40, 42, 44–46, 48–49, 51–52, 54–57, 65, 67, 70–71, 75–81, 83, 85, 88–89, 93n43, 96, 100, 105, 109, 113–14, 116–17, 119–20, 122–23, 128n49, 132–34, 136–37, 139–45, 149, 152–53, 155n21, 160–77, 179–81, 183n28, 186n78, 187n86, 188
Mosaik-Kollektiv, 14, 20n53, 27–29, 37–39, 46, 48–49, 51, 56, 62n91, 77, 83, 139, 142, 161, 164–66, 169–71, 174–76, 180–81, 187n86
Müller, Helmut, 49, 51
music, 46, 83, 90, 191
  beat, 90, 186n80
  jazz, 87
  rock and roll, 46, 90

National Socialist, 179
Nazi, 7, 67, 81, 88
Nazi legacy, 34, 68, 89
Nazism, 54, 78, 86
See also Third Reich
Native American, 81–84, 86–87
Neos, 29, 31, 73, 77
  Greater Reich, 77, 79–80
  Neosian Union, 74, 77, 152
nephews, 24, 26, 70, 132, 139–140, 154n1
Netherlands, 172
Neues Leben, 119
New Economic System (NÖS), 47
niche society, 2, 9–11, 48, 64–65, 88, 97, 99–100, 107, 112, 117, 119, 121–23, 128n49, 135, 146–47, 152, 166, 177, 179, 189–91

Nischengesellschaft. See niche society
nostalgia, 177, 182n9

Old Shatterhand, 81
Orient-Südsee-Serie, 24, 30, 46, 48, 140, 166
Ostpolitik, 174–75
Otto und Alwin, 83

panopticon, 6, 192
Pat (character), 54, 104–6, 132, 134, 145, 150–52
Patenbrigade, 106–8, 126n32, 127n40
Pats Reiseabenteuer, 13, 53–54, 56, 66, 101–3, 104–6, 108, 110, 115, 124, 128n49, 134, 145, 147–51, 158n59, 172
pedagogy, 87
Peer Tyla, 73, 77–78
petitions. *See Eingaben*
picture book, 40, 56, 60n63
Pludra, Benno, 36
popular culture, 49, 56, 81, 83, 88–90, 94n65, 111–12, 127n43, 135, 154n11, 157n52, 157n54
postwar, 8, 36, 67–69, 89, 125n24, 128n47, 133, 145, 173, 188
privacy, 2, 9–11, 46, 48, 65–67, 88, 98–100, 112, 117, 121, 123, 146, 172, 190
private sphere, 4–9, 65, 96–99, 101, 106, 108, 116–18, 121, 123, 128n49, 135, 146–47, 189–90
proletariat, 3, 29, 33, 134, 143, 150. *See also* working class
propaganda, 1, 3, 65, 78, 85, 98, 158n65, 160–2
  cadres, 87
  propagandistic content, 54, 66, 189
public sphere, 4, 9, 12, 19n48, 64, 89, 97, 105–6, 113, 123, 189
  ersatz, 2, 9–13, 106–7, 114–15, 190–92
publishing regime, 2–3, 13, 24, 27, 31, 34, 49, 57, 77, 90, 106–7, 122, 132, 136, 142, 146, 149, 152, 159n75, 160–61

Quick et Flupke, 41

"Rabbit film," 49, 93n53, 127n40, 127n43. *See also* Eleventh Plenum

racism, 71, 79–80, 144, 166, 173, 179–80
radio, 11, 47, 88, 90, 134, 186n75
"real existing socialism," 3, 151, 180
Rechtstaat, 177
Red Star, 30
Red Western, 84, 86, 90, 93n53
Red Woodstock. *See* 10th World Festival of Youth and Students
Regulations for the Protection of Youth. *See Verordnung zum Schutz der Jugend*
"reluctant loyalty," 113–14
Republikflucht, 42–43, 128n49
Rietschel, Lona, 16n4, 142, 174
Ritter-Runkel-Serie, 47–48, 137, 167–68
Ritter Runkel von Rübenstein, 47, 137–38
Römer-Serie, 25, 29–30, 46, 48, 187n86
Russian Revolution (October Revolution), 23, 73

Schlegel, Harry, 53–4, 102, 105
Schmitt, Erich, 30
Schmutzliteratur, 27, 38, 42, 54, 100, 163, 180
Schund und Schmutz, 3, 15, 145
Scrooge McDuck, 23–24, 26, 28, 69–71, 79–80, 132, 136, 139–40, 142, 149, 153n1, 160, 167
Seduction of the Innocent, 179
"sequential art," 39
Sheriff Teddy, 35
"shlock," 164, 171
Sinus Tangentus, 29, 31, 73, 75–76
Social Democratic Party (SPD), 7, 42
socialist personality, 3, 6, 8, 10, 14–15, 18n28, 19n45, 22, 32–35, 37, 40, 44, 49, 51, 53, 65, 71, 85–90, 96, 105, 108, 110, 120, 122, 124, 132, 135–36, 145, 162–63, 177, 188, 190–91
Socialist Realism, 18n28, 31, 33–34, 41, 44, 46, 52, 90, 127n43, 162, 166
Socialist Unity Party (SED), 2–4, 6–7, 9, 22, 30, 32–35, 41–42, 45, 47–48, 59n40, 64–68, 75, 87–88, 90, 112–13, 120–21, 126n30, 133, 146, 150–52, 158n54, 159n75, 160–61, 166, 168, 172–73, 175, 177, 186n80
SED regime, 2, 4–5, 8, 10, 65, 81, 90, 96–97, 99–100, 106, 111, 113, 117,

133–34, 143, 147, 151, 161–62, 171, 177, 180, 186n83, 188–89, 192
SED state, 4, 6–7, 10, 12, 15, 18n28, 21, 34, 43, 51–52, 54–57, 64–65, 76, 83, 97, 99, 111, 120, 124, 146–47, 176, 180, 189–92
Söhne der großen Bärin, die (Sons of the Great Bear), 81, 84
Sommer, Theo, 99
Sonnenallee, 90
Soviet Bloc, 1–2, 9, 15, 23, 31, 33–34, 73, 78, 84, 90, 117, 128n47, 150, 159n75, 178–79
Soviet Military Administration in Germany (SMAD), 6, 42, 67
Soviet Union, 3, 11, 23, 29–31, 33–34, 53, 71, 73, 87, 162, 171. *See also* USSR
Soviet Zone of Occupation (SBZ), 7, 41–42, 67, 78, 87
Space Race, 29, 71, 81
"speaking socialism," 106
  on socialist rhetoric in letters of complaint, 10, 108, 174, 185n71
Spur der Steine, 93n53
Sputnik, 29, 32, 71, 73, 75, 81, 83
Stalin, Joseph, 11, 30, 61n70
Stasi, 4, 6, 10–11, 64–66, 113, 121, 126n30, 131n87, 134, 146, 151–52, 161, 171, 180, 186n83, 189
  secret police, 4, 42, 64
Steinchen auf Steinchen, 164
storytelling, 13, 23, 39, 42, 45–46, 56, 141–42, 149
  device(s), 40, 55, 137, 141
Struwwelpeter, 41–42, 52, 69
superhero, 67–68, 141
  genre, 36, 41, 68–69, 145
Superman
  character, 69, 179
  comic, 20n52, 67

Tarzan, 145
technology, 29, 31, 72–73, 75, 83, 87, 104–5, 141, 144, 150–51, 159n69, 163
television, 11, 51, 65–66, 83, 87, 99–101, 111, 125n20, 127n40, 127n43, 128n49, 129n64, 134, 147, 152–53, 168, 190–1
Thälmann, Ernst, 120

Thälmann Young Pioneers (JP), 22–23, 26, 33, 36–39, 43–44, 52, 54, 56, 66, 78, 85, 94n65, 100, 106–7, 109, 143, 164–65, 189
Theater im Palast der Republik (TiP), 83
Third Reich, 78, 81. *See also* National Socialist
Third World, 71, 141, 144–5. *See also* Developing World
thoroughly ruled society, 64–66, 97, 113, 177
Tintin, 41, 70, 149, 158n65
travel, 14, 24, 37, 80, 128n49, 132–35, 137–47, 149–53, 158n57, 191
  restrictions, 133–34, 152
  space, 29, 31, 37, 72, 76, 80–81, 84–85, 90
  time, 29–30, 37–38, 139, 151, 178
Trommel, 22, 108–9, 113, 119, 122, 188
Turba, Kurt, 45

Übermensch, der, 179
Ulbricht, Walter, 8, 10, 31, 42, 45–47, 49–51, 87, 90, 120, 134, 146, 172, 180
Uncle Sam, 80, 139
Uncle Scrooge
  character. *See* Scrooge McDuck
  comic, 70, 132, 136, 138, 183n28
United States of America, 1, 14–15, 23, 29, 34, 36, 41, 52, 54, 67–68, 71, 73, 79–80, 93n43, 121, 127n43, 128n47, 130n66, 139, 143, 162, 167, 175, 189
  Civil War, 79–80
  frontier, 84, 86, 143, 172
"unity of economic and social policy," 113, 119. *See also* Eighth Party Congress
Unkultur, 67, 90, 170, 175
Unrechtstaat, 186n83
Unser Sandmännchen, 135, 153, 168
USSR, 31, 47, 73, 90. *See also* Soviet Union

Verlag Junge Welt, 8, 13, 16n4, 22–23, 26, 37–39, 44–45, 48–49, 53, 56–57, 65, 67, 89, 96–97, 101–2, 114, 117, 131n87, 135, 153, 161–62, 164–71, 173–80, 188–89, 191
Verlag Neues Leben, 23, 26–28, 30, 34, 37, 69, 88, 132, 154, 161, 164, 173, 184n48

Verordnung zum Schutz der Jugend, 8, 21–22, 26, 33, 35–36, 43, 56, 68–70, 133
Vietnam, 105, 107–8, 127n40
Volksarmee, 121, 126n32
Volkskammer, 98, 172
Volkspolizei, 22, 68, 102
Vontra, Gerhard, 84–85
Voyage of the Red Star Pioneer Troop in Wonderland, 30

"welfare dictatorship," 113–14, 116
Weltraum-Serie, 12, 28–29, 31–33, 37–39, 44–46, 48, 70–73, 75, 77–81, 83, 85, 88, 139, 152, 153n12, 163, 165–66, 169, 187n86
Wertham, Fredric, 1, 21, 36, 67–68, 94n61, 179
West Germany, 14, 23, 26–27, 33, 35–36, 88, 133, 144. *See also* Federal Republic of Germany (FRG)
Westernization, 160, 167
Wild West, 88, 143
Winnetou, 81
Wolf, Christa, 171
working class, 5, 33, 38, 51, 54, 79, 94n61, 142, 163. *See also* proletariat
World Federation of Democratic Youth, 107
World War I, 69, 80
World War II, 1, 14, 20n52, 32, 39, 42, 54, 67, 73, 81, 84, 92n38, 105, 133, 160, 166, 189
Wort-Bildgeschichte, 55

Youth Communiqué, 45–51, 90, 119, 146, 172, 180

Zeitgeist, 12–13, 64, 85, 87–89, 94n66, 96
Zhukov, Innokenty, 30
Zimmermann, Gisela, 164–65

www.ingramcontent.com/pod-product-compliance
Lightning Source LLC
Chambersburg PA
CBHW071340080526
44587CB00017B/2908